Ignite *Your Life* Conscious *for* Leaders

Thirty-five outstanding stories by individuals dedicated to consciously inspiring the planet through individual leadership

FOREWORD BY

JB Owen

Founder of Ignite, JBO Global and Lotus Liners.

PRESENTED BY

Amy O'Meara, Ana Sofia Orozco, Ana Cukrov, Anay Patel, Andrea Gontkovičová
Anne Tucker, Ashley Avinashi, Beth Medved Waller, Carol Benson,
Catherine Malli-Dawson, Christina M. Ghose, Claire Wild, Damian Culhane,
Dana Shalit, Emily C. Ross, Francesca Ciaudano, Hanna Meirelles, Ivana Sošić Antunović,
Jamie Takahashi, JB Owen, Joanne Hughes, Karyn Kerr Pettigrew, Katelin Gregg,
Katja Glöckler, Lori Lennox, Maggie Reigh, Matej Šimunić, Meena Kumari Adnani,
Michael D Lynch, Nancy L. McFarland, Natalie Matushenko, Nitasha Sarin, Sam Beard,
Sara Feldman, Sherry Brier, Vicki Graham

Published by Ignite and printed by JBO Global

DEDICATION

Many harbingers of despair believe that the world is in crisis. They see humans with their technologies and excesses threatening our very existence. Others foresee a bright future where the untapped powers of our minds, bodies and consciousness are elevating human behavior. They see a tidal wave of infinite discovery, new compassion, and self-empowerment reconnecting ourselves to nature and the Universe. They believe that we are on the verge of a new era greater than The Renaissance and The Enlightenment, filled with possibilities and opportunities never before considered in human history. Many believe we are on the brink of The Conscious Revolution.

Thirty-five of those visionaries and risk-takers have shared in this book. They represent the energy, consciousness and heart that is sweeping the planet in a scale never before seen. Let us salute them. Enjoy them. Join them. Learn from them. Their heartfelt leadership is leading the way.

Special congratulations to JB Owen, her team, and her vision. She's a powerful world catalyst recognizing and mobilizing this growing wave of hope.
— Sam Beard
Creator and Chair of Programs for 8 United States Presidents.

Author Testimonial

"When I first started working with the IYL team, I realized immediately how professional they are. Every member of the team adds value to the publishing process — a truly multi-talented approach. I was encouraged to explore new writing techniques to unlock my creativity. I was able to share and test my story with like-minded authors and an executive team to get feedback. I was able to go deeper into how to make the writing more impactful and how to ensure the story flows. At times, the experience and coaching was cathartic — helping to process my own journey and how to share that in a powerful way. The technical support on how to ensure the story appears on the page was invaluable. It took my ordinary good writing to a phenomenal level.

Thank you to all the IGNITE publishing team. I have felt encouraged, supported, challenged and fulfilled in sharing my story to a wider audience. I am truly grateful for every member of the team's input and for empowering me to share my story.

If you are considering writing or sharing your story with a wider audience and to truly become a published author, then IGNITE is definitely the best place for you. Take your writing from good to phenomenal."

— Damian Culhane

"Writing my story for the Conscious Leaders book helped me understand the impact I can have on others. The process was equally profound and deeply rewarding. Connecting with the other authors through the mastermind sessions made me feel like we were creating a mosaic, and my story is one of the many tiles that makes up the whole picture. I am honored to be published amongst so many other conscious leaders who are set to change the world and make a difference in others' lives. I thank JB Owen and her team for bringing this gift to the world. I have no doubt it will ignite many others in their quest to become more conscious in their daily work and personal lives."

— Catherine Malli-Dawson

"I'm honored to be a part of this book series that reminds the world that EVERYONE has a story to share that can positively impact others. It's a brilliant concept that encourages people with a message to make the time to put their thoughts into words. The remarkable process removes the stress, time and logistical constraints that publishing a solo book presents. And the Ignite team (editors, publisher and fellow authors) almost instantly evolves from strangers to cheerleaders to family."
— Beth Medved Waller

"The Ignite publishing process has been seamless and easy for me. Writing and sharing my story of transformation helped me break through a writer's slump and reignited my enthusiasm to help others in an even bigger way. I enjoyed the opportunity to work with three editors and I am honored to align with JB, Peter and the team to offer inspiration and tools to ignite love and joy around the planet. I am so grateful for all of the support and connections!
— Maggie Reigh

Vishen Lakhiani and JB Owen

FOREWORD BY
JB OWEN

I first met Vishen Lakhiani at an event called Awesomeness Fest in Puerto Vallarta, Mexico. It was an emotional marker for me to attend that event as I had convinced myself it was going to signify a change in my life and be the start of something radically new. I met dozens of amazing people and had countless "ah-ha" moments, all thanks to Vishen and the speakers, trainings, and experiences he and his team brought together that weekend. Vishen was the leader of this transformative program and his message was all about stepping into a new realm of consciousness within yourself.

I didn't actually MEET Vishen during that event. I SAW him up on stage numerous times and noticed him hurrying by, in and out of the jam-packed conference room. I knew OF him, and many of the other participants had spoken with him, but the closest I got was standing beside him while waiting in line at the buffet. I tried to strike up a conversation, but his star-appeal was a bit daunting and I didn't want to sound silly commenting on the asparagus soup or the never-changing Mexican weather. I let our encounter pass by because I was worried he wouldn't have time for me or value what I had to say.

The next year at the same event, taking place in Costa Rica this time, I mustered up the courage to chat with him. I wanted to share that two of my friends (whom I had met at the event the year before) had fallen in love and were on their honeymoon that very day. Yet when I approached him, he kindly asked for a minute as one of his team had just walked up with an important matter. I backed away slowly, feeling like he was much too busy to talk to me and my news wasn't that urgent. Later that day, I saw him again. As I ventured closer, his phone rang. I quickly diverted myself to the left as if we were simply passing each other in the hall. A third opportunity for conversation arose, but when I began sharing my news, he stopped me and said, "Is it possible this can wait? I've got an urgent matter to attend to," and he walked off.

I'll admit my feelings were a bit sensitive. I wasn't thrilled with his response, but I overcame my disappointment and walked up to him one more time that day while he was on his computer at the back of the conference room. I approached him with trepidation as I didn't want to be rejected again. I kept thinking he wouldn't have time for me and I should just abort the whole idea. Rubbing my hands together, I walked over nervously, wanting to share my news. Except before I finished my sentence, he looked up and said, "I'm in the middle of something. Can this wait?"

"Never mind!" I blurted out, feeling fed up with all of his excuses and his dismissive behavior. I hastily turned and walked off. He stood up and called me back, but I just kept walking, calling over my shoulder, "Don't Bother!" I was not impressed and was frankly somewhat hurt by his behavior. I walked back to my seat and sat down to watch the next speaker, who was about to take the stage. For the next hour, I sat there feeling rattled, upset and utterly rejected. My emotions had been triggered and I felt deeply resentful toward him.

When the speech was over and we all rose from our chairs to give the speaker a standing ovation, someone tapped me on my shoulder. I turned around to see Vishen standing right there. "What did you want to tell me?" he asked, mere inches from my face.

I was still fuming inside and again said, "Never mind."

"Why never mind?" he asked, puzzled, and giving me his full attention. "I can listen to you now. What did you want to tell me?"

Something inside of me felt obstinate. "I've tried to talk to you three times today and each time, you have been too busy for me. Obviously, what I have to say isn't important to you." I wasn't using my kindest voice. I started packing up my things, ignoring him as he had ignored me.

"That's not entirely true," he replied calmly, "But obviously you've created this situation and made your interaction with me aligned with your belief system."

"What?!!" I was flabbergasted. My chin almost hit the ground. Who did this guy think he was blaming his rude behavior on? I scoffed and furrowed my brow, completely speechless and at a loss as to what to say next.

He noticed my silence and continued, "Whatever you believe about yourself is what you made happen."

"You're putting this on *me*?" I asked in utter disbelief. "You were completely unavailable every time I approached you! This is NOT my fault."

He smiled, took a deep breath, and with great compassion replied, "You might want to explore that a bit more."

I was dumbstruck... annoyed... and internally pissed off. I couldn't comprehend his meaning and felt appalled that he had had the gall to say that. Our conversation ended and I was left turning in the wind from our unpleasant encounter. I spent much of that evening replaying it in my head, going over every word. I was filled with a sense of injustice for how I felt he had treated me. But his statement of *"Whatever you believe about yourself is what you made happen"* kept playing over and over in my mind. In fact, it echoed in my psyche for close to six months.

What I have come to know now (but didn't know then) was that Vishen was doing what he always does... leading ME to look within myself. His words were meant to provoke thought, instill insight and inspire reflection about the most important thing... my belief systems. He planted a seed in me that began to germinate. An idea I had not previously considered began forming, molding a new neural pathway in my mind. I started looking at my actions differently and analyzing my results. I saw myself from a birds-eye view of how I predisposed my outcomes based on my predetermined thoughts. By analyzing my attitude before and after an encounter, then questioning my state of mind, I saw how I could affect the overall outcome of any situation.

I quickly noticed that when I believed things were going to happen a certain way, they often did. Good or bad. If I had formed a firm opinion of how things were going to unfold, nine times out of ten, they usually went that way. I realized I absolutely had control over my outcomes if I went in with the right attitude from the start. It was liberating and fun. I was, as Vishen says, *bending reality* with my own internal thoughts and predetermining my results.

As I dove deeper into this concept, I started peeling back the layers of why I had so much habitual thinking. Where had I learned those thoughts? And, what triggered me to think that way? I found a lot of answers rooted in my childhood, in the lessons, ideas and concepts that had been put upon me. I also saw how I formed opinions and bought into ideas that became the framework for how I conducted myself as an adult. After much growth and introspection, I re-evaluated my conversation with Vishen and, to my delight, FINALLY understood what he was trying to show me.

I had grown up a latch-key kid with two hard-working entrepreneur parents.

Their businesses required them to work 15 and 16-hour days. Most afternoons, after school, I would take the city bus to my mom's office and linger there, waiting for her to finish and drive me home. I'd spend hours loafing around and passing the time until she was done. I distinctly remember feeling like she had no time for me, that she was too busy and that what I had to share... she wouldn't find important.

I spent most of my childhood feeling this way with both my parents as they were always so busy dealing with customers and employees, completing tasks and spending hours focusing on important papers that had to get done.

Often, I would creep into my parent's office, too timid to bother them. More often, I felt they didn't have time for me and assumed they were too busy, so I'd just veer away and avoid contact. If I did get the courage to share with them, I often felt nervous... the exact same feelings I experienced the first few times I approached Vishen.

I was astonished to admit to myself that I had potentially predisposed meeting him with all the thoughts I had in my head from childhood. I super-imposed those opinions on him by feeling he wouldn't make time for me. That he was too busy to hear what I had to say. And that is exactly what happened between us.

At long last, his words of *"whatever you believe about yourself is what you made happen,"* made sense. I realized what he was trying to tell me. I saw how my aloof reaction and upset behavior was a reflection of how I felt as a child. It was based on my interactions with my parents. I also recognized that even before speaking to him, I had a preconceived idea of what was going to happen and that his "busyness" would result in him treating me in a certain way: the same way I was treated by my parents. I set the whole experience up to mirror the feelings I had as a kid. It was life-changing to see the obvious connection and how it was affecting me in my life today.

In that first encounter, I learned who Vishen is. He's a person who changes lives by awakening you to the next level of your own consciousness. He has spent years working on his own awareness and belief systems so that he can authentically share with others how to do the same in their own lives. He has built a world-class company that offers life-changing programs. And, he has collected the works of countless other leaders to create a platform solely aimed at raising the consciousness of the planet. His mission is to create connect-edness by bringing people together through conscious thinking and mindful intentions. To me, he is the epitome of a Conscious Leader and someone who leads himself before leading others.

Six months after our second encounter, I saw him again in Greece. He was at the back of the conference room, speaking to some other participants. From a few feet away and with no indication from me, he stopped talking to turn in my direction. He gave me the biggest smile... because on my face, was my biggest smile. He excused himself from the conversation and walked toward me. Without a single word passing between us, he walked up to me and we hugged; a deep, caring, welcoming hug that seemed to speak words itself. My heart wanted to thank him and my intentions were pure. Little needed to be said; yet, everything was stated.

He had liberated me from decades of ineffective feelings and limiting beliefs. I felt transformed. I was free to see every encounter at face value and begin every interaction based on the outcomes I wanted to create. Our conversations from that day forward have been one of friendship and camaraderie. He gave me valuable leadership insight that I will forever cherish.

Two years later, when I emailed Vishen to ask him if he would marry me and my fiance in Tallinn, Estonia, I had already decided in my mind that he was going to say "Yes!" His response was immediate, and it was exactly that. Vishen did the work to officiate our wedding in front of hundreds of other like-minded, conscious individuals. My 12-year-old son led me down the aisle toward Peter — a man who is the greatest example I have ever seen of one who loves and leads courageously in his own life.

That was one of the happiest days of my life, and it all started with a thought, an idea and a "knowing" that to have a better life starts with leading your life exactly in the direction of your own dreams. To be a leader starts in the heart. It percolates within and then permeates outward, spreading magically to others. Having a conscious intention is like a beacon; the Universe hears you and then provides. I have learned by watching Vishen over the years that leadership is subjective. One can lead from the heart or from the head. You can lead by force or by example. Vishen has taught me that leading in love is the truest form there is; and that by being conscious of how you lead, you graciously inspire others to do the same.

I am forever grateful for Vishen for leading as he does. He is an example of someone who consciously leads from within WHILE being a leader for so many others. He represents that leadership and consciousness work beautifully together.

Vishen Lakhiani, JB Owen and Peter Geisin. Photo taken by Kersti Niglas: July 14, 2017

Learning to Lead

Throughout this book, you will read numerous stories of people stepping into conscious leadership. They may not be the epic sort of stories you see in movies or on dramatized news channels. Instead, they will be the heart-simmering accounts and mind-centering realizations of awakened individuals *discovering* their role of leadership. These are the stories amplifying the quieter side of leading because each true leader ultimately leads themselves. They use their understanding and inner knowing to propel themselves forward and seek out new and different ways to do life better. They listen to their inner guidance and trust their deep intuition. They desire to elevate as many people as they can and aspire to lead by motivating others to rise higher than where they are themselves.

This book is filled with many examples of how conscious leadership can be done. It is jammed full of realistic examples of every aspect of cohesive leadership. It shows how being a leader takes not just strength and perseverance, but self-worth and self-conviction. How knowing oneself and honoring that is the true reflection of valuing everyone. Leaders lead most effectively by example. Conscious leaders exemplify that ten-fold. They step up first, give full out and always have open arms available. The new paradigm of leadership rests in the heart of leaders devoted to *IGNITING* the planet. This book is designed to inspire all individuals who are stepping into and embracing that gifts of true conscious leadership on a global scale.

Enjoying Your Leadership

In the upcoming pages of this book, you are going to read many stories of men and women leading themselves by leading others. You will see the "supportive" leader and the "compassionate" one. You'll witness them impacting many and clearly see their determination to impact themselves. There is no "right" way to lead. Many in this book have felt tremendous pain and been brought to their knees through hardships. Others have been hurt, abandoned, lost, and ignored in their quest to embody their leadership role. All have had to struggle and rise up from difficulties. None were simply given the keys to any kingdom. They worked tirelessly to become leaders of their own lives first. They vowed to push through any obstacles that might have held them stuck so they could be conscious to encourage each and every one of you.

While collecting these stories, we observed a kindred spirit emerging. The pages were not filled with big, flagrant examples of one person controlling many. The messages were not centered around accolades or achievements. Few, if any, bragged about awards or recognition. Most, if not all the stories, shared the common theme that Conscious Leaders lead in a unique way. They go inward before they go outward. They think before they do, weighing all the options before making a clear decision. Most importantly, they ACT accordingly. They find the Source within them and they discover their own Inner Strength. They search relentlessly and ask nothing of anyone else that they are not willing to do themselves.

We also noticed that the photos of individuals with arms crossed, in power suits, behind a big mahogany desk were stereotypical and unrelatable. The new vision of a Leader was showing up in casual clothing with a genuine smile. They wore pride on their faces and had a twinkle in their eyes. Our leaders were pragmatic, eclectic and sincere. They took leadership seriously and cared less about how they looked or how they were perceived. What they set out to do in the world made all the difference, not how they looked in a photograph. I applaud each and every one of them.

Destined to Lead

We began a deep exploration into what leadership truly is. What does it mean to lead in a conscious way? What is true conscious leadership? How does one define leadership in general? How do consciousness and leadership come together? You are about to find out...

My wish is that when you read through these stories, you are deeply transformed by the examples of leaders guiding others through guiding one's self. I hope that your mind opens and your self-awareness awakens to how powerful you are on your own leadership path. That you feel the strength within the sharing and the supportive intentions behind it. Each author wrote their story so that you may relate to the conscious journey within it. Every story was written with the hopes of lifting you up in your own leadership discovery; designed to encourage you to take the reins in your life and not only hold on, but ride it full out, with the wind in your hair and no desire to slow down or look back.

We all know that it is one thing to lead under necessity and strife, but it is another to lead with love, compassion, and collective consciousness. You will see throughout this book that self-realization is the common theme. Devotion, empathy, and consideration are constantly present. Intuition, self-love, self-growth, and divine purpose are the four corners of the lives each one of these authors has created. Their leadership is in leading themselves first before they ever felt they could lead another. That is what makes this book so unique and unprecedented. They have lived it first. It isn't a theory or an idea. They do more than consider it, they have become it; and now they have written about it to encourage you.

As you turn the pages, you will find each story begins with a *Power Quote*. It is like a mantra or a battle cry. I believe every leader should have one. It is a statement that pushes you to do even more and makes you think a little deeper. It is what your bumper sticker would say, or what you'd write on your office wall. Power quotes are that sentence or phrase that you might repeat over and over when the tears are flowing from both life's hardships and it's rewards, and each Power Quote is designed to remind you of what you have inside — *exceptionalness*.

Next, you will be able to read their *Intentions*. These are the author's goals and aspirations — what they wish their story will do for you. It is a personal message, filled with meaning and purpose. They want to IGNITE You to begin living your most extraordinary life and they share what they hope their story will prompt in you. Their intentions set the tone for their message and are designed to both awaken and elevate your thinking.

Then, the *Story* follows. It is an account of each author stepping into leadership and consciously awakening to the *Ignite* moment that started their new awakening. We all have *Ignite* moments in our lives that change us, define us and set us on a new path or trajectory for life. These stories are those moments, told in the most genuine and heart-felt way. They show that we all have *powerful* moments that not only define us but ultimately transform us.

Once you have finished their inspiring stories, you will find a list of *Ignite Action Steps*. These are the tangible things they did to support and define themselves. Each author shares easy-to-do, practical tips for you to try and implement immediately. They are the processes and practices that worked in their lives. Each one is different and unique, just like you, and is proven to yield magnificent results when done consistently.

We all know actions speak louder than words; never is that more accurate than in leadership. Action IS the key. To move the needle forward in your life, we encourage you to try one new action step each day and do it consecutively for 30 days. We have offered you 35 different action steps to try, so find the one that works best for you. Each one is potentially the step that could change your life forever. Start with one that calls to you the strongest, and follow through to see magnificent and significant change throughout your life.

Take note, others may be looking to you for leadership. Your kids, siblings, friends, neighbors, and even your spouse may be watching to see how you lead so they can imitate and follow you. This is the moment to step into new conscious realizations in your own life and make it rewarding. You get to decide how to live and how you will transform yourself. Make the most of it. Let these stories remind you that you can do anything, be anything and accomplish anything you choose. You can happily move forward and find your bliss. Your life can be absolutely wonderful on every level; you just have to decide first and then move consciously forward in that direction.

Lead with Heart

We know that many people read compilation books to be inspired. If you feel that your story is still unfolding, or you're trying to figure it all out, we are with you. We have all been through hardships and go through them numerous times in our lives. Our stories show our successes in spite of all that. We still waffle, like everyone else; we have just practiced and re-practiced using our leadership muscles to pick ourselves back up. The greatness behind of all of these leaders is behind you now. We support you full-out and will cheer you on as you uncover your own leadership skills. We all extend our hands should you need a bit of support, some advice or a friend to confide in. We offer ourselves should you ever want to reach out because something we said resonated with you or what we shared was exactly what you needed to hear. Please know we are all accessible and eager to connect, so please feel free to find us.

Leaders need to stick together. We need to support one another as we rise and flourish. We need to help each other along the way. For everyone to benefit, everyone must help. On your road to leadership, you will be challenged and confronted; but if you are true to your inner knowing, those challenges will be met with the purest intentions. A leader is someone who takes a chance, follows their heart and overcomes obstacles along the way. Seek out all that you need so you can make powerful decisions about your own life. Focus on you, your aspirations, and talents. Accentuate your gifts and shine your light. Give all you can to your expansion because you are worth it, 100 percent.

I am ignited by the idea of you turning the next page and reading the many stories of consciousness and leadership. I am excited that you are about to read about another person stepping into the very essence of their own life. It might be filled with success or hardships. It may be riddled with conquest or failure. Either way, their stories are a gateway to the next possibility for your own life. You can be inspired by what they shared and decide to go out and shine, or feel energized to go forth in your life with goosebumps on your arms and a zeal in your step. That's the real essence of life. That's what makes it juicy and exciting. It isn't all or none; it's how you lead yourself through and emerge on the other side of your own volition.

The stories you are about to embark on are all our stories. They supercede race, culture, age and even gender. They are the human story, the experience of being a Being on this earth. They touch at the very heart of belonging, connecting and sharing. They are raw, real and unrestricted... that's what makes them so amazingly engaging. They cut through all the "stuff" we want people to see and shine a light directly on the heart of who we were born to be.

Ignite was created to ignite others and impact humanity. Our mandate is to do more, share more and spread a conscious positive message to as many people as possible. We believe in the human connection. We believe that power comes from being heard, being seen and belonging to something greater than one's self. We invite you to Ignite others. To let your story be heard, share your experiences, and find your voice. We pride ourselves in bringing people together, offering a solution, giving back and doing something good for the planet. That is the mission and purpose behind IGNITE. There is power when one person touches the heart of another and a spark begins, be it inspiration, love, support, encouragement, compassion or belief. We all can be a leader in living a kind and gracious life.

May you have many ignite moments that transform your life into the amazing person you were meant to be.

JB Owen

Please know that every word written in this book, every letter in these pages, has been meticulously crafted with fondness, encouragement and a clarity not just to inspire you but to transform you. Many people in this book stepped up to share their stories for the very first time. They courageously revealed the many layers of themselves and exposed their weaknesses like few leaders do. Additionally, they spoke authentically from the heart and wrote what was true for them. We could have taken their stories and aimed for some "brule" defining perfection, following every editing rule; but instead, we chose to leave their unique and honest voices intact. We overlooked exactness to foster individual expression. These are their words, their sentiments, their explanations. We let their personalities shine in their writing so you would get the true sense of who each of them is completely. That is what makes IGNITE so unique. Authors serving others, stories igniting humanity. No filters.

SAM BEARD

*"To move any mountain, all you need is vision,
persistence, two toothpicks and a starting line."*

**My 50-year message is simple; and it is working for more than one million
people ages four to 104. I wish for the reader to see my public service story as
an open invitation with a step-by-step roadmap. ANYONE CAN DO WHAT
I HAVE DONE. My intention is to encourage everyone to believe they can
do what I have accomplished, in their corner of the world. Accept my GIFT.
Think BIG! Think I CAN! Create a SIMPLE PLAN. GET STARTED!**

GET OFF YOUR ASS AND MAKE A DIFFERENCE!

At age 12, in my heart and core, I wanted to help others. I was the do-gooder
of the three Beard boys. If someone was bullied, I befriended them and made
them the class hero. Service has guided my life for 68 years.

Often, I relive the worst day of my life… I am 29 years old. I am working
for my idol, Senator Robert Kennedy, in Bedford-Stuyvesant, an inner-city
poverty area in Brooklyn, New York. Our shared dream is to open opportunities
for all Americans and end poverty.

The Senator is shot and murdered.

I am in tears. My life as I know it is over.

The nation is in tears. I don't think I can go on.

At the bottom of despair, I remember the message of the Kennedys: that
one person CAN MAKE A DIFFERENCE.

With no money in sight, I returned to my one-room apartment and launched a nonprofit.

Over the next 20 years, I had the honor of creating and running programs for four US Presidents — Richard Nixon, Gerald Ford, Jimmy Carter and Ronald Reagan — working through our nonprofit National Development Council (NDC).

The NDC President Ford and President Nixon initiatives changed African-American and Hispanic business lending in America. In 1968, all the banks of New York City refused to lend $1 million to Blacks and Hispanics. In banking terms, they were "red-lining." Across the country, Blacks and Hispanics were 16 percent to 19 percent of America's population. They owned 1/1000th of one percent of America's business assets. My nonprofit energized more than 3,000 volunteers. They helped hundreds of minority-owned businesses. In two to three years, the New York banks were lending more than $50 million a year to minority business owners. This success attracted the attention of President Nixon and led to my first presidential initiative. This resulted in the largest transfer of resources into minority-owned financial institutions in the history of America. At that time, there were only 36 banks owned by minorities.

It all began when my mentor suggested I make a program for the President in 1969. I was 29 and I laughed at him. Me, phoning up the White House to say, "I have a program for the president, put me through." Then, one sentence changed my life. My mentor said, "If you don't try, you'll never succeed." So I went to Washington and was tenacious. I learned I had to repeat myself, and my vision. In 18 months, I was in the White House. Not with the president, but with Len Garment, who ran everything for domestic policy.

My success began when I met Alan Steelman, the director of President Nixon's Minority Business Council. He was my age and I connected with him. After almost two years, he trusted me. Together, we went to the White House to meet Len Garment in person. I expected just the three of us to be in the meeting. Suddenly, there were 40 people from different departments and jurisdictions; 20 sat on my left and the other 20 sat on my right. Len Garment started the meeting, "We like your idea," he stated. All 40 people suddenly had big smiles on their faces, as if they had just created a program with the president of the United States. Garment continued, "You have proposed a $50 million deposit increase. We want the president's goal to be $100 million."

My response started with, "But…" All 40 people turned and stared at me. "Who is this young kid screwing up our presidential program?" must have been on their minds. I told Mr. Garment, "Walking over to the White House with no money in my savings account, the largest number I could think of was $50 million. If you allow me to be the chairman of the program, I am not going to fail. Period. Can we announce $50 million and I will do everything in my power to get you the $100 million?"

He laughed, "Nice try, it's $100 million or nothing."

I said, "Fine, I agree." That was the end of the meeting. I had learned how Washington worked.

I never saw those 40 people again, and off I went to work.

President Nixon's 100 Million Dollar Minority Bank Deposit Program

In 1969, there were 36 Black and Hispanic banks with total deposits of $405 million. They were lending $60 million to minority businesses.

Conversely, the "white" banking system had total deposits of $800 billion, claiming they were lending $100 million to minority businesses. Since they weren't lending $1 million in New York, there was no way that number was correct across the country. President Nixon's goal was to increase the deposits in the minority banks by $100 million dollars in total. The Nixon program increased deposits in the minority banks by $255 million, which was the largest transfer of financial resources to minority-owned financial institutions in the history of America. Because of our program, the minority banks tripled in number and the deposits reached more than $2 billion in the next few years.

I was on a roll, and carried on with the NDC President Carter and Reagan initiatives. NDC's Carter and Reagan programs led to the creation of more than 10 million jobs in low-income communities.

Once I had done one presidential program, I realized I could keep doing it. Few people can honestly state they created and chaired programs for eight presidents of the United States. My attributes were simplicity, positive energy, big ideas, and persistence. Thousands of people have this capability. I laugh. I had no competition. I was the only person who thought I could create a program of this magnitude. And so I did.

I did what I enjoyed doing. Looking back, my initiatives started with an idea and a tiny pebble. As I and my team pushed the pebble down the hill, it gained momentum and became a landslide of success.

Founding the Jefferson Awards with Jacquline Kennedy Onassis

Since I had worked with Bobby Kennedy, I would see Jackie Kennedy once or twice a year. In 1971, at a cocktail party, I was talking to my friend and saw that Jackie was walking across the room. As she got closer, I looked behind myself to see who she was going to meet. I was standing next to a wall. I realized she was coming over to see me. I was anxious, but not overwhelmed.

Jackie said, "You have a reputation for getting things done. What ideas do you have now?" This was in the middle of Watergate, and I responded, "I think there should be a Nobel Prize for Service in America." Much to my delight, Mrs. Onassis went on for 10 minutes about what a great idea that was. I did have enough gumption to say, "Jackie, I will call you tomorrow morning and, if you agree to chair the project, I will set it up."

She agreed, despite being bombarded across America and around the world. I was elated and once again went to work.

In 1986, I appointed a new president at the NDC to continue running Economical Development, making myself the chairman. I set off to do other initiatives, such as running the Jefferson awards with Jackie Kennedy and seeking to add savings accounts at Social Security. The NDC was paying my salary and I built up my pension over a 40-year period.

A Second Personal Crisis and Meditation Taught An Old Dog New Tricks.

28 years later, at age 75, the NDC president said the pension I had built up was not mine and there would be no more income coming to me. I didn't sleep or work throughout the one-year legal battle that ensued. I was devastated. Suddenly after working for 40 years, everything was gone. Ugh. Ouch!

I felt I didn't deserve this. I picked myself up and went back to work.

From all outward appearances, at age 75, I was viewed as a "success." I helped design and implement public service programs for eight U.S. Presidents. My resume was filled with how I took ideas from ground zero, building them up into major programs affecting millions of lives. My career accomplishments stood out and, on the home front, my family and three children were thriving.

Just one problem… the interruption of income and the loss of my pension created debilitating stress. My life was turned upside down. The solution came in a form that was astoundingly simple and profoundly life-changing: Meditation.

I am very thankful, as that conflict set me on a whole new and transformational path. I am hardly the stereotype for anything that might be considered woo-woo. A graduate of Yale and Columbia, I am more Brooks Brothers than tie-dyed. I had a childhood where sitting was frowned upon when you could be up and being more productive.

The die was cast within me. All these influences, from parents to schooling, presidents to mentors, all combined to teach me to *"think big."* They went out of their way to support me. I feel the Universe delivered them. I learned from others how to turn ideas into actions and actions into movements.

My curiosity about that mystical, spiritual and emotional dimension (to which meditation provides a gateway) persisted through the decades — no doubt dropping hints along the way that maybe I should do something about this deficit in my life's patterns. My whimsical mind found notions like reincarnation and past lives exotic and fascinating, but far afield from my lapsed Catholic upbringing. I read up on therapies that used hypnotism to help patients pop into past lives and heal from trauma. I even spent two days with a noted expert seeking to uncover possible past lives. Basically, nothing worked. I did get a flickering image of a Roman soldier with leather armor, a skirt, sandals and a sword — like Kirk Douglas in the film *Spartacus.* This could have been an image of a past life, but I really concluded that my urge to have a successful outcome might have conjured it up, since Kirk Douglas was on the Jeffersons Awards board.

I was also given some tapes to help relax the mind that, in retrospect, I'm glad I held onto. Years later, when the onslaught of stress came full force, I took out those dusty tapes and used them to see if I could get some relief. The sonorous voice and relaxing music helped calm my nerves and allowed me to work productively three to four hours a day while wading through strident and toxic negotiations to resolve my situation.

As I became more experienced in these daily, one-hour meditation sessions, I found to my surprise an added bonus that I could also seek guidance to help restore my life. As I began listening to the intuitions I was receiving, I found that I had uncovered what is best described as a direct path to my own intuition.

The basic idea of using meditation to reach an elevated level of consciousness was certainly not new to me. A half-century earlier, I had read about calming the mind through meditation to connect to higher energy. But every time I tried, I calmed my mind and fell sound asleep. Since insomnia was never an issue for me, I didn't see much benefit and quit. The point of meditation is to reduce stress. When you reduce stress, your brain grows and the prefrontal cortex opens up to creativity, intuition, compassion and flow.

Coincidentally (or maybe not), an old colleague who I had not seen in 10 years called and said he was coming to town. When we met for coffee, I shared my crisis with him. To my surprise, my friend was a global expert in the untapped powers of the mind and self-realization. Without hesitation, he virtually unlocked the door to a whole library of books and life-changing seminars. I devoured the list of books and began attending various seminars both in the U.S. and abroad.

All the while, many remarkable things started happening, many of which defy logical explanation. It is safe to say that what came in the wake of my crisis has been an unfolding adventure into the realm of human potential that has been more exciting than anything I've experienced in my life. The exploration into my psyche was eye-opening. My priorities were backward. Career, family, friends — instead of family, friends and career. I uncovered all types of personality flaws that had been tempered by my predominantly left-brain existence and career activism.

The more I meditated, the more I learned and gradually began filling in the gaps. Our parents are our first teachers, but typical of their generation, they were hardly the hugging, touchy-feely types. So, to make up for that, I am learning much later in life how the longest and hardest (and the most rewarding) journey for me is the 18 inches from my brain to my heart.

I am becoming more adept at how to better love, empathize and connect with others; to understand their minds and better listen to their priorities. In short, I am learning emotional intelligence. I greet each day with gratitude and excitement about newfound possibilities. I want to do whatever I can to spread the word. This is my new life's work. The next big program I build will cut to the chase and will be the most important one of all. With all that meditation has given to me, I know my best work lies ahead.

June 24, 2019 — My 80th Birthday — A New Beginning

For my 80th birthday, my family took me to a Georgia resort to celebrate. I was asked many times what it feels like to be 80. I had never thought of that. Before my speech, I had my answer. In my first 80 years, I had finally learned how to be a better husband, father, and friend. In my career, I had learned how to collaborate and move mountains. At age 80, I was at the starting line and raring to go. In the next 20 years, I will certainly have the biggest impact I have ever had using forms of mindfulness, compassion and service to CONNECT and ELEVATE human behavior.

I am living proof that you can teach an old dog new tricks! What new tricks do you want to learn? You too can develop a life of service, expand your consciousness, step into leadership and move mountains. GET STARTED!

Ignite Action Steps

Step One: If you are simple, joyous, and positive, people will like you.

Step Two: Ask. "What is my IDEA to MAKE A DIFFERENCE?" Listen to your heart and intuition to find your passion.

Step Three: Create your plan, taking no more than half an hour. Again, trust your intuition. Ask. What three or four things do you need to do to carry out your plan? Keep it simple.

Step Four: Get Started. Be persistent. Engage a team. Change your plan as you proceed.

Sam Beard - USA
President, GIFT Global
www.GIFTGlobal.org
www.SamBeard.org

LORI LENNOX

"Sometimes, it is hard to know what to do;
but once we know, it is even harder not to do it."

I share my story in hopes that some piece of it, some part of it, might evoke your own deeper question so that you might ask yourself, "What is my truth? How can I serve? What is the yearning of my soul?" So that you, as I did, can find your way home.

A VAGABOND AND A CROOKED COTTAGE

My dad used to tell me I had a 'vagabond soul.' He said it was one of the things he loved most about me. Given I was around seven years old when I first heard this, I had to look up the definition: Vag-a-bond *n: wandering from place to place without a fixed home.* As a child, I was always looking for truth, to make sense of the world, to make sense of myself *in* the world, for harmony, peace, and goodness. There are plenty of 'Lori' stories about that girl. The girl who would take off for hours in the streets of our town or deep into the woods behind our house, learning about life and humanity that way. She was a most curious seeker, wishing she could make it all better and right; a quest beyond her years. That's the backstory, with the foreshadowing. Now, we fast forward.

In the late 1990s, thirty years later, I was living a good life. Many would say I was living the dream. I'd arrived to sought-out destinations, long ago mapped, and to measures of success all along intended. I was following the only path I could see, informed by my life's conditioning and society's script. I had quite a flourishing corporate career working for best-in-class companies; a rising star, consistently elevating as a leader. I'd created stability, security and comfort. Security, a non-negotiable necessity to me, matched by my steadfast commitment to super-responsibility. I was always the girl (who became the woman) reaching for rungs, higher rungs, new rungs, new ladders. Less of a climber and more of a reacher, mostly to that which seemed out of reach. I'd get there to that next rung, that next place; barely. I would stabilize, and then catch up to all that it asked of me. And then I'd reach again. I'd done it. I was doing it. Success! By many of my preconceived notions, I had arrived, materially evidenced by the trimmings, my fancy cars, my lovely things, my titles and corner offices. Abundance, indeed. "Looks like you're living the dream!" "Yes," from the outside. On the inside? Generally "yes" too, for a long time... Until I wasn't.

I can recall in the memory of my cells the dissonance that began to grow in me at this time. Starting as a seed and spreading into a bed of weeds; taking over the landscape of me.

I began to feel vacuous, in the empty kind of way. At first, a small nagging wanting my attention. An unsettledness. A question that was stirring. One that, for a while, I couldn't specifically grasp or identify. It was just there, day by day, turning month by month... this growing, gnawing feeling of a hole inside of me.

But my life was so perfect. "What the heck is wrong with me? Look at this life. I am extraordinarily blessed. Yet, I feel like I'm stagnating and pushing my life up a hill. What's wrong?"

It was like I was a character in a movie and all looked so good on the screen, yet the heroine was silently suffering within. Earning a self-awarded gold star by keeping her discomfort all to herself. She was the woman with the perfect life, after all.

Along came what comes when we are living in the questions and mining for answers. Or, at least, when I am. When I am looking for answers, particularly to my own puzzles, I begin to ask everybody questions, lots of questions... looking for a thread to pull, a resonance to resonate with, a dot to connect to, a light bulb to shed light on the elusive. Me, the seeker of truth, curious, committed to the inquiry. Me, the vagabond soul, always needing to know what is true. *It is the process of my life.*

I ran into an old friend. I hadn't seen her in over a decade. She had radically changed careers since I had seen her last. More importantly, she was radically happy. "Wow, how did that happen? How did she choose this? How did she discover this holy grail of hers?" She shared... She'd spent time with a career consultant and he had led her to the discovery of this new path of work, and to her purpose. *Purpose?* This was in 1998, a time when these newer-age terms were not yet mainstream, or at least not familiar to me. Purpose, a concept entirely foreign yet mysteriously comforting to the seeker within. "Interesting. I'm curious. I'll call him."

I called him that day.

I spent three months with this character of a gentleman. I wish I could thank him to the heavens, but sadly, I don't even remember his name. I remember his office. It was more like a den, disheveled and mismatched in a hodgepodge kind of way, with a dog. The dog was always in his office, too. A golden retriever; I remember that much. My inner narrative, "I'm not so sure about this. Thousands of dollars for this endeavor. Out of bounds, out of comfort zone. Am I being super-responsible?" I wondered. At the same time, I had an equally strong conviction that this was where I needed to be. An inner echo: "Once you let go of fear, the truth will appear." Every morsel of my being needed to be in this den with this dog and this man, perhaps an angel for whom I have no name. I was doing card sorts, assessments, essays, and plenty of other odd exercises. Our contract was for him to deliver to me a suggested vocation that would leverage my gifts, align with my values, and meet the desires I had outlined for my life.

"Leadership Coach."

Coach? "Yes, coach. In a business setting." I'd never heard of such a thing. This was a while before coaching became a more conventionally accepted or validated profession.

"Really? I can have a *job* that is in service to others, that helps others, that is in the center of my wheelhouse, without going back to university to seek a Ph.D. or another multiple-year specialized degree? And this can be an abundant career?" Yes, he assured me. At my next and final visit, he handed me a hefty binder full of material on leadership coaching as a profession.

I was excited; I was on fire; I was inspired. I did extensive research on this prospective career path. I was ready for it to be a big "yes," and a big "now!" The binder became my treasure; its contents my path to freedom. And then, just then and right then, I was recruited by a world-class high-tech company in Silicon Valley. I was offered an incredible leadership opportunity with millions of dollars in equity as a reward. These were once in a lifetime opportunities; everyone in the Valley knew this. Here was my invitation. Five years to be fully vested. Five. I can do it. This was in the early days of the dotcom boom. Unimaginable wealth was being realized by the day (on paper) by a lucky number of *right place, right time* people – and I could be one of those. I actually wouldn't have done it just for me, for I was dispiritedly weary of those ladders. But for my family? Without question. To be able to take care of them – my mom and dad and sisters – I couldn't say no. YES! Definitely, reluctantly, I said, "Yes, of course."

Do you know what is weird? At least to me, because I don't understand why I did it?

I threw away my binder.

Perhaps I had to let it go subconsciously to fully step in.

I began living the dream that wasn't my dream. Stretched, uncomfortable, successful once again, blessed financially and otherwise. I don't forsake the good nor the gifts for a single moment. I met my future husband, the father of my son at this time. So, of course, I was exactly where I was supposed to be. Life is graciously reverent and perfect that way. No matter how dissonant I was in my work, no matter how much I wanted to be creative and free in my *purpose*, it was clear that I was working toward a different purpose. 'Focus and look forward'. We were living a lovely life, the best of times in many ways. My partner and I had a flat in Paris. We didn't live there full-time but used it as a working base. We were both global leaders in our businesses, needing to be in Europe often. It was a pure juxtaposition. It was part magical, part hollow; a different bubble, this one of effervescent promises with hues of future dreams.

Then, the bubble burst.

We were in Paris. It was the spring of 2001. For weeks, our stock price had been plummeting; no more "riches by the day on paper." We awoke one morning to news of another sizable overnight loss. The value of my options was now lower than when I had joined the company. Of course, all my comrades were shaken, but as for me, I was struck on a different level. I was overwhelmed with an urgent need to reckon with my truth. So I took off, as this wanderer often did, into the streets of Paris. I walked for hours, for city blocks, for miles. The voice, the stirring from years before, was demanding my attention. I walked and walked and walked, and let it all come.

Am I willing to trade stability for joy?

Am I willing to trade predictability for passion?

Am I willing to trade securely living in dissonant mediocrity to living in my truth, in the uncomfortable unknown, for at least a little while?

Am I willing to live on the precipice until I find stable ground?

Am I willing to trade clinging to the old to reach for the bounty that is my calling?

Am I willing to believe in me? To jump with no net?

Somebody once said to me, "You can wait to find your wings before you jump, or you can jump and find them on the way down."

Wait or jump? Wait or jump?

Four hours of walking later, I was lost on the streets of Paris. In 2001, there were no smartphones with maps and a GPS. I love those French'ies, but with my poor French... well, no one would help me with directions. I viscerally remember the scene. In time, I found my way back to the flat. Lost and then found, literally and metaphorically. The vagabond soul was heading home as if for the first time. Heading home to herself, this time. I was clear.

I guess there really is something to springtime in Paris.

"I am done," I shared with my partner. "I can no longer say no to my soul. I won't. Not for another day." When and whether the stock options would ever return to a level of value for me, didn't matter. "I am done."

Everyone thought I was crazy. I mean, like, *everyone*. This was a time of economic crisis, chaos, and loss; fear and scarcity for many, most especially in the valley where I'd planted my roots and tethered my hopes and dreams.

"What? You're going to do what? So many are losing their jobs and you're going to leave your coveted, high paying, secure career?" I'm fortunate that through most of my life, people have generally believed in me. But not this time. Most people generally thought I was bonafide crazy. No one gave me permission.

That was just the beginning.

I could not have imagined what was to come. Or perhaps more accurately, how I was to un-become. To un-become to then become.

All I could see from where I stood on the precipice was that I would be stepping into the path of coaching as a profession; specifically, leadership coaching. I would extensively pursue training to become the best coach that I could be.

But first, to let go.

I rented out my home. Sold my "too fancy, anyway" car. Gave away stuff. Downsized, simplified, to earn this right, super-responsibly, within myself, to make this bold move. I moved into a crooked cottage, cobwebs and all. I knew it was crooked because when I dropped anything cylindrical on the floor, it would roll to one side. I loved my crooked cottage. It was my refuge, my sanctuary, and my launchpad, all in one. Of the many homes I've lived in and loved, it was my favorite. It was the symbol of my courage and my freedom, and the place of rebirth.

What I thought was to be a vocation, and determinedly, a successful one, became an evocation – an unpredictable yet perfect shake-up of my existence.

It was the beginning of a perpetual awakening. I'd thought it would be a rather linear parlay from being a leader to coaching a leader, but I had yet to understand the depths of the responsibility I was stepping into. I had yet to grasp the opportunity that came with standing in service to another. As I stepped onto this path of transformation in order to help others transform, it became clear how much work *I* had to do. My inner work. My ego work. To walk the talk, to be the teacher, the guide, the coach. Otherwise, I'd be a fraud. This deep excavation is not for the faint of heart. Once we wake up to full accountability of self, it is hard to run and hide from ourselves, no matter how much we might want to.

I could not have imagined this by-product of my reckoning with my own truth. To be wide open… to undo, uncover, dissolve and dismantle my unconscious unconsciousness… In many ways, I had to die unto myself to rebirth into this privilege that I had claimed. To teach, I first had to become the student. To guide, I had to become the coordinates of the compass. To coach, I had to know how to be THAT kind of leader. A conscious leader who leads others to their own consciousness, evolutions, and transcendences. This was then, and this is still now. I will always be a work in progress; an awakening in progress. The journey is endless.

I'm often told by my clients what a difference our work has made in their lives, in their leadership, and in their wisdom, resourcefulness and success. As much as that humbly brings me joy, another truth is the reflection that each brings to me, them as teacher and I as student, us in a parallel process, is a gift beyond measure. In elevating my clients, I elevate myself.

The butterfly effect is a small change at one place in a complex system that can have large effects elsewhere. With leadership comes utmost responsibility, affect, and impact.

My work is my growth and my passion. My leadership is my privilege. No more crooked cottage, although most definitely, it is minted as a lighthouse in my memory. Whatever I had let go of has been returned to me in volumes. I've been able to help my family still, perhaps more from wisdom and in service, than in any other way.

There is so much more to come. I am now an activist of consciousness as I expand my work and leadership into other realms. The vagabond soul made its way home to the place inside that existed the whole time. It wasn't about finding my way to something or somewhere else; it was about finding my way to who I am.

It was a journey of a thousand miles to get me here, no different from yours. What would you do if you listened to the whispers (or the clanging bells) of your own soul's yearnings? What would you be willing to let go of? To un-become? To become? To find your way home? What would be your first single step to set free the vagabond in you?

IGNITE ACTION STEPS

- **Self-Inquiry:** If you fully believed in yourself, what would you do or try? What are you willing to let go of and un-become? In what ways are you hiding from yourself? To what are you attached? What is your unique gift to bring to the world in service?

- **Take a single step…** The first step.

- **Become a student of consciousness.** Find your teachers. (Because *"once you know what to do, it is harder not to do it."*)

- **Be the witness behind your thoughts.** Live in the habitual loop of discovery, awareness, action, and accountability, and repeat. This is how new realities are formed.

- **Be present and grateful** for the blessings of you and of now.

- **Take a walk** in the springtime in Paris?!

Find your way home.

Lori Lennox - USA
Executive Coach, Speaker, Author, Consciousness Activist
www.lorilennox.com

JB OWEN

"Lead with Love."

It is my intention that this story awakens something new inside of you. That, from it, you see the importance of stepping into your life intentionally, with conscious awareness and clear direction. That you rise to your greatest potential and lead with your truest heart. That something I have written stirs your soul, unleashes your desires and unharnesses your deepest wishes, far beyond what you knew before. That, by reading it, you find the leader that lies within you, marching forth with all the love you have.

HOW YOU PLAY THE GAME

I remember my 18th birthday quite fondly. It was three days after I graduated from high school. It was hot that June weekend and the air seemed to crackle in the mid-afternoon heat from the beating sun. I was happy to be both free and liberated, all in one fell swoop. I was done with school and eager to step into adulthood.

For my birthday present, my mom bought me a ticket to a 4-day event called The Pursuit of Excellence. It was not a typical gift for someone my age. My friends were getting cars and travel vouchers; class rings and computers. I wasn't sure what to expect from something that had both the word *pursuit* and *excellence* in the title, but I was willing to give it a try. I went eagerly out of respect for my mom and out of my own curiosity as to what "excellence" was all about.

I was the only one there under 30 and I felt the wide gap in ages between myself and my closest peer. Most of the others stood around drinking coffee and chatting while I stuck close to the door. I hated coffee and hadn't mastered the art of small talk, so I found myself playing with some lint at the bottom of my pocket. Quite quickly, I felt out of place. I shuffled into the main room, sitting close to the back. The event started out harmlessly enough with everyone getting to know one another while sharing ideas and thoughts on how to improve their lives. The female facilitator was a stunning woman in her late 40s, both articulate and well poised. I admired her immediately, so I took copious notes of all the things she suggested.

On the third day of the event, after the dinner hour, the facilitator told us we would be playing what she called, "The Game" for the rest of the evening. She split us into two equal groups and divided us into two separate rooms. She then explained that we had to ask trivia questions back and forth between our groups to score points. The questions also had to be unanimously agreed upon by everyone. The team with the highest number of points would win, and we had to reach a certain number of points to end the game and go home.

Immediately, a handful of people took charge of our group, firing off tough questions and dominating the conversation. Some of the less aggressive people sat back and simply watched; not getting involved or saying very much. Some participants thought only about strategy, wondering how best to ensure a win, while others wanted it to be easy going and let the opposing team score more points to make it so they would undoubtedly win. That upset the few who were competitive and high pressured; they were determined to win at all costs and couldn't even comprehend giving the other team any kind of advantage.

The discussion went on for an excruciating 40 minutes before our team came up with a question for the other group that we could all agree upon. It was a fair question, not too easy or too hard. The consensus was to test the waters first and see what the other team would ask us so that we knew how hard of a question to strike back with. As our answerable question went off to them, we listened intently to the one we got in return. It was an extraordinarily difficult question that no one in the room knew the answer to.

This provoked a harsh debate by everyone. Some were mad for being too kind to them with our weak question. Others wanted revenge and plotted to come up with an even harder question they would never know the answer to. Some were blamed for making it too easy, while others began jostling to take charge and fix what the previous leaders had messed up. A few got their feelings hurt and shifted to the back of the room, while others checked out completely and stopped paying attention to the diehards that were bent on scoring more. The game went on for hours with questions going back and forth repeatedly. Some were obvious give-away questions while others were exceptionally hard. Eventually, it was close to midnight and our group had grown both frustrated and disgruntled. People were losing their patience and wanting to forfeit the questions just to go home. Others were cheering endlessly to keep going, while a few were nurse-maiding and counseling the ones who were pouting and pissed off at the more aggressive leaders.

Before a winner was fairly declared, the facilitator came back into the room to give us an update. She calmly told us that the game was over... and no one had won. A few participants shouted out, disgruntled for not continuing to a win! Some grumbled under their breath about how the game was rigged and no one could succeed. The majority of the group cheered with delight at the prospect of finally going home. A gambit of emotions ran through the group, from frustration to relief, then disappointment to anger. People were both happy and mad at how the game was ending and had strong opinions about who they felt had actually won.

I noticed that there seemed to be a lot of attachment to either winning, declaring a tie or forfeiting an outcome altogether. People disagreed and debated with one another as to how they would have done it differently or what they would have accomplished if they were in charge. There was a lot of blaming and finger pointing. Overall, few were happy with having spent so many hours playing a game with no obvious winner or loser. Most were tired, fed up and emotionally drained.

I wasn't sure what to make of the entire evening. My life to that point had consisted of biology classes and cheerleading practices. I had never observed adults in teams, trying to make group decisions amidst personal opinions and social dynamics. I had seen my parents disagree, but more often than not, they settled things amicably based on facts and priorities. That evening was filled with opinions based on ego, comparison, and one-up-manship. I saw people splitting off into small sub-groups and bad-mouthing one another, while others ignored the group or cheekily tossed in sarcastic comments just to rile everyone up.

As an observer, I noticed there was a clear delineation in how people interacted. There were the leaders, the detractors, the sympathizers and the clowns. People instinctively took on one of these roles right out of the gate. They naturally led with grace and ease, or they started out cynical and suspicious of the rules and guidelines. I witnessed individuals immediately jump into making sure the group was happy and that everyone had a say. They wanted to ensure feelings were recognized and no one felt left out. A small cluster of people ran the humor wheel. They joked around endlessly, vying for comical relief and doing little more than keeping the team entertained and laughing.

What was even more fascinating were the roles people adopted once they felt frustrated or disappointed. As the hours ebbed on, there were some who started out with one attitude and then suddenly switched to another. The guy who began the game as a leader quickly became a detractors as he was teased and questioned about his early decisions. Another, who was called out for being too sensitive by wanting to let the other team win, turned into a clown, mocking the whole process and being foolish to get attention. A woman who was at first rejecting everything we proposed turned into a leader when the group got frustrated and wanted to quit. I saw others consoling and commiserating with whoever they were sitting beside, only to then get up and move to a different chair next to someone they resonated more closely with. Two men who had agreed at the start shifted onto opposite sides of the spectrum and flung insults back and forth. People moved from taking a lead and including the whole group to getting mad and wanting nothing to do with anyone. One person even left the game without permission from the facilitator and despite everyone insisting they remain.

It was a marvel to watch it all. I saw human behavior at its finest and its worst, confined in a single room, with no clearly defined boss, nor any actual roles or responsibilities. As the youngest there, I was both perplexed and mystified. I didn't fully understand what got people so riled up with one another, nor why winning and losing was such a trigger. My head was spinning with all the opinions and my heart was pounding in anticipation of what would happen next.

In perfect personal development fashion, the witty facilitator only smiled kindly at all of us. She let the conversation and disappointment die down before she spoke what I consider to be the first (and one of the biggest) Ignite moments in my entire life.

She said, "How you played this game… is how you play life."

That sentence was like an explosion in my head. I realized I had sat in my chair that entire evening and not said one single word. Hours had passed, votes had been made, decisions had been debated... and I had no input into any of it. I just sat there like a stump on a log, observing, watching, analyzing, but not participating. I didn't contribute. I didn't add anything. I certainly didn't disagree with anyone. I didn't think of a question, have an answer or come up with a single thought the entire evening. In fact, what I had done was let everyone decide *for* me. I was easily persuaded, voted with the majority and did what others suggested. I wanted to fit in. I didn't voice my opposing thoughts because I was content to let the "older people" decide. I thought I was too young to have anything valuable to say and felt insignificant compared to the smarter, faster-talking men. I shrank, feeling inferior to the older, well-dressed matrons in the room. I thought my questions were silly and my answers would obviously be wrong. I doubted myself, and assumed no one would want to hear what I had to say.

I saw, for the first time, how I was playing life.

I let my age be a downfall instead of speaking up. I allowed my fears of being disliked crush my insights for a solution for the group. I was letting others make decisions for me instead of making decisions for myself. I was judging, assuming and predisposing my outcomes before they happened because I felt my age was a hindrance. I wasn't taking charge of my own life. Instead, I was literally sitting on the sidelines.

I saw then how my behavior had a ripple effect out into my life and the people around me. Up until then, I was acting out and adhering to the many cultural and societal rules I felt were expected of me. Never before had I felt awakened to questioning those ideas in a way that wasn't rebellious, but instead, intelligent and deliberate. I asked myself, "How successful would I be if I continued down that path of compliance?" I had big plans for my future and recognized that how I was "playing" the game was not going to get me what I wanted out of life.

I left that evening fundamentally changed. At the prime age of 18, just setting out into the world, I saw a 360-degree view of what was possible around me. I got a first-hand look at what my life *might* be like versus what I *desired* it to be. Watching all those people in that room was like a foreshadowing of my own future. I questioned how I acted and asked myself who I wanted to become, based on my own volition and not the well-meaning of others. It was a lot of retrospection for a newly-graduated teenager, but it was the best reflection I could ever have done for myself and my life to come.

Eleven days after I graduated from high school, I left my small town and moved to the big city. I broke free from the confines I was in by leaving a three-year relationship with a bad-boy boyfriend. I walked out of a dead-end job and began studying fashion design — a career I was laughed at and ridiculed for wanting. Living on my own was a struggle. I had an empty fridge and no money to put gas in my car. I forged new friendships, started a career-making job and asked intelligent questions whenever they were needed. It was a constant push outside my comfort zones, paying attention to how I acted in all situations.

I noticed if I was being bossy, weak, afraid, fearful, or making others' needs more important than my own. I took control of my life and, each and every day, became a student of how I was indeed playing the game.

I graduated with honors, receiving a degree in Fashion Design from a well-known school in an even bigger town than the one I first moved to. I landed an incredible job with a top couturier after agreeing to work for free for a month to prove my worth. I started my own fashion label and sold clothing and jewelry in some of the top stores across the country. Within a few years, I began working in the film business as a costumer and quickly advanced to Set Supervisor and Shop Steward. For over a decade, I was fortunate to work on movies with A-list celebrities and award-winning directors.

I continued to observe how I was showing up and behaving. When I first started working in film, I was like an eager puppy running around the set, doing more than was required, and loving every second of it. There were other crew members who had been doing it for years and their attitudes were marred and jaded. I promised myself if I ever got like that, it was time for me to quit. If I couldn't show up full out and play the game with all my might, it was time to move on and do something different.

Fifteen years later, I was at the height of my career, standing on the rooftop of a 30-story building beside a world-acclaimed and Oscar-winning director, watching the sunrise on the horizon after working 21 hours non-stop on a film about human mutants and the world sinking into apocalypse. And I knew my next step had arrived. I had become marred and jaded. Playing the game had turned both unfulfilling and inconsequential. Making movies with insignificant plot lines and unnecessary violence felt unrewarding and hollow. I wanted to have more impact and meaning in my life. I needed to do more than observe myself and just pivot. I felt ready to step forward and fully LEAD the game I was in.

From that second Ignite moment, I vowed to begin living as an even more exceptional version of me. I took bigger risks and challenged myself even more. I did the opposite of my habits and went on the true *pursuit* of finding a new meaning of *excellence* in my life. And this time, I wanted to do it while being fully conscious and clear about what steps I needed to take to get there. I studied the great books in personal growth. I took class after class, seminar after seminar, immersing myself not just in learning but in Being. I awakened my mind to new concepts and ideas, and surrendered old paradigms and outdated beliefs. It was a reckoning, to say the least, with the words "How you played this game… is how you play life."

I had to ask myself if I had been playing all this time? What did *playing* actually mean? With who, how, where and why was I playing at all? Was I inept at playing? Or was playing a fabulous excuse? The entire contrasts of my identity came into question and I had to decide if playing meant doing, being, pretending or placating. There was nowhere to hide, nowhere to sit on the sidelines in my mind. I knew that if living the greatest version of me was to happen, I had to lead myself out of the confines of my very own making.

Today, if you met me on the street, you'd see a woman deeply in love with her world, her family, her husband and her friends. You'd also see someone who doesn't lead others, but instead, leads herself. My greatest strength comes in knowing exactly who I am and how my talents and shortcoming accentuate and punctuate my life. There'd be a sparkle in my eye and a spring in my step, for I have walked the journey of a thousand miles in my own skin. I have led without leading and have forged on by using my own tears to wash away any of the so-called "failures" I may have made. These have been the lessons I have learned while playing The Game.

"How you do one thing is how you do everything. How you show up is how you show up. How you play today is how you play every day... and how you BE in the game of life is how the game of life will be for you. Know thyself and you know everything. Live fully and you have won."

IGNITE ACTION STEPS

Sit down with yourself in your favorite place and ask yourself...

How do I play the game of life? Listen, write, record, reflect, and be 100 percent honest with it all.

Then, keep what you like and do whatever you have to do to get rid of the rest.

JB Owen - Canada
jb@igniteyou.life
Founder of Ignite, JBO Global and Lotus Liners
igniteyou.life & lotusliners.com
jblovesyou

CAROL BENSON

*"Life's plot points are often disguised as opportunities
for you to have a life of more delight."*

My intention for you, dear reader, is for you to rewrite your life, noticing any Ignite Moments, to embody your full potential. To let the genius of *you* lead by finding your flow in creative expression, financial freedom, more authentic connections and inspirational delight.

REWRITE YOUR LIFE

"What?! Me? Uh uh, I don't think so. My creative introvert wants to run the other way. No way, not me! Find someone else."

Since this compilation is called *Ignite Your Life for Conscious Leaders*, let me start out by being fully transparent: I never set out to be a leader. Wasn't in my life's game plan. Didn't even occur as a potential career choice. Surprisingly, it's evolved like a trick package with layers and layers of endless wrapping paper hiding the prize. You know... a combination of fear (What if I don't like it?) and excitement (Never would have chosen this; but somehow, it works).

You see, when leadership opportunities came my way in the past, I would feel a lot of resistance. "No! Not me! I want to be behind the scenes! That's what I'm good at." At least, those are the thoughts I wanted to believe. Despite my resistance and fearful beliefs, admittedly over the decades of my life, I've had glimpses of my *Unexplored Inner Leader.*

When it showed up in small ways, like a challenging situation way beyond my professional experience in a job, I went for it. Full-on. My response was, "No worries; I can do it."

> "A boss has the title. A leader has the people."
> *Simon Sinek*

Barely a year out of graduate school, I was offered a top position supervising twenty speech-language pathologists who had many more years' combined experience than newbie me. Uncomfortable, though knowing it was foolish to decline the offer, I went for it. Figuring it out, acting as if I knew what I was doing even when I didn't have a clue. Not exactly "impostor syndrome," but something akin to it became ingrained in my nature. People began viewing me as a leader long before I did. To me, it still felt like a remote, unthought of possibility.

Instead, I felt drawn to become more conscious by connecting with a higher spirit and expressing my creativity. My logical mind wrestled between doubts of having a steady career path and doing what made my soul happy and my heart sing,

The safe career path seemed to rob my essence. Staying true to my mothership guidance system nourishes me to feel fulfilled, thriving and happy. I recently learned which of my talents paves the way for me to ease into my flow state: the natural, effortless unfolding of least resistance, focus and enjoyment.

> "Your focus determines your reality."
> *Qui-Gon Jinn, Star Wars: The Phantom Menace*

For a long time, this wasn't the way of my life. Many times, it felt as if I were trapped in a sad story, seeking happiness in all the wrong places. You see, I had dreams of becoming a writer. I ached and avoided doing what didn't nourish me from the inside out.

Do you ever have dreams you didn't believe possible? That was me. I kept hearing in my mind the voices of my parents, siblings, even friends. A chorus of doubters singing a song I thought true for a long time. One part fear, harmonies of self-doubt, and a refrain of "I'm not good enough." Ironically, I began emerging as a leader. I now activate entrepreneurs and business owners to uncover their dreams. You may be wondering how this came to pass. It took a while to figure it out by trial and error at a time when I was still doing my best to fit into a career box. (You may also know about *that* box.)

It's a box you choose when you follow a linear path of what's expected of you, like declaring a college major with a predictable guarantee of financial results. I still hear my dad's voice, "You made a wise choice."

Did I waste time blocking my genius and not freeing it from the box? Waiting before shining a light for others to unlock their own dreams? From my perspective, heck no! It's all been a gift; although topsy-turvy, frustrating, and slow-going at times, it has been worth every minute.

Rewriting my life became a profound practice. As an avid reader, music and art film fan, storytelling has always had a profound impact on me. Stories lure you on a journey, explaining and providing meaning to situations or experiences. It's a meta-narrative thrill when allegedly unrelated and random events become organized and explainable. The human experience resonates with the emotions of characters, protagonists, antagonists and supporting roles.

When my children were small, my ex-husband saw me. Saw who I really was when no one else in my family did. He surprised me, offering me the chance to stay home with nanny support so I could spend a few hours daily hiding out in my home office to write, and not return to the drudgery of a 'fallback' career. What a gift! I am grateful for his support. I became a prolific writer. Once obstacles were removed, dreams started showing up by having the time to write eighteen screenplays, two novels and placing in the top ten percent of top screenwriting competitions.

On a lark, I submitted a screenplay sample with my hopes high that I would be chosen to attend a 10-day retreat in Maui. Well, I was accepted into a 10-person screenwriting mastermind intensive with renowned expert Christopher Vogler. I was beyond excited, since I was a raving fan of his screenwriting book, *The Writer's Journey*, based on Joseph Campbell's brilliant book, *The Hero With a Thousand Faces*.

A quick overview of this "Hero's Journey" model begins when the protagonist is called to an adventure, then faces a challenge, triumphs over it and then their world is restored back to normalcy. Think *Star Wars*, *The Wizard of Oz*, and *Spider Man*. After many obstacles, the hero discovers themself in the end. The retreat I attended had a long-lasting impact not only on how I view story creation, but also making sense of my own life and how I grow *me*.

Upon returning from Maui, it's as if a doorway marked 'Enter' had swung open for me to pursue my long-desired dream. I even met a muse, Sam. He was a grizzled, martini-drinking New Yorker, seasoned journalist turned screenwriter; my beloved writing mentor. He pushed me to go beyond the suburban mom-world comfort zone.

Sam said, "Carol, stop being small! Get out of your own way, little grass-hopper. No more '*being a mom*' excuses. Time to fly." He gave me new keys to explore my writing chops; to develop 'rhinoceros' skin; to show up as me. I took the challenge by giving myself a push to step out of hiding, to become a different type of leader and to expand beyond motherhood.

My own hero's journey called on my inner protagonist to do a rewrite. I answered a *call to adventure*, way beyond the edge of comfort, to write a screenplay about a teen runaway and her mother. Well, the mother part, I knew inside and out, but I had never experienced the runaway teen world. With Sam prodding me, I hung out weekly at a local park, interviewing homeless teens for developing a teen character. I wanted to understand my character's motivations and write accurate dialogue. Suddenly, I couldn't settle for being parched of creativity, intellectually stale or living my life in ranges of monotones.

Was I scared? Oh yes, I was at first. I left my purse at home and stuffed my car keys, license and phone inside the hidden pockets of my jacket. Holding tightly to my coat, I arrived bearing gifts of dollar bills, tampons and protein bars. Pretty quickly, the teens began to trust me and candidly share their stories. My own empathy was deeply activated by their raw honesty and vulnerability, and allowed me to authentically show up and fully engage with them. Their voices left etchings still echoing in my memory.

Eventually, this one screenplay did the rounds in Hollywood for three years. I had to emerge from behind my laptop to fly to L.A. (where I had once lived) for several pitch meetings with producers. I was, again, completely out of my comfort zone. Acting as if I was confident and already a successful writer, I pulled it off without shyness getting in my way for face-to-face meetings. I held my breath for this screenplay to be green-lit for production. That hasn't happened yet, and I say 'yet' with a smile on my face; putting that screenplay out there opened the door to a few really well-paid writing gigs.

Listening to these two contrasting inner dialogues in my brain became a potent Ignite Moment: 1) the inner critic saying, "I'm not enough," and keep-ing me in the neutral mom-zone; and 2) the inner champion urging me to stop hiding and playing it safe.

Shifting gears to become more of myself by exiting safe roles and speeding through uncomfortable edges, I found I was rewarded when I took chances. I veered from my "go-to" path of disbelief, self-doubt, not feeling good enough, and all the other negative mindsets influencing past decisions, and stepped into making my dreams became real. Instead of safely behind the scenes, I claimed a plot point story twist to become a hero in my own life journey, not a version of roles others thought I should follow. I was rewriting my life and charging forward on my unique path of least resistance.

Let's pause. Please take a moment here to ponder how your own life has given you a wild ride of plot points and character archetypes. What chorus have you been listening to? What dialogue do you routinely say or think? How does a life disruption grow you?

I invite you to take a wide-angled perspective of how your life story richly weaves into your unique experience; a series of many Ignite Moments taking you to where you are right now.

Rewriting my life as a conscious leader allows me to contribute to others as a coach, speaker, trainer and author. I began taking more personal risks, like applying for two coaching certification programs in no way related to my clinical or writing background. *Way* beyond my comfort zone. Self-doubt panic, "Who am I to think I have what it takes to be a candidate?"

There were hundreds of applicants. In the end, I was one of only thirty-seven selected to become a trainer with a very well-known global brand and be thrust into a public spotlight, as if the universe was prodding me to shed my former character's identity shell.

Another Ignite Moment flirted with me when I felt drawn to apply for a conscious business certification training. My husband, Paul, with a hint of a knowing smile, asked, "You sure about another certification program?"

A reality-check opportunity happened. Okay, was I having a FOMO (Fear Of Missing Out) moment as a serial learner and seeker? In all honesty, I heard a strong "Yes!" message inside me saying I really, really needed to do it. So I did.

Feeling a bit like being back in graduate school with peers, followed by a faculty review of my final project, I crafted a framework for businesses to shift into a more conscious business model by focusing on individual growth as well as local and global contributions. It included skills such as presence, engagement, mindfulness, kindness, transparency, gratitude, generosity, unity, compassion and even forgiveness.

A full-blown and powerful Ignite Moment blatantly got my attention. During the virtual presentation, I was nervous. Self-doubt was churning inside my gut, glued to the full volume thought-noise distracting me from being present. Then, as if a spotlight brightened, during the rubric-scored live-panel reviews, I witnessed my role models sitting with their jaws hanging open. They were astonished by the practical ease of my project. "Sheer brilliance" was the feedback.

Boy was I surprised! Receiving recognition for being creative!? This project allowed me to be my authentic self. No pretending or trying to impress others. *I was enough.* Some people call it hacking ideas. I call it distilling information and creating a new and unique perspective. This project let me taste a *free-to-be-me* moment as I watched most of my doubts about being seen as someone with expertise go out the window. Poof! In its place, I found an inspired and delighted confidence for sharing ideas; a new paradigm for doing business and for contributing in ways I had never felt the freedom to do before. I was listening to a different chorus.

Is self-judgement getting in your way of having a life of happiness? Is your box misshaped? Is it too puny for you to expand into your unique potential? Does feeling safe and secure blindside you into decisions that keep you small?

Understanding my life story and the motivations behind the many story-glue moments that ignited me helped discover my life's magic potions. These multi-layered life story experiences have sprouted many unplanned leadership skills and abilities. I have discovered how to turn unexpected situations into a path of least resistance by flowing with my natural genius zones. I was lit up!

What lights *you* up? For me, it's knowing I can inspire others to grow into their fullest potential of ease, happiness and feeling empowered by their natural genius-zone talents; to confidently walk with less resistance in their lives.

No more being stuck inside a box that is preventing my joy. I shifted my life story paradigm into living each day as a leader, not a follower. It's part of my daily practice to actively, moment-by-moment, rewrite any parts of my life that are needing some attention. I do my best to choose a path of least resistance; to be more in the flow of authentically showing up. It's an exciting, creative and fulfilling path to rewrite and then conduct my own life symphony. I invite you to rewrite your own life areas that are needing attention to level up. Actualizing your choices! Seize opportunities for a life of pure delight for you!

IGNITE ACTION STEPS

HINT: Boldly ask two trusted friends to answer these next two questions about you:

1. What story genre does your current life look like? A tragedy? A romantic comedy? A madcap adventure? A thriller? An endless drama? A Lifetime story? Damsel in distress? A memoir? Boring and predictable? Fantasy fiction? Circle one or two, or add your own.

2. What character role have you been playing for much of your life? Rescuer who saves the day? A giver? A taker? An entitled brat? A know-it-all? Someone needing saving? Living a life of fantasy? A bleak realist? A negative naysayer? A comic relief jokester? A femme fatale? Anxious and fearful? Carrying around baggage from the past? Victim? Survivor? Good little girl? Sexy Super Woman? What other roles?

Underline all that apply.

THEN: Independently do these next four questions:

1. Make a list of all the dreams you have for living a life of delightful fulfillment.

2. Make a list of all the *Shoulds* and *Not do's to delegate to others*; then, make a list of all the things you love to do.

3. Sum it all up to describe what story, characters, repetitive dialogue and plot points you've been living.

4. Are you satisfied with your current life legacy? What story do you want to tell now?

BONUS: List all the Ignite Moments in your life. Have fun!

Carol Benson - USA
Speaker, Author, Trainer
Itdoesntfeellikework.com

ANDREA GONTKOVIČOVÁ

"Care about others and they will care about you."

We prefer and remember experiences filled with emotions, be it fun, love, surprise, fear or uncertainty. Becoming a leader is a process of realization of not only what moves people's bodies, but most importantly, what moves their hearts and inspires them to contribute. There are more than seven billion people on Earth, but only a few worth following. You can choose to become one of them in your family, work or among friends. Have a dream. Make a plan and work on it. Our lives are a sequence of things which happen as a consequence, not as a coincidence.

LEAD WITH HEART AND GUTS.

Life is a story, which unfolds gradually, but its elements interact amongst each other. You don't know when and how. Thus, be consistent and clear. Be grateful for people who support you on your journey and pay this forward. Inspire and lead others with heart and guts. The intellect is not always the answer.

I was born and grew up in the tallest mountains in Slovakia where the summers are short and winters cold. That made everybody focused on the core, and beautifully straightforward and modest. My mum and dad were experts on chemical industry and worked in one of the most important and modern factories in the country at that time. I went to the local school where the atmosphere was friendly and family-like. Everybody knew everybody and their families, so the teachers, parents and kids had a full family album on each other with the "executive summary" at the front. Teachers were called endearingly by name and were truly interested in our feelings, state of mind and situation at home, including our siblings and parents. They were full of jokes but also available for an intimate discussion and personal advice, if needed. We honestly cared about each other and had a good time.

It really did not matter who needed help. One day, it was a student looking for a drive back home or some additional cash to pay for tomorrow's lunch. Or the other way around, a teacher needing help with picking up her little child in the kindergarten.

In spite of this safe, family atmosphere, the teachers were academically demanding and supported each child's development to their full potential. The academic schedule was packed, lessons were very focused, and progress was measured regularly. Humanities and natural sciences were taught at a very high level with the goal of readying students to be successful representatives at various competitions as well as preparing them for their future secondary and university studies.

I remember vividly the photo wall at the entrance to the school filled with pictures of students with the best academic results and winners of various competitions. It was not only a big contest to get your pictures up there but, of course, a huge stamp of recognition for those who succeeded and a motivation for those who had not yet appeared there. School gatherings were another platform for acknowledging success as the Headmaster or his Deputy would summarize the recent achievements of school representatives at various events in the region or at the national level.

I enjoyed this positive but competitive environment and took it as an opportunity to learn new things about the world and the way it functions. I think it was the warmth and support I felt that liberated me from the potentially unhealthy pressure and fear, which sometimes blocks people from walking the unknown route or taking risks. I progressed academically, succeeded in various competitions and successfully represented the school. And all this with a lot of fun and enjoyment.

I was a very good student. I also represented the school in the region as well, so my picture was on the photo wall. However, as I was growing up, finding out how the school ran and who was giving direction started to intrigue me. I looked for answers and discussed it with people whom I respected. I was curious to hear what they thought. I chose those whom I admired for their abilities to make complex things simple. One of them was my teacher of the Slovak language arts. She was a walking example of an extremely demanding but also very warm and fair individual. I spent hours with her, preparing for various reciting and drama events. This gave me an opportunity to discuss everything that was on my mind. I asked her questions like: "What is the Headmaster doing and why do I see him only rarely?" or "Why do all the teachers meet every Monday if they spend so much time together during the week?" or "Why do I need to participate in extra activities if it does not reflected in my grades?"

She explained to me in a simple way that what I saw happening at school, including the family atmosphere filled with healthy competition and ambitious, success-oriented students, was a part of a bigger strategy. She said: "We care about our students. We want to give you the best foundation for your careers and future lives. We love seeing you grow into happy and successful humans. At the same time, our Headmaster cares about us and supports us, the teachers. And this atmosphere of caring and ambition creates a fertile ecosystem, allowing us all to be happy and continue learning."

This was confirmed by my math teacher, another person on my list of people I admired and respected. She looked like a princess to me with her long, blond hair and beautiful dresses. She walked calmly and with a smile on her face. Her tone of voice was soft and composed. She made the most complex mathematical problems look like simple tasks and math became just a game. Nevertheless, this beautiful princess was still demanding and firm. She motivated us to tackle difficult math problems, take on new challenges, and improve. She often shared examples of her students succeeding and enrolling in top schools in the region, always concluding with how proud she was to have contributed to their success.

All in all, I was super lucky with my elementary school. It gave me strong academic foundations and my first insights into the recipe for leading people forward and having them perform their best.

I started to realize that things happen as a consequence, not as a coincidence.

After growing out of this school, I moved up through college to university, finishing my studies at rapid speed. With time and experience, I picked up other truths about life, such as, while there are many highly intelligent people who can work out the most difficult intellectual logical conundrums, not all of them have the ability to bring others along. There are actually only a few who can make the results of those conundrums relevant to somebody else and unite a team around a good cause.

With this information, I stepped into the next stage of my life. My first job was in a small educational company. I was responsible for building the international relations. However, I soon realized that the company was headed by an absolutistic leader who lacked a clear vision and drove the small team, including me, in constant chaos and mess. After several weeks of trying to understand, I still had no clue as to what kind of international relations I was expected to build, with whom and with what purpose. Days were spent in endless meetings and the mood was miserable. No decisions were made unless the top boss was present and they changed frequently. There was no progress foreseen neither for people nor for the business, and the overall environment was negative and destructive. I did not enjoy this and moved on within a few months.

I then went through a series of interviews with several companies. The biggest one was an international company with 80,000 employees in 180 countries, with more than 100 years of business history. In the context of my humble international experience with a small team, this looked overwhelming and too big to be true. Many questions came to mind: "Are these statistics possible?" and "Can somebody *lead* 80K people across 180 countries for 100 years?" I also wondered, "Will I be able to blend into this diverse international team?" and "Do I want to do it? And what's in it for me?" I remember clearly riding the elevator as I was being escorted to the office of the general manager. While I was extremely curious, I was also afraid that what I was doing was too daring and risky. I was stepping beyond what I knew and felt comfortable with. Luckily, that doubt soon disappeared.

The initial seconds of the interview gave me some answers and with the first joke, a connection was established. I experienced a flow of intellectual horsepower, curiosity and fun. I made up my mind in an instant; I wanted to join this kind of people and discover how to have people care and move for the same cause. More importantly, I also decided that, one day, I wanted to grow into the top leader of a company like this myself. This was a gut feeling without any material inputs or guarantees. I just felt it.

I joined the Slovak team and started my business career. The complexity of my tasks and the level of my impact increased in line with my learning curve. I was benefiting from the opportunity, being guided by top business professionals and strong and inspiring leaders. I moved from the small Slovak market to a bigger one in Czech, and then started leading a dossier at the European level. While my role and the sizes of my teams continued growing, I got repeated confirmations that the recipe for creating and leading the most successful teams and the happiest people remained the same: mutual respect and support with a clear understanding of what we all want and determination to get it.

And yes, my gut feeling about joining this group was right. More than 100 years of history made them real experts in uniting their teams around one cause all around the world and leading them forward. Whether it was in the area of inventing and producing great products, getting their customers excited about their choice, or providing them the support they longed for, this company, with all its intellectual horsepower, curiosity and business appetite, took a very courageous decision and started putting itself on the global map of companies which are truly transforming human lives in the 21st century. In addition to my happiness in being a part of this team, I also fulfilled my 20-year dream and became one of the top business leaders in Central Europe. But just before that, my big Ignite moment was to come.

I received a call from a person I did not know. She was working for one of the biggest publishing houses in Slovakia. They are also the organizer of an annual competition for extraordinary and successful women in nine categories, such as business, art, media, science, education, etc. The lady called me to share that the nomination committee, including, among others, the President of Slovakia, the General Director of National TV and Radio, and top representatives of Academic world, had chosen me as one of the three finalists for the category of business and management. I thought the call was a joke, one of those from the morning radio program where they want to see your reaction to something really crazy and have the whole world listen to it live. So I held my horses and thanked her calmly. It was only once I received this information in writing, in its whole magnitude, that I realized what had happened. Out of millions of professionals in Slovakia, the committee had chosen *me*.

I immediately started thinking about how I wanted to play this, and concluded that this was far greater than me. This was about all the people who had helped me get to where I was today. Family, teachers, friends, colleagues, bosses, fans. And it was also about those young people who had big dreams but were not sure about their right to have them. I decided to frame my nomination as a confirmation that big dreams are allowed and young people, irrespective of where they come from, should trust their foundations. I was a walking manifestation of this. And not only me. Through the time spent together with other nominees, I gradually discovered that, while in different categories, our stories were somehow similar. Big dreams, strong aspirations, hard work, and in some cases, the opportunity to learn and be inspired by others.

The 28 finalists had amazing lives and were an enormous wealth of inspiration. Ladies who had brought beautiful soprano arias or the sound of a lyrical harp to the eyes and ears of many Slovak music lovers for years; others who devoted their lives to bringing young kids to art, such as the founder and manager of the boys' choir; a lady reporter who had exposed her life to investigate various cases having a major impact on the shape of the Slovak society. Two of the most encouraging ladies were an elementary school teacher focused on the Roma minority and a founder of a school on the island of Madagascar. Imagine the poverty, chaos and lack of support they experienced; and in spite of this, they decided to lead in their area of expertise and do the best possible.

Getting to know and understand each other was a much smoother and more natural process than I had foreseen. All the ladies were already so fulfilled and sure about the cause of their lives and none of us got hijacked by the potential competitive spirit of the process we were going through. Quite the opposite, in fact. We built an environment of mutual trust, recognition, respect and admiration. The journey to the awards was so unexpectedly enriching, helping us all to grow beyond our areas of expertise. We created a conscious, friendly bond, ready to be activated whenever we choose.

The Awards ceremony was live; shot by the national TV and the announcement of the winners were intertwined with cultural program that helped us relax. Nevertheless, my name came up twice, as the winner of the category business and management and of the top award, Absolute Slovak Lady of the Year 2019. It was a huge surprise to me and an obvious opportunity to share my message with approximately 1.5 million other people. I had a flashback to my childhood and was grateful and humbled for those who supported me along the way. More importantly, I knew I had consciously made a decision that I wanted to lead in such a way that the journey would be easier for others.

As I held my award, I shared, "Slovakia has a wealth of talent. Each of us can be successful at home and in the world. I encourage you all to have big and courageous dreams. As long as you can dream them, you can have them come true." I was so happy and grateful that I could share this message live with all those people watching it.

This continued with my home compatriots. The mayor of my little mountain town called me and announced that she would like to award me with the Prize of the Mayor from my hometown. I saw this as an opportunity to celebrate my journey with those who supported me from a very young age. It was the ultimate opportunity to inspire those who were in the early stages of their lives and thinking about where to take themselves. I got tears in my eyes and lost my voice for a while. I was truly touched. The weight of both of these awards grew exponentially. I was filled with gratitude, love, happiness and appreciation.

I felt that the level of my emotions was even higher than those linked to the Absolute Slovak Lady of the Year. There is a saying that nobody can be a prophet at home, and thus, the recognition by people from my hometown has a truly special value. I would have my mum and other family, my old-time friends, teachers, neighbors and all those people who have known me for so long there with me. And I was to share the stage with my elementary math teacher; this beautiful, gentle and princess-like woman who was among the first in my life to have taught me NOT to give up and to be kind and supportive to those people who are seconded to our hands. She was also recognized by the Mayor for her lifetime contribution to the education and growth of the town's kids.

I believe that we all can lead with both heart and guts; that each of us has a role to play in life, whether we are a teacher, parent or business owner. We can all be leaders and consciously decide to encourage, support and inspire others to become their truest potential. When you care about others, they will care about you. This is what true, fulfilling leadership looks like. Sometimes we get; sometimes we pay forward. Make your life dynamic in all your greatness and keep going. That is where you will find the real reward.

IGNITE ACTION STEPS

Life is an opportunity to write our story and leave a mark on this Earth. Time is of essence; if you care and want to be efficient, be clear about what you want in life and go after it. Have your dreams. Don't be afraid to think big and be daring. Identify and learn from the best people in your profession and leadership. They might not be famous, but they could be super important for solidifying your back bone and overall balance. Build your foundations well and rely on them. Geography, or the size of the place you start your journey from, does not matter; it's all about the quality. As long as the principle is correct, it is easy to multiply the numbers. If you can lead a team of 3, you have all the prerequisites to lead a team of 300 and more. You can lead in any area you choose; and rest assured, all of them count, be it education, art, minorities or business.

Andrea Gontkovičová - Slovakia
Business Leader, Absolute Slovak Lady of the year 2019
www.pmi.com

MICHAEL D LYNCH

*"Being in alignment with what's most meaningful to YOU –
that's TRUE SUCCESS!"*

I see many people entranced by the idea of climbing the corporate ladder in their pursuit to find success. I know it only too well – I have been there myself. My intention is for my story to help you clearly see that success doesn't come gift-wrapped in the boardroom, in praise from work colleagues or a boss, from a promotion, or from the numbers in your bank account. True success comes from within and is only found in your heart.

SUCCESSFUL LEADERSHIP STARTS AT HOME

I used to believe that being a successful leader meant working hard and climbing up the corporate ladder. That would allow me to retire early and then finally begin to live a life of freedom and fulfillment. This belief aligned with what I learned as a child: Working hard and making sacrifices were the keys to achieving success.

My dad worked around the clock at times, when I was young, to ensure that everybody had a constant supply of one of the modern world's basic needs, electricity. He worked on the power lines and I vividly recall a time where he missed our family Christmas because of wild storms. He did whatever was needed to support our family and create success, and every small salary increment was quietly celebrated as another milestone was achieved.

What I had learned about success at home was only reinforced further through my own experiences in childhood. I worked hard at school; the result was good grades. I worked hard at sports to overcome the disadvantage of a small skinny frame and my lack of natural ability. My dad stood in the yard for hours throwing the cricket ball to me as I tried again and again to catch it. When it came time for the kids' cricket practice, I was always the first one there. When the men's cricket practice started right after, I was the only kid who stayed around and I was often the last to leave. Eventually, all that hard work paid off when I was selected to play in the top men's cricket league in my area at 15. Throughout my teenage years, I also challenged myself in Tae Kwon Do. It was a huge win for me when I earned a black belt at the age of 15, one of the youngest in the academy to do so. Who would have thought this small, skinny kid could break wooden boards and ceramic tiles with his hands and feet? Hard work and dedication seemed to pay off.

When I joined the corporate world, I already knew that if I put my head down and worked hard, the results would take care of themselves. For years, it seemed to play out just as I expected and I embarked on a steady rise through the corporate ranks. My hard work was seemingly catapulting me toward the success I desired. The long work hours seemed totally worth it, as I was well on my way: Achievements, promotions, business class and 5-star hotels, and a multiple six-figure salary.

And who could argue? I had opportunities to live and work all over the world with all the expat trimmings. I was being invited to exclusive events, meeting world-famous sports stars, and responsible for managing the risk on over $70 billion in annual revenue. It seemed to be all the confirmation I needed.

However, at the peak of my corporate power, severe stress and anxiety showed up unannounced. I clearly remember the day that changed my life forever. I was at work juggling many competing tasks, tight deadlines, and feeling completely overwhelmed. It was just like any other normal day, really; except this day was different.

I was sitting at my desk when suddenly I was dizzy, my vision blurred; my physical body felt numb. My heart felt as if it was pounding out of my chest. I didn't know what was happening to me. Was I having a heart attack? I felt so scared. All I knew was that I had to get out of the office. Somehow, I managed to pick myself up and leave.

It turns out I was having my first anxiety attack. How could this possibly happen to me? I was building such a successful corporate career. I prided myself on being able to work extra hard and multitask with ease in order to achieve so much.

After that day, the stress, anxiety, and the unavoidable numbness that came with it followed me everywhere. I had to give all I had just to maintain where I was at. My mind never stopped; I constantly felt exhausted. There were days my brain was so foggy, I couldn't even focus on my work. I'd wake up every day feeling like I needed to sleep for a week. I knew my body was telling me to slow down, but what would my life be... without this success? So I pushed, as hard as I could; occasionally too much—triggering another anxiety attack—but most often just enough to keep myself right on the threshold of falling apart. I was like an 8-cylinder car running on only 2-cylinders. But I was talented and determined; I managed to get by focussing all my efforts and energy into my career. Giving everything at work meant I had to make sacrifices and prioritize my career over other areas of my life, including my family, and my SELF.

It would mean that, by the time I finished a week of work, so stressed out and anxious, I had nothing left to give. I wanted to take time out on the weekends to relax. To try and escape from all this pressure and struggle. My wife at the time, after a week at home taking care of our son, understandably wanted to go out; so, I would always say yes. What was the point, after all, of living in the Netherlands if we couldn't jump in the car and go explore the nearby countries of Belgium, France and Germany?

There were several times I'd be driving along the freeway with my family in the car when the anxiety and numbness would overwhelm me. I no longer had clarity and couldn't focus on the road. I'd have to pull over and get into the passenger seat. I couldn't even drive a car and it made me feel like such a failure. It took so much energy just to manage the stress and anxiety. To keep it from completely consuming me. Yet I saw no way out. I HAD to keep this up if I wanted to continue to be successful. *Because success is what we all want in life, right?*

Then my marriage fell apart and everything seemed to come crashing down on me. As if that wasn't enough... Being the father of a 3-year old son who was at the prime age of learning, growing, loving, and playing with me every morning and night, and I all of a sudden had to say goodbye to that. It completely crushed me.

My family and closest friends were half way around the world in Australia, and often asleep during my deepest, darkest moments. I felt so genuinely alone. This feeling was so overwhelming at times that I sent a text message to the few friends I did have in the Netherlands, desperate for a reply so I could feel a connectedness with someone. I'd go to bed each night with the photo of my son and his mother beside my bed, crying myself to sleep, praying that some minor miracle might bring us all back together again.

My lack of awareness at the time had me blaming everything outside of myself. I had hit rock bottom and felt like a complete failure. At this, the worst point in my life, I couldn't see the $70 billion dollars I was protecting anymore. I couldn't see the business class and 5-star hotels. All I could see was not one failed marriage, BUT TWO FAILED MARRIAGES! Yes, I had now failed at marriage number two.

A rare moment of clarity for me. Amongst all the blaming of my ex-wives for what they contributed to the downfall of our relationships, I started to see how the common themes of LONELINESS... and LACK... and FEAR played out. I realized, through both these relationship breakdowns, there was one common thread: It was ME.

It must NOT be about them, I thought. It HAS to be about ME! I was so ashamed. There must be something wrong with me.

I clearly recall the moment in the fully furnished apartment that I had hastily moved into. The local area was foreign to me, the furniture was foreign to me, the weather was cold, and there was just me occupying the whole three floors. It was eerily silent and I felt so alone. I realized at that very moment that I could continue to play the victim and think "poor me," I could go out partying and drink myself silly, I could continue to deny this upheaval in my life... OR... I could explore what role I had played in creating this situation and make changes in my life to ensure it never happened again.

I made the decision that I would come straight home after work every day, have a single glass of wine while I cooked my dinner, and just learn to be by myself. At first, it scared the shit out of me. I started reading and writing every night. I got into this routine and decided that I would not go out drinking or socializing with others until I was comfortable in my own skin, at peace being all on my own. It was a daunting goal and seemed like a difficult road ahead, but it was the start of the journey to recovery for me.

I started writing a blog at the time. In my first post, titled *Finding the Right Path*, I wrote about owning my role in what had happened and wanting to be a better person:

Life is an unusual journey. – I have made many mistakes in my life, the biggest and most damaging only recently. Yet despite the intense pain and hurt arising from knowing I have inflicted the same upon others, this time it is different. – This time I could not hide, flee or deny. This time I had to stand, face the truth and accept the consequences. This time I have to pay a heavy price and pay these dues openly. – This time it is like my eyes have finally been awakened. This time I can finally see to the core of the problem that has been burdening me for most, if not all, of my life. This time I am ready to deal with this problem head on so that I can leave it behind once and for all. – This time I will move forward to a happier and more fulfilling life.

Soon after my son and his mother moved back to Australia, I received an offer to move to Singapore. I had a big decision to make and I knew I had to do what was best for my own healing and growth. Moving to Singapore would present a struggle to stay present in my son's life. On the other hand, how could I learn to take care of myself unless I was truly on my own? I believed the best way to teach my son to be happy in life... was to learn to be happy myself.

I made the agonizing decision to move to Singapore 6,150 kilometers and an eight-hour flight away from my son. I had to learn to be a bit selfish to allow myself to become the person I was meant to be and also a positive role model for my son. I travelled back to Australia once a month, red-eye flights both ways, just to spend a valuable three days with him.

I realized that this life I had been living, this life of a corporate leader, was far from what could be called a success. This definition of success I'd carried throughout my life could not really be mine. Perhaps I'd just borrowed it from somewhere else. I mean, how could it possibly be mine if I'd found *success* and still felt SO EMPTY?

I had to work out how to find the courage and strength to get myself back up from this place of emptiness. How could I stand in the middle of my shame and be brave enough to face the world again? I recognized that it was not about me being unable to handle stress and anxiety, or ending two marriages, or failing as a father. It was not even about me having to choose between work and life! It was simply about me learning how to love better and stronger. It was about finding and living the RIGHT version of success; the version where I am truly a successful leader of life.

But how was I supposed to press reset when I had to be brilliant on the outside but was scared on the inside? How could I cry, when men aren't supposed to cry? How could I give myself permission to redefine success? Because this *success* I had been chasing, this *success* I had borrowed... this was NOT the SUCCESS I wanted to live. I DIDN'T CARE about the billions of dollars, I DIDN'T CARE about a six-figure salary... Not as much as I cared about being loved, and loving, and most of all, being at peace with the man I am in the dark of night when nobody's looking.

I found my way to this really strange practice called meditation that, years ago, I would have judged. Because it was so strange, I went all in and wore all the Indian garments. In hindsight, it wasn't a good fashion statement; but at the time, I didn't care. If I was going to step out of my norm into "strange" to liberate myself, then I was going ALL IN.

I began to take better care of myself and create more balance and stillness in my life. What had seemed like a crippling situation at the time turned out to be such a gift as, slowly, the dark clouds in my mind subsided. There, in the stillness, I found the piece of me, as I found peace with me. I found the essence of me that knew my version of success could only come from within *me*, nobody else, and it meant far more than just a career. It was — and still is — about being in alignment with what is truly important in my life.

I began to rebuild. Gradually, I found more enjoyment and meaning in everything I did. I experienced moments of real happiness. Not only did the stress and anxiety eventually disappear, but I began to enjoy more success across all areas of my life, including... wait for it... in my career.

After vowing that I would never get married again (I mean, who would blame me after two 'learning' marriages?!) I met the woman of my dreams... so, YES, I'm married again, and THIS time, it's for a lifetime. I'm now living happily with my beautiful wife and daughter in the picturesque beachside town of Byron Bay, Australia. I've created a life for my family and for mySELF that is full of meaning and purpose; a life that I would never have dreamed was possible a number of years ago.

The move back to Australia means I am much closer to my son. We are less than 50 km away from each other now. No more red-eye flights required. We still have some healing to go through together, but we see each other far more often and he adores his new little sister just as much as she adores him.

I am a different person, a different husband, a different father. A different human. I am more patient, more loving, more understanding. It seems worlds away from that crazy, stressed out, emotionally anxious guy I used to be.

I've awakened and I've found that what we crave in the future is accessible to us NOW if we are willing to slow down to gain more clarity, challenge our existing beliefs, and use the space it creates to do the things that we previously believed one had to wait for.

Once I learned how to more consciously lead my life, the happiness and freedom I had always been chasing came far more naturally and easily. I now know without a doubt that being a successful conscious leader starts at home. It has nothing to do with promotions or salary. It is about the way you show up with your wife, the way you show up with your kids, and most importantly, the way you show up with yourself.

Before I wanted success with the big *S*. Now, I just want to be the safe space that helps people redefine success so they can truly learn to be leaders of their own lives. I'm on a mission to help others to adopt a definition of success that DOES belong to them, to realize there is more to life, to empower themselves and to create change. I lead them toward balance, freedom and fulfillment.

I encourage you to redefine your success outside of your career. This brings you more peace, enjoyment and self-love. Let go of unnecessary stress and anxiety; instill calmness, clarity and confidence. Create connections, build loving relationships and be inspired to make YOU your most important priority.

Ignite Action Steps

- **Slow down:** Allow yourself regular time out to be still. Use meditation, be in nature, or just have quiet time to reflect and allow whatever needs to emerge to do so. When you slow down and give yourself space from the everyday noise of life, that is where the magic happens: You allow insights, inspiration, and intuition to arise.

- **Connect:** In those moments of stillness, ask yourself what is most meaningful to you in life. If you could truly live the life you wanted, what would your unique version of success be in terms of self, family, friends, career and contribution to society? Don't think it! Allow it to arise from deep within and write it down.

- **Keep the flame alive:** Now that you know what YOUR success is and you've ignited that spark of passion inside, you have opened yourself up to opportunities you may never have thought possible. What can you do today to keep it alive and take small steps towards being a truly conscious leader of life?

Michael D Lynch - Australia
Conscious Business Coach
www.michaellynch.com

KARYN KERR PETTIGREW

"Your work is meant to be an expression of you. When you express from your radical intersection, your power is multiplied."

It is my intention that reading this leads you back to your intuition and the choice to (re)claim all of you. You are a divine being and ALL of the things that animate, excite and call you are meant to be an active part of you. Embrace them and stand in your unique transformative power.

HIDDEN PATH TO YOUR POWER

It was a Tuesday in September when my daughter said, "Mommy, I don't want to go to school today," eyes wide, resisting me as I held her hand and walked to her classroom. This was so unlike my daughter. She was five years old at the time.

"Hey pumpkin, what's wrong? Do you not feel well?" She looked at me and then down to the ground, simply shaking her head. I felt her forehead and asked if she felt sick.

"No, I just don't want to go." She was virtually in tears. I looked at my watch; I had seven minutes to make my train.

"How about this," I suggested. "Try to go this morning. I will talk to Mrs. Morrison. If you still don't feel well in an hour, I will ask Amma to come to get you." She looked up and nodded her head okay. It was a tough call for me because kindergarten was only for half a day.

I made my train, barely; sweat stinging my eyes from running the last block. In the midst of trying to collect myself, I didn't initially notice the people on their phones. There were *a lot* of people on their phones. I ignored the tingling on the back of my neck and went on to find a seat. It was only 22 minutes to downtown. I finished applying my makeup and drank my tea. The buzz of people talking never dissipated. It felt weird.

As we were exiting the train, I realized there were a lot of people still in the station. My walk to the office began to feel like I was swimming upstream. More and more people were walking toward me away from downtown. What in the world was going on? The tingling on the back of my neck returned.

I finally looked at my phone. I had missed several messages. One of the three from my office read, "The city is in a state of emergency. All 911 liaisons are to report to the city's control center immediately. I ran the rest of the way to my office, unsure of what was happening. There were so many people in the street. It was already the makings of an unusual day.

At the time, I was the director of marketing and communications for Chicago's natural gas utility. Part of my job was to help them become customer-centric as the industry deregulated. Instead of thinking of the customers as a gas meter, we were bringing humanity to the forefront. It was a job that I took seriously and I knew it would be an interesting challenge. The rest of my job was to serve as a primary contact for media and public relations. Basically, if a pipe blew or if there was a gas-related incident, either my boss or I was responsible for responding to the media. I had been called into the field dozens of times.

That day was September 11, 2001. Terrorists had just attacked the US World Trade Center and the Pentagon. It was the first and only other modern-day attack in the United States since Pearl Harbor over 60 years ago.

When I arrived at the office, all but about 50 key employees had been evacuated. Critical Chicago services were on high alert as potential targets; however, we couldn't abandon our work centers completely. City services like electricity, gas and water were essential to maintain. It didn't help matters that our sister offices and the one next door were three of the tallest buildings in Chicago.

Fortunately, emergency service action plans were in place from the Y2K/millennium preparations. It was a very long 72 hours. The 9/11 attacks impacted the nation and devastated the lives of millions. It changed the nature of safety precautions and travel around the globe. It also punctuated a deep gnawing discomfort with how I was serving the world.

I realized that my daughter had known something wasn't right that morning.

She wanted to be home where she felt safe. She was completely plugged into her own intuition and awareness that something was off.

Missing so many of the clues that morning made me realize how out of touch I was with my intuition. I was so caught up in D-O-I-N-G things as a wife, daughter, mother, and star employee that I was losing myself. Everything felt external. I was disconnected from things that had meaning, with no real animation in my day-to-day life. Almost like being on a treadmill. Lost and cut off from my calling.

Shortly after 9/11, I connected with a mentor, Sonia Choquette, who suggested that I had a talent for healing others through the use of intuition. Her recommendation finally acknowledged an awareness I had been feeling and ignoring for a while. I was doing a great job at work but not loving the work I was doing. I became a voracious reader of all things metaphysical, spiritual, and religious. From the Bible to the Tao, from the mind-body connection to its connection to quantum physics, I was a sponge; trying to absorb and understand as much as possible. For two years, I read, attended lectures and had mind-bending conversations about the nature of reality.

And then I hit the wall.

Being on call for emergencies and with a household to maintain and two young children was tough enough, but when combined with a dramatically waning interest in my day-to-day work, showing up as the Karyn they had come to expect was almost impossible.

I started making little mistakes. Nothing career-ending, but not the caliber they had come to expect. Just before the holidays, my boss took me out to lunch.

"Karyn, what's going on?"

A dead pause from me.

"You're not really acting like yourself. You seem distracted at times. A little off your game. You are in a position to be promoted and you can have any job. What do you want next?"

I wasn't prepared for these kinds of questions.

"Why don't you go home for the holiday? Rest up and think about what you'd like to do."

I wasn't ready to divulge any of my thoughts. I was a little worried about how my new explorations would be perceived. My new interests were not as common as they are today and I wasn't ready to share what I was discovering.

I took Christmas vacation and thought hard about what I wanted to do. Every time I tried to convince myself that it was not a good time to leave the company, I would get a little nauseous.

The truth was, I wanted to open a wellness center so that I could help people see that it is possible to get off the treadmill. I wanted them to understand the connection between what they were thinking and what was showing up in their bodies. I had the desire to help move humanity forward. I knew I could inspire businesses to operate in a more humane way.

So, I decided to quit my job.

No, it wasn't quite as clean as that. I had had deep discussions with my husband at the time. We were both nervous, but we knew that something had to change. I had lost over 15 pounds as well as the sparkle that everyone had come to know as my can-do-get-it-done attitude.

The first day back from vacation, I took my boss to breakfast and with tears of gratitude and fear, told her of my plans to start a wellness center. I wasn't leaving for a new company, I was leaving to honor my spirit. My calling.

With a slight crack in my voice, I told her, "I'm happy to stay for three months so we can get things in order." I think that timing was not only to help her but also to give me time to wean myself from decades of programming about "having the right kind of job."

We attempted to keep my plans quiet for the next three months. I'm not quite sure how the "cat got out of the bag," but about four weeks after our conversation, people began to stop by my office to whisper that they "knew" about what I was I up to. Many of them would quietly close the door and tell me how they wished they had the courage to do what I was doing. I was nervous but relieved, and it became the beginning of conversations with others about how to live from the heart.

I did leave three months later, but I didn't open a wellness center. I started writing a book. Six months later, it was published. *I Quit and Choose Work that Aligns with My Soul* was a narrative workbook which told mine and others' stories of hitting the wall but consciously choosing to follow the soul.

The book led to talks, presentations and coaching. I was fully immersed in my heart's work. It opened the world for me to become a conscious leader. Everyone in my family benefitted. I was able to be present without exhaustion. I spent time each week in my children's classrooms. I found community and friends who spoke my language and didn't think I was strange. I (re)discovered my intuitive wings.

One of my clients at the time was taking on a new Chief Operating Officer role at a business incubator and knew they were looking for coaches. It was a perfect match. The next thing I knew, I was coaching five entrepreneurs per year through the program. While I was hired to be an executive coach, I was not able to leave my business training at the door. What happened next can only be called the emergence of my radical intersection.

As I worked with the entrepreneurs, I began to notice a correlation between the problems they were having in their business and the personal blocks they were experiencing. It was almost as if someone was skywriting for me because I could see the links and patterns energetically. I developed a program that aligned the seven Hindu chakras (energy centers in the body) with the key functional areas of an organization. For instance, if someone shared that they were having marketing trouble, especially with attracting the right customers, I knew that there was likely to be a block in the entrepreneur's fifth chakra, the one governing expression. From there, we worked to uncover what wasn't being said and expressed.

The chakras align with business functions as follows:

7th Crown Chakra — Inspiration/Mission: Is the business, idea or action inspired, drawn from an animated space?

6th Third Eye Chakra — Vision: How does the vision unfold in its richness?

5th Throat Chakra — Marketing Strategy: What is the language used to express the organization's brand and positioning? Is it accurate, defining, differentiating?

4th Heart Chakra — Operations: How do the ideas become action?

3rd Solar Plexus Chakra — Human Resources: What process and structure will support creativity, innovation, emotional freedom, openness, and respect?

2nd Spleen Chakra — Customer Service: How do we prepare the front line to be responsive and inspired to serve?

1st Root Chakra — Sales Strategy: Who is our ideal customer and how do we best meet their needs?

If you look carefully, you will see that there is a sequence or flow in the body from the seventh chakra to the first. The same is true in an organization, from the idea or inspiration through to the very first sale. Discovering this parallel flow led to interesting conversations when clients had sore throats, stomach bugs, low sales, or trouble finding the right customers.

That work led to my four-part Blind Spot process, which ultimately evolved into my concept of the *Radical Intersection*. Your Radial Intersection is the place where your loves, gifts, strengths, callings and wonder converge. It is where you (re)claim and activate all aspects for your most powerful self.

To me, conscious leadership is best executed from this place. The place where you stand in the glory of all that you are, leaving nothing off the table. People suffer because they can't figure out how or have been led to believe they cannot integrate some aspect of themselves. The attorney who loves photography, the fireman who wants to teach — these things can seem unrelated and without correlation. But it is impossible for these facets to not work together if you allow them to align within you.

You are the divine union, the point of convergence. Just as we imagine nothing that we are not prepared to pursue, you are drawn to nothing that cannot come together in you. Your job is to work at bringing them together. Sometimes, this will be through a hobby; other times, it will be in your daily work. In either case, you must not ignore these callings. They make you...you! And they lead to your greatest power.

My radical intersection combines my love of travel, fashion, beauty, empowerment, entrepreneurship, working from anywhere, saving the planet, and helping others. Each day is an opportunity to dream, express, create and just be happy. I am fortunate to have launched two businesses from this special place.

When we are fully integrated, serendipity is our constant companion. Things align. Doors open. We can reduce the effort but increase the effect. That is your birthright. You are the only *you*. The world needs exactly what you have to offer!

This is how I see peace happening on the planet. One by one, with each of us finding our way to the activation of our unique attributes. When you are in the flow, there is no anxiety, no resistance, no need to compare your life to anyone else's because you are content. You claim your life. This becomes your hidden path to power.

IGNITE ACTION STEPS

WORKING TOWARD YOUR RADICAL INTERSECTION

Grab a pen and paper, or your journal, and answer the following questions.

There are no right or wrong answers. Pay attention to things that seem to "pop" into your mind.

Ask yourself the following:

1. What do I love?

2. What are my gifts or talents? (Think about what your friends would say.)

3. What are my strengths? (Those things I love to do and do well.)

4. What callings do I have? What callings have I ignored?

5. What am I curious about?

6. What are my aspirations?

7. What do I think should be different in the world?

Once you have answers to the questions above, see how many of them are integrated into your daily life. If they are not, spend some time figuring out how to add more of them in. Work with a friend or partner on this exercise. I find that companionship is a helpful motivator and just plain fun. If most of your responses are already active in your life, congratulations! And thank you for living from your radical intersection!

Karyn Kerr Pettigrew - USA
Founder of ZoeGoes
ZoeGoes.com

ANNE TUCKER

"Everything you create starts with your energy."

I am aware that my life and what I create in it are a reflection of me and my inner landscape. The first place I need to start is with my own energy. What I wish is for you to come to this awareness faster than I did; to save you some of the struggle. Rather than spinning your wheels trying to change your outer world, look first at your inner world. The changes you make there will flow naturally into your life.

WHAT YOU MAKE, MAKES YOU

When my son's 4th-grade teacher asked for volunteers, it was clear that all the parents were expected to volunteer for something. So, I signed up to be the class Virtue Mom. I thought I was picking the simplest option. The year before, I had signed up to do the class auction project and that was a ton of work, so Virtue Mom seemed like a pretty easy job by comparison. I had to come to the school once a month and teach a 30-minute lesson on virtues to the kids.

I had no idea that this choice was the first step that would lead me down a path of total joy and then complete frustration, and finally, to my own deep, personal growth.

I could have made being Virtue Mom an easy job. I could have fulfilled my duties just by reading a nice picture book to the kids that the librarian recommended and calling it good. But I'm never happy just doing the regular thing. Once I get started on something, I tend to get carried away. Within minutes,

I'd dismissed the book idea and thought instead, "Wouldn't it be fun to create a board game about virtues?"

Well, I was right — making a game was fun. But it was anything but simple. My kids and I invented what is arguably the coolest board game ever. Using parts from Home Depot and a photo printer, we made a 3-dimensional, spinning board game. A stack of 60 cards gave the kids funny tasks related to different virtues that would move them through the board. I called it The Virtue Game.

On the day that I finally brought the game into the classroom, the crazy 3-D boards were a sensation. The cards we'd made had the kids laughing so much that teachers from neighboring rooms came in three times to ask us to quiet down with no success. It was a home run. At that moment, I moved out of the intellectual exercise of creating the game and I was shocked into a feeling of gratitude at seeing their joy... the impact of the game was so uncomplicatedly beautiful, and I had done that. Me. Every time they drew a new card and reacted to the silly tasks, I saw how delighted they were and it felt like Christmas morning when I was a little girl. I was stunned and delighted to see what was happening, to see their genuine delight, and to recognize that I could create that over and over again.

After the third kid came up and asked me where their mom could buy the game, it slowly dawned on me that, not only had I made something that made character education fun, I had also created something I could sell.

I loved the idea of starting a business with the game and with total joy, I immediately jumped into the process of producing it. First, I had to work the kinks out. That meant testing and revising it again and again in different classrooms and at different schools in the area.

At one point, I brought it to a character education conference in Canada and when the event organizer invited me to show it to the whole group, I spent hours in my hotel room with yellow duct tape and glue sticks, trying to get enough boards constructed and cards cut out for everyone to play the next day. The whole process was a crazy by-the-seat-of-my-pants adventure, but every time I watched someone play the game, I felt the joy of it and I was inspired again.

After a little research, I learned that producing my 3-D game board was too expensive, but I realized that the real value was in the funny cards anyway, so it became a much simpler card game. While progress didn't exactly happen in a straight line, everything I needed seemed to show up as I needed it and I was able to get the first shipment produced. I was in business! I was wildly optimistic and completely unaware of the challenges I was signing up for.

From this fantastic high, my new business and I began a sad, slow, steady descent. Selling the game wasn't easy. I tried everything. I did ads, articles, in-store demonstrations... I got press interviews and hired distributors. Almost all of these very time-consuming efforts led nowhere. It was incredibly demoralizing. They'd get a little bit of traction, but only if I was there to hold each sale by the hand — in other words, they never reached any scale and the sales were limited to how many resources I personally put in.

My entire life, I believed if I put in the effort, the success would come. I relied on this belief to fortify myself and draw up the courage to step out into the world. But *this* process was like the gradual unwinding of all that armor so that, in the end, I was left naked and winded. As one little defeat after another piled up, it gradually eroded my trust in myself and in my ability to make things work out as I intended.

Google ads would lead to a few sales, and while these sales led to some great unsolicited 5-star reviews on Amazon, I was just breaking even with each purchase and I was burning through my inventory. I went to a trade show and sold games to a dozen or so independent toy stores around the country. A dozen stores is nice, but nowhere near what I'd hoped and confusingly low, since the game was voted one of the best new products by the other exhibitors. I even had two other vendors competing to try to buy the rights to the game from me.

I was in the back of an airport taxi cab coming home from the trade show when the most promising of the two vendors called me with his final offer. It was low. Very low. I asked him if he realized that I would be giving him my business at a loss, that all that work and inventory would result in nothing for me. His offer seemed heartless, but to him, it wasn't a passion, it was just a business. It made me feel like what I created was not even value-less. It was a liability. I floated up out of my body and couldn't feel anything except the hollowness in the pit of my stomach. It was the death of a dream.

What was so tantalizing and frustrating about these small deaths was the reaction of the people who did buy the game — people LOVED it. I got love letters from teachers, parents, and school counsellors asking me to make more cards. I would see on Amazon that people were coming back to buy three copies at a time to send to people as gifts. The game even won a few awards. I just couldn't get enough buyers to look at it to sustain a business. Are you depressed yet? Because I was.

I try to learn from my experiences and this one had some important lessons for me. Going back and looking at it now, something stands out to me that I couldn't see then. In all of the information I'd created to sell the game, there was no mention of *me* at all. I wasn't anywhere on the website — not even my name. It was as if the game had been invented out of thin air and did not have a real, living person behind it.

Even before I created the game, I felt uncomfortable making myself visible — it made me feel exposed and vulnerable. I was so resistant to being seen online that I avoided setting up a FaceBook account for months. When I couldn't avoid it any longer and I had to post a profile picture, I chose one where the camera was upside-down and I was wearing a pointy paper party hat. My head looked like a scoop of ice cream in a cone and you'd have to turn your computer upside down to see my face.

I was hiding. I didn't want to be seen in such a public way. The problem was that my game business was an extension of me. I created it, my energy was the blueprint, and if I was hiding, then my game was, too.

I didn't understand this and the failure of The Virtue Game ate at me. Every time I thought of starting something new, The Virtue Game hovered in the back of my mind. After trying so hard in so many ways to make it work, the only remaining variable I could blame was me. I thought my energy must be blocked in some way, but I didn't know why. I began to search for ways to find and heal whatever it was in me that was preventing me from succeeding with my business.

I dove into self-development with the same abundant enthusiasm with which I approach most things. I was opening up to energy work and hypnotherapy, and I was learning to see myself through a new lens. I began to understand that this failure, and all the other hardships in my life, had happened *for* me, not *to* me. That it was all perfectly designed to show me where I was holding myself back and to help me grow.

I felt like I was becoming a better version of me. And I liked it. But the more clearly I saw myself, the more I seemed to fall out of resonance with the people around me. My friends didn't seem to want me to change and I began to feel more and more alone. Desperate for connection, I sent an email to eight women I knew to see if any of them were interested in having a discussion group about personal growth. Not a single one responded. That was especially hard. I really wanted to talk to others about my experience. I needed to be around people who were exploring these new ideas, reading interesting books, pushing themselves to grow. People I could learn from and share my journey with; who could see me for who I was becoming. The people I'd relied on up until then weren't able to move forward with me. I wanted to find people who could.

It's funny how all things have a purpose. If I hadn't felt so isolated, I would've never been motivated enough to do what I did next. Since I didn't know how to find the community I was looking for, I decided to step way outside of my comfort zone, become visible, and see if they would find me.

I started a public meetup. I rented a beautiful theater space right in the middle of downtown. I wanted to attract people I could learn from, so I decided to make the meetup a monthly speaker series. I called it Wisdom Soup.

Since I had no idea if anyone would show up, I decided (like a kamikaze pilot diving straight into my fear) that I would be the first speaker. I'd done a lot of public speaking for work, but that was a safe, known context. I'd never put myself out there publicly like this, to people I didn't know, in a context where I was showing up as *myself*, open and vulnerable, talking about things *I* care about.

There was the very real possibility that no one would come, which would mean that I could stay hidden, but then I would still be alone. So when the big night arrived and 25 people I'd never met before came in and sat down, I was overjoyed and just so grateful. And maybe just a little bit terrified.

Three years later, Wisdom Soup has evolved into a vibrant community with over 870 local members and more who join us each month remotely from around the world via the live broadcast. We've continued to meet regularly every month and we even have a big annual event called the Wisdom Soup Spirit Summit that sells out every year. Wisdom Soup has been the community and friendship that I was looking for, and so very much more.

It turns out that there were a lot of people who were also searching for the same kind of community and when I finally decided to make myself and Wisdom Soup visible, they found a home, too. The community has grown to be important to so many and it belongs to all of us. The people who are a part of it have found teachers, healers and friends that have transformed their lives, and the impact of this community ripples out from each one of them.

What I learned is that creating something like a game or a meetup doesn't stop when your product gets shrink wrapped. Your finished product is just the beginning, the seed. That's the part I'm good at. But creation is an expression of divine energy and if you want to bring something new into the world, you have to follow the same rules and steps that nature does.

I needed to help that seed sprout and support it through all the stages of growth into its fullest expression; to grow it into a tree that bears fruit that others can eat. When I was trying to bring The Virtue Game out into the world, I needed to access a type of creative energy that was new to me, that would draw attention to me, to my energy, and then create community and support around it. And as long as I was determined to hide, I was blocking the flow of that energy through me. Later, when I started Wisdom Soup and I consciously decided to push myself out of my comfort zone, I stepped into that unfamiliar energy and the community and the support that had been missing before suddenly appeared.

Growing a business motivates you to push yourself into the energies you don't know. You encounter difficulties you never imagined. You find roadblocks where you least expected it. And those roadblocks have an unsettling habit of being located firmly in the center of the places where you are holding yourself back. Where you're hiding, or doubting, or under-valuing yourself... that's where you'll run into trouble.

When you put yourself, your energy and your life's purpose out there, by stretching your boundaries with self-compassion, it's one of the best pathways to personal growth that I know. There are always parts we bump up against and struggle with as we're trying to create something, and that's the point. If life were smooth and easy all the time, we wouldn't grow. This planet is a healing place, but not in a relaxing, spa vacation way. We come here to be challenged so that we can become aware of and work on our issues.

Whenever you decide to throw your hat in the ring, you are becoming more of who you really are as a divine creator. Your false starts and moments of despair, and even your failures, aren't really failures at all. Just by trying, you are already succeeding at what really matters. You're succeeding at becoming you. And the more of you that you can embrace and allow to flow through you, the more that you will love your life, because your life is a mirror of the beauty inside you.

IGNITE ACTION STEPS

Seeing yourself clearly isn't something that comes naturally. When things go wrong, you might think you're just having a really bad day. But in fact, you may be bumping up against limiting beliefs or unprocessed emotion and not recognize that the negative experience you're having out in the world is coming from inside of yourself.

For example, if you feel unseen or unheard in some way, take a look at your profile picture. Is it a clear, bright, authentic photo of you? Or is it a picture of your dog? How comfortable are you with receiving the attention or recognition that you might feel is missing?

To put this in action, close your eyes and feel into your desire to be seen and appreciated. What would you like others to recognize about you? Is it your creativity, your loving heart, or your integrity? Or is there a talent or interest you have that people don't know about? Then, post a photo of yourself on social media that you feel reflects this gift. As you do, notice any feelings of vulnerability that come up.

You can use your work in the world as a mirror of your internal state to give you information about where you have limiting beliefs or unprocessed emotions. When you bump up against obstacles or when events trigger you, you can access this wisdom by reverse-engineering what happened.

Open your journal and ask yourself, what is happening right now that feels like a block or trigger? Then begin with the question, *"What would I have to believe in order to create this?"* Begin writing, even if you aren't sure of the answer at first. Your writing process can help you to explore and unwind your subconscious beliefs.

Anne Tucker - USA
Founder of Business Energetics and Wisdom Soup
www.AnneTucker.com
www.Bizenergetics.com
www.WisdomSoup.com

FRANCESCA CIAUDANO

*"Don't snooze on your Life — it is waiting for you to wake up beyond
your current reality and take you on a journey of wonders."*

**I'm a fugitive writing to show you how to escape without physically leaving.
When a sentence is decreed, we have choices: to learn, grow and break
free from the chains. Or the freedom of reliving it over and over again till
it suffocates us. Allow what is within you to surface. What will surface is
there to set you free. Together, we can stage a jailbreak. Read on.**

A HERO MUST ALWAYS RETURN HOME

I'm here in front of this annoying white coat. What does he know about
me? How can he just tell me that there is nothing to do and my condition can
only get worse, unless… unless what? Unless I decide to change my life? Who
is he to judge me? What does he know about the life I conduct? I built this
masterwork piece by piece, muscle after muscle. This is exactly what I wanted.

I shut the door behind me and start the search for another white coat.

Those shaky legs, those pus-filled skin-eruptions, that heart exploding in
my chest are not my property. I don't accept them. Next registration counter,
next waiting room, next white coat comfortably seated on their blue chair, a
desk separating us. The story repeats. Another doctor trying to convince me
that the only exit is to change my life and ingest some man-made chemical
pills. Well, that's not an option I can entertain.

The scene goes on with a few more white coats and similar outcomes until a friend recommends I try an alternative called Ayurveda. It requires a minimum of three weeks' treatment and a trip to India. How could I possibly take so much time away from work? Utterly unrealistic and totally impossible, the suggestion is immediately dismissed. I walk away from the idea but cannot walk away from the reality of my condition.

The darkness of my most hidden chamber has just gotten darker. At this point, the sense of obligation towards my job is surpassed by fear. My mind is not functioning. I'm barely able to drag myself out of bed in the morning. I reluctantly listen and book and flight.

Arriving at Trivandrum airport in India, I get in the taxi, my legs trembling in pain, my body agitated and tense. We reach some palm trees and a purple gate, entering an exotic-looking yellowish building. I go in and drop my luggage on the floor, waiting for my first encounter with the doctor. An assorted array of beings seems to be housed here, communed by dull appearances, green robes and glasses they carry around. I meet the doctor, who hands over my robe and my first glass full of some stinky potion. I understand that detention is starting for me, too. Not exactly how I had envisioned spending three weeks of my life, as I've never taken so much time away. My racing mind could not accept to waste this precious time in a hospital-wanting-to-be-a-resort in India, surrounded by sick-looking "holiday-goers."

How could I possibly have known these stinky concoctions and green robes would mark the initiation to a new me? A trip to my essence for which I have no ticket nor itinerary?

Locked in my room, it's 3 AM, and the space is colonized by morbid shadows, unwelcomed vivid nightmares and strident sinister noises. Unable to sleep, I let my mind take me back in space and time; I step down from a stage holding a significant advertising trophy in my hands. I'm enfolded by people. They are loud and overjoyed. Ecstasy is all around. They are all celebrating for me but, I soon realise, without me. I'm numb. Undeniably proud, but lacking that deep sense of happiness I was promised to feel once such an achievement became mine. Didn't I put in titanic efforts to get here? Didn't I always dream about getting what I have now? In the midst of those celebrations, I stand still, looking at myself, observing my own extremely successful life through other people's eyes. The promised happiness is powerless to fill the void. Silence. Empty silence. There I was, supposed to be celebrating my success, but nobody handed me a ticket to the party so I sat and watched from the sidelines.

This glimpse of my own emptiness cannot possibly mean much more than just a bad day, a bad mood. Tomorrow, I'll feel again. Tomorrow, I'll surely be in a celebratory state.

The job continues; I go on denying the signs for weeks, months, years. I am gradually contributing to my own disintegration. I can't see the bars yet. Getting immediately busy, sunrise after sunrise, just to be unconsciously pulled down into Alice's Underland, with the only difference being that magic, white rabbits and wonderful tea parties have been replaced by late nights, no proper eating habits, stress and constant anxiety. A wasteland of stones with no King or Queen of hearts.

"Make it happen" would become the mantra my team recognized in me, no matter how many people got burnt along the way. Me included. Completely unaware that I had walled myself in for years, feeling tired and incomplete; but in truth, never realizing that I was only looking for better food, a bigger cell, and not yet a way to escape.

Constantly concentrated, never attentive. An immense dispersion of energy accompanied by an unnoticeable misinterpretation of the "happening." In reality, I hadn't truly ever paid attention. Concentrating on myself and team performance, I excluded everything and everyone else until my new body conditions forced me to move from concentration to attention. Until overwork, overstress, overthinking knocked me down to the floor and commanded my attention — to see a new reality that excludes nothing.

The palpitations, the panic, the white coat... my eyes are open again, in this room in India, to finally fall asleep.

I wake up after a few hours to the anxiety of not being in control. The freedom of using my phone was taken away. No more emails, phone calls, contacts with the outside world — all withdrawn. Constantly short of time, I never thought I could spend it on my own with no accessory to help my mind escape. I could not eat what I liked to eat, speak to who I thought I had to speak to, work on what I considered important to work on. No beach, no pool, no exit from this hospital dressed up as a resort. In all of this, day after day, I'm not getting any better. My skin condition worsens and the repetitive darkest nights turn me into a sleep-deprived being. I'm ready to pack and go back home to my comfortable living, but anyone who knows me well is aware that giving up is not in my vocabulary. I know it too. So I decide for the first time, when I'm at the innermost cave of this adventure, to give it a try. Stop fighting for control of everything. Let it go. I breathe in, deeply... moment after moment... realizing that, consciously, I'm not even in control of the most profound thing that keeps me alive: my breath.

Seeing the true extent of my imprisonment, I stop denying and began to look for a way out. A way out, where the only possible direction is beyond the confines of the visible. A way out that takes me in. With this newly found acceptance, gradually my environment changes, lightens and the nightmares leave. There is silence, but this time it is not a cruel, empty silence — it is a silence that draws full attention.

The surrounding walls crash, leaving me standing in a newly defined space which I *see* for the first time. Stepping with naked feet on the ashes, I walk away from the stage, *free*. I was not in control of the script any longer, but perhaps I never truly was. If I had been in control, as I had always thought, then how could I have possibly broken down, ending up in this place far from home, alone, trying to treat a condition that was caused only by my mind? A demand from the same mind I thought I had control of. What if my conviction of being in control is what turned me into a convict? Was I really responsible to orchestrate the entire script of my life, or was the drama something over which I had only limited jurisdiction? What if there was another script? One where I was not so much in control of the outcome but in control of a new opportunity?

I recognised, for the first time in 17 years, that I had really never questioned, never allowed myself the chance to sit quietly in my own presence. I had passively accepted the societal and commercial truth of happiness: being readily available at the next rung of a successful career ladder... of the next recognition... beautiful house or exotic holiday... I had chased all of it, with all my strength and determination, as I thought this was also my truth. But now, this determination of pursuit and the illusion of control are replaced by silence that creates attention; new attention that broadens my narrowed focus to wider possibilities. Nothing is excluded anymore. Mind moves from the inactivity of just believing *what is* to the stimulating possibilities of *what could*. The realization is both painful and liberating. Painful, as energy and time was spent looking in the wrong direction. Liberating, as now I get out of my head and step into a new world-view, accessing and discovering new aspects of reality, which were hidden to my previously limited perception. Grateful to all *what was* and ecstatic to allow myself to discover *what could* and turn it into my new *what is*.

24 hours are left before I will be shipped back to everyday life. It was the moment I had been dreading when I landed in India, anxious about three weeks not possibly being enough to heal me. The job was unfixable. A prison. I would have to quit upon my return home.

Sitting on this terrace, facing the bluest ocean and the greenest forest, with a glowing new skin and no sign of the conditions that brought me here, my new self is anxious to pass through the gate and board on a plane. I'm ready to get back home. I freed myself from the prison.

Back home in Dubai, walking through the grey clinical corridor, I put my hand on the knob and push the door open; I breathe it all in. As I'm getting into the next supposedly-to-be-difficult meeting, one of those I used to fear, there is no anxiety, no sense of frustration. Nothing seems familiar anymore, but all feels natural.

As the days pass, it is clear that I have reconstructed myself and the rebuilding process has forever changed the way I would lead my life. I actually SEE people for the first time, not just as task-performers but as the flesh and soul that are behind those performances. I intellectually knew but never truly understood. My mental model was tuned to the wrong frequency; a frequency that turned down feelings, put our whole-being on pause while in office and expected machine-like human beings. That's the price we pay for our career, our financial security, our nice car, our glamorous travels. We couldn't afford all those luxuries just being ourselves, could we? Just being myself would not take me up the ladder to success and the expected happiness. But that, my friend, is just an illusion... the illusion of our mind, the illusion of having it all under control.

My new conscious viewpoint was becoming multidimensional. I had missed recognizing the soul of the organization; a spirit that went beyond the numbers, the profit, the sales and awards. The only way to get out of the toxic and disengaged environment was actually to get inward. To its people. To its heart.

Businesses are made and run by people, yet we easily and damagingly disregard their centricity; the fact that they have a spirit, a soul. No wonder 85% of employees* are disengaged at work and in search of meaning. We need to realize that if we keep looking for meaning outside of us, we will never find it. It's interesting that we can wander the world in search of purpose and meaning when they are something we create — not something to be trailed after in a futile treasure hunt. The fact that such a staggering percentage of the workforce is disengaged is, in my view, a clear signal that many are not ready to look within themselves to find purpose.

We are victimizing our positions by expecting something or someone else to solve our misery. It's our responsibility as leaders, managers and employees to drive the change, within ourselves first and then in our social space. A space where decisions are to be taken from a different truth. Routines to be un-routined. Culture to be re-empowered. Humans to be noticed. Eyes to be seen. Focus to be enlarged. Real connections to be revalued. Acceptance to be extended and difference to be celebrated.

I feel so profoundly changed without having left the job I considered the cause of all my miseries and frustrations. Moving from a pure transactional, performance-oriented work to a relational-people one had given me a purpose. I had managed to leave without leaving.

Three years have passed since my trip across the ocean to India and into the depths of me. I have become a more powerful, effective version of myself. A constantly newly born person, wife and friend. I revalued the delivery-chain of performance at all costs and redefined my role in it. I learnt that when you lead differently, people have no choice but to participate differently. Silence unveiled the culprit of my self-imposed trap while self-questioning taught me that, to truly leave, I had to face my internal limitations with courage. With this realization, the true elixir of my quest became fully unwrapped.

A difficult relationship, a stressful and unfulfilling job, these are to be faced without physically running away through finding yourself first. I staged a "jail-break." Not hard, once I knew the bars were of my own making.

Staging your own "jailbreak" requires going within. It is the path to free-dom — to not carrying the cage with you to your next job or to your next relationship... Like any hero's path, a journey cannot be complete without returning home.

This is the core of truly transformative leadership: finding your truth, facing it and bringing that new person back to your environment. To create a life of full potential, you only have to follow the thread of the hero's path.

IGNITE ACTION STEPS

Strip yourself raw
Watch your thoughts floating gently...and let them go
Free yourself — know you are not your thoughts
The space you never knew was there will reveal its full power

Are you ready to "jailbreak" or are you just looking for better food and a larger cell? Curious to know what your true life potential is? If you are, it requires constant practice. Sign-up to a daily membership plan to your own mental gym. The practice is extremely simple but not as easy as it might sound.

1. **Silence, silence and more silence.** Daily. Silence is the true elixir to wellbeing and happiness. Only if you allow silence into your Life will it be able to show you its full wonders. Twenty minutes of daily mindfulness

meditation is required. *Sit comfortably, close your eyes and pay attention to your breath naturally coming in and out through your nose. When you notice you are thinking, bring your attention back to your breath without judgment. This is all you need to do.* Remember the power is in being silent and observing your thoughts and breathing. (*See resources for more info.)

2. **The regular practice** will allow you to become more aware and start noticing the mental models that make up the walls of your cell. What are the situations that trigger negative emotions and discomfort? Start noticing them objectively; then, understand their source. This process will transform you deeply. Each of us will go through it in different ways. There is no work-for-all formula; however, if self-enquiry is not enough, there are plenty of courses, books and workshops that can help you on this journey. Find the one that resonates with you.

3. **Knowing** is not enough to truly break free — you need bravery.
- **Be brave** to trust and take action.
- **Be brave** to give yourself the chance to live the life you feel right for you — and not the one the people around you expect you to live.
- **Be brave** to know when your direction needs to change.
- **Be brave** to go against logic, to fail and succeed.
- **Be brave** to break the box you are fitting into right now.
- **Be brave** not just to speak your words, but to live your truth.

Finally, transformation is meaningless if aimed to please your own ego. Ask yourself how your journey can benefit others. Be the hero that comes back home. Lead from this new core. You'll notice that. Once you change the way you captain, people have no choice but to change the way they travel along with you.

Do you dare to be the hero of your life?

Francesca Ciaudano - United Arab Emirates
Marketing Professional and Conscious Leadership Advocate
cfrancy2015@gmail.com

ASHLEY AVINASHI

"Bring ALL of you. The world is waiting."

It is my wish for this story to remind you that showing up as our true selves, in our vulnerability, connects us deeply. Connection leads to trust; trust to an opportunity to inspire. As you allow yourself to be loved and be seen beyond the parts that have been hidden away, you will be led to your truth and light. Spend time exploring your authentic nature and gifts, and honoring your bumps and bruises along the way. The struggles are here to teach you just what you are made of.

BORN AGAIN: A RETURN TO TRUE SELF

When we become disidentified with the roles we take on to earn love and approval, space becomes available to create with infinite possibility. When our own pain is transmuted, we meet our truest purpose.

Sometimes, in a lifetime, we are given an opportunity to reinvent ourselves. As we gather the wisdom that has come from courageously transforming our inner limitations, we step into meaningful service for those around us who have faced similar thresholds in their own lives. The path opens as we bring true selves forward, and accepting ourselves in all of our humanness helps deepen our compassion for those who have yet to recognize their own light.

My own compassion originated in witnessing the sufferance my parents carried from their lineage, and from their cultural and societal framework.

Despite this, they did all that was possible, within their capabilities, to raise us well. They instilled a great resilience and work ethic in us, and a profound sense of community. Being of East Indian origin, helping and supporting the collective was a part of our daily lives.

From this foundation, I created the *perfect* life. Well, seemingly perfect, as per the formula for success. Through hard work and focus, I found my way into thriving positions of acknowledgment in almost every aspect of life. In my high school years, I was nominated captain of our running and rugby teams, council member and top overall student. I earned a full scholarship to the university of my choice. This path of leadership continued into my adult years, first as a recruit for a fast-track management program, and later, as a thriving sales and investment expert in one of the busiest real estate markets in North America.

From a young age, I had my heart set on following the family lineage, that of entrepreneurship. My exposure to business formed the framework by which I aimed to lead, much of which was unconscious. I carried a desire for perfectionism. A deep-rooted habit of workaholism. An attachment to external validation. There was a sense of idealization in managing "all the things."

Everything seemed to work just fine. My goals expanded over time and I surpassed each and every one — in areas of career, fitness, travel and more. Yet, at some point in this cycle of over-achievement, my energy became increasingly depleted. There arrived a sense of meaningless purpose in the busyness. I was on autopilot, which limited my ability to pivot as needed. Daily tasks such as driving a car felt robotic and disconnective, yet I motored on, empty and confined to my own mental prison.

Little did I comprehend that my desire to stay on the hamster wheel would lead me to a heart that was starved; a heart that deeply desired connection beyond the external metrics. Unknowingly, I was lost in patterns of proving myself to the world around me. The undercurrent of my behavior, not known to many, including myself, was driven by a need to be seen as good enough, and be loved for all that I did. Despite the *ideal life,* I felt enslaved to the personalities I wore on the outside.

With time, I came to see that my path was not my own. It was one that reflected the overwhelming commitments I had made to those around me. I was exactly the way I promised I would be — strong, resilient and able to handle anything. Yet, as much as I felt I was leading my best life, there was a striking void in my heart. How I was perceived was what fueled me, and the cycle had become unsustainable.

Experiencing motherhood was the turning point. Through my children, I started seeing parts of myself that I had never witnessed before. I had strategically been hiding in life by overworking, over perfecting, over everything. The children started seeing through my patterns. They challenged me to stay in my heart, though my intellect often interfered. The resistance of staying on the path I had created was too great to ignore. I hadn't given up on proving my worth since my earliest years, so taking space to slow down and reflect was foreign to me. I started percolating on what all of this was for. My earliest years of life had taken me into deep transcendental practices and connected me to a world beyond what the mind could perceive. Yet, my adult life felt propelled by the narrow vision of what I could control and manufacture on the outside of me.

I started to pause. A period of deep contemplation shone a bright light on how I was not leading with my heart. The one thing I wanted — to be authentically connected in a meaningful way — was what I kept myself from through many distractions. Like others I had seen in positions of leadership, I, too, had not resigned from my attachment to external outcomes. I, too, was exemplifying old patterns based on survival; rooted in fear and lack. I was still carrying the competitive spirit that I had witnessed in corporate life; one that focused on aggressive growth tactics rather than purposeful impact. I, too, was leading with an empty cup.

What I saw with time was that I was unknowingly playing into the old leadership paradigm. Where was collaboration in this *new-age* model? Why did it feel we could hold it all ourselves? Why did it seem that we could create without being very intentional about *how* we were creating? The old model was geared to self-indulgence rather than shining our individual light *to raise* the collective.

I felt conflicted with each step, knowing that I had poured my soul into all that had been created thus far. The path of overachieving felt predictable and easy in some ways, yet I knew that my trajectory would have to change. The ways of traditional success and validation from the external world no longer fueled me. I had community in the sense that I knew it to be, yet I no longer saw myself within it. I felt deeply ashamed for what I had come to learn would fulfill me. A paralyzing sense of aloneness plagued my days— badly bruised by moments that had me question the purpose of my entire existence.

I had spent many months at this point, cutting through waves of emotional turmoil and silence. Being away from all I identified with was the only relief I came to know. Even through the uncertainty, the pain of not being true to myself had magnified and was excruciatingly difficult to unsee. What were once whispers held a definitive grip on every decision. I was seeing through my hustle for worthiness. My sense of self betrayal was agonizing. The foundation of beliefs upon which I lived my entire existence was upheaved. What I had come to know a *happy* life to look like was a mere illusion. I was fighting my own death before it had arrived. *Until it did.*

Another weekend arrived where I ventured into the abyss of uncertainty. The hiking group I was scheduled to climb Mount Gardiner with had not arrived; they had missed their ferry to the island where we were scheduled to meet. My heart was set on finding answers through exploration that day. I wanted to run hard and fast, to take space for me, to scream from the mountaintop at all of the disconnect I was plagued by.

My brief run through the woods and past a beautiful sanctuary hadn't quenched my thirst for adventure that day. So, I proceeded to the base of the mountain that I had anticipated climbing with the group. Inquiring about directions at the base, I was cautioned not to go up without a compass and some company.

As I parked my car, my nerves escalated. My intuition screamed that I proceed with caution while my physical self and soul were hungry to feel more deeply; to see more. Without any further thought, I hastily started running up a marked trail with only car keys in my pocket. In time, I understood the premise of the warning. The valleys on the mountain were deep enough to lose yourself in. What I had hypothesized would be under two hours to reach the peak felt to be three, four or possibly five. The trails became more sparse along the way. I had no sense of time. No watch nor phone, no water nor emergency equipment. My survival instincts had been peaking for months now and the rush of uncertainty amplified it. As I was sinking into fogginess from sheer exhaustion and lack of hydration, I arrived at the summit. There, I found a small group of hikers who too had had bouts of panic as they navigated through the valleys.

An overwhelming desire to find my way back rushed over me, as though I had been abruptly planted in a video game and my time was running out. I was dreadfully anxious to return before dark. Uncertain of the trek back, I found myself scurrying hastily down steep inclines without much caution. I trusted that I would find my way back before dark if I moved quickly, just as I had done throughout my life.

I encountered some streams which became wider as I attempted to descend. The skin on my legs exposed, cut open by the dense brush. I found myself scrambling across larger rocks while taking note of animal droppings. The trails certainly were not marked here. Any semblance of a path led to a dead end. I began to recall all of the dead ends that had come about in my life, those which offered a glimmer of hope — yet void of fulfillment and peace. "You can do this, Ashley. You will make it," I shakingly affirmed out loud. Over and over and over, "It is not your time yet."

I was so lost. Distressingly, I made my way up and down the valleys with what little energy I had. Entirely panic-stricken, I saw vacant cabins along the way, perched above the water's edge. In my increasingly depleted state of awareness, I thought to break through a window and take shelter until the following day. It was as though my life's fatigue had culminated into the utterly feeble being I had become. I had one last thought of dropping down to the ocean below with no reserve to ascend again. Perhaps a distant boater would notice me as I flailed for help in the ocean.

I had been calling out for help for what felt like several hours, shedding endless tears. My body did not have fuel to carry on. All the exhaustion accumulated through my years of *running* had caught up to me. I acknowledge that I had driven myself to my edge. In fact, for 38 years, I had been challenging many thresholds, racing out of my comfort zone, without slowing down to listen. I was shaken to the core as I attempted to digest my reality. My entire being was ready to give up, writhing in physical and emotional defeat. The totality of my being surrendered in that moment, preparing for a goodbye that would only be witnessed by the great force of nature.

Unconsciously, I was completely naked; face-to-face with the inadmissible polarity of this human experience. In the trenches of deep suffering and disconnect, I had been seeking a hint, a clue as to why I found myself on this planet. I had been awaiting an opportunity in which I could fully express the pain of having lost my truest self in this lifetime. Right then, I received the message that I had come alone and would go alone.

I said goodbye to all that I knew in those moments of taking my last steps. I envisioned my children growing into adults who would courageously live from their hearts. I thanked my parents for all they had shown me. Briefly, I basked in the hope that my physical parting would serve in reminding those who knew me to take care of themselves first. For all those, especially mothers, who had abandoned their own sense of self in exchange for love and approval from those around them. I took the last steps I could manage and collapsed to the ground as a bleak, defeated mass.

I wouldn't know how much time had passed, but there came a moment in which a very potent energy started moving through me. It brought me into a sense of peaceful knowing that I could not recall ever experiencing through my many years of self-inquiry. My eyes ever so subtly opened to the light that enveloped me.

My greatest recollection of those moments was a declaration to the Universe that if I were to return to the physical world, I would stand in my fullness. I would choose to live life differently. I can also extract from this experience a strong proclamation that my time in asking what the Universe could do for me was over. These moments were a definitive pivot towards living in contribution of humanity; my calling into service in a way that would be rooted in seeing my own light and fully embodying it to lead others to theirs.

Intriguingly, a path was before me, gently stroked with sunlight. The faint trail was visible enough to reassure me that there was a way home. A way into salvation.

The stream of light led me to a road, and beyond the road, to a home. Not fully aware of my state but feeling guided, I made my way across the road and fell to the doorstep. I was gently greeted by a woman with an angelic presence. She appeared to comprehend what had happened, sharing that a hiker had once before arrived at her door in a parallel state of shock, after losing his way.

I lay my beaten body down on her couch. I took my first sips of water, hydrating the heaviness that had led me to this experience. My heart sat in deep relief, yet my mind in disbelief. It was then that I was finally met with a great sense of knowing that I had a place in the world.

Over time, I became disidentified with the need for rigid roles, responsibilities and my old pain patterns. They had been deserted on the mountaintop. I embodied a tender luminosity, knowing my value was not in who or what was validating me on the outside. The layers of deep-rooted beliefs in not feeling to be enough were stripped away. I came into a deep sense of trust and gradually felt the dots connect. I realized a knowing that reminded me that, no matter what I choose for myself, I am more than worthy of joy and abundance. That I, too, am made of love. That this journey had been a calling to reclaim the forgotten parts of me so that I could fully show up to this life.

And this is how my purpose was born. To support just how we can keep the magic alive within — that which we are born with. Releasing much of my own deep imprinting and experiencing my transformation was needed before I could lead others to see the magnificence within themselves. This was my path to the stillness and disidentification from all that I thought I needed to be. With that, my most expansive self was invited to come forward — a self fueled by my truest nature and by my own life experiences.

My greatest inspirations have been those who work from the light within themselves. The universe *will* carve a path to infinite possibility for those willing to trust. It is your turn to believe that sharing yourself in all of your wholeness is the place from which you will shine your brightest. Bring ALL of you. The world is waiting.

IGNITE ACTION STEPS

- **There is only one of you in this world.** Lead as your authentic, whole self. Own each part of your story with vulnerability. This is where people find safety and connection. Your vulnerability will give permission to others to step into theirs.

- **It takes a great deal of courage** to stay the course in the way of self-discovery. The old patterns will try and pull you back. Trust that it is all working for you.

- **Only we ourselves know** where we are meant to travel in this lifetime. When you listen from within, you will be guided to your greatest life purpose.

- **Allow yourself to grieve** as old ways of being are shed and life invites you into more. Self-compassion is essential to opening to the path.

- **Your life outcomes will be reflected** by the frequency with which you have created. Be mindful and intentional about how you are stepping into your vision.

- **Yes, even leaders need support** and true community. Don't walk alone. Reach out and allow yourself to be seen in your humanness.

Ashley Avinashi - Canada
Raising Humanity Founder
www.raisinghumanity.com

SHERRY BRIER

"Rock Your Life: Be Daring, Dazzling and Divine."

I hope you come to know that the world is waiting for who *you* are. There will never be another you. My deepest wish is that you allow yourself to be seen, heard and find joy in an unlimited world of possibility. It's never too late. Believe in yourself and *do it for the world*.

CHAMPION FOR BEAUTY

Do you know how sometimes you feel like something big is about to happen? Something so momentous that you feel this tremendous pressure? I never gave birth, but I imagine it's something like that. The feeling that something is about to begin; something new wants to be born into this world. I felt that feeling about seven years ago: I knew I wanted to be of greater use on the planet.

I love teaching dance. My entire being feels ecstatic and free, and the music opens me to another world. Choreographing and directing my dance company feels like a sacred trust. Having my own dance studio where we come together and create beauty and community by dancing is a divine blessing. I'm able to take women who feel shy and awkward to a place where they see themselves as beautiful dancers who share their joy with the world.

But something was brewing. I kept asking Spirit what it was that I was supposed to do. I wanted to serve more people; to be a brighter light in the world. Then, I heard someone say, "The thing that breaks your heart the most is where your service lies." I realized then that the thing that brought me to my knees had always been the plight of women and girls around the world. I am horrified that girls aren't allowed to go to school, are married off at a young age against their will, and as grown women, are not able to go out into the workplace. As a warrior against wasted potential, I'm outraged that half of the human race is treated with varying degrees of suppression, abuse, and tyranny. Imagine what all that unleashed woman-power could create!

I recalled the saying, "Ask, and you shall receive; knock, and the door shall open." So I asked Spirit what I was supposed to do to support and motivate more women. I wanted to give them the courage and space to reveal their knowledge and wisdom, which is so desperately needed in the world today. I wanted them to know that they do not need to remain as hidden treasures. The answer came to me in a vision — downloaded in its entirety — name and all. I was to create Women Rock Project. It would be the largest online video library of women's wisdom. There would be hundreds of videos of women telling how they had overcome obstacles to live the life of their dreams and give back by inspiring, educating, and motivating other women.

And so I began.

I was astounded that I was doing it. There were so many new skills I had to learn, so many new people I had to bring into my life. It was a complete expansion of my personal energy. To date, there are over 500 videos of women on WomenRockProject.com. I received so many emails from people about how the project was such a revelation for them. I felt so much joy in my heart that I was able to reach more women and be of service in the world. To see so many women giving back inspired me to do even more.

A few years into the project, my life became very difficult. My sisters and I brought my 95-year-old mother from the East Coast to California to care for her. My health started deteriorating to the point where I could barely walk and I had to stop teaching almost all of my classes. It was devastating. I'd been teaching dance every day for almost 30 years. I didn't realize it then, but my life was about to change.

It all began on a vacation in Tel Aviv, Israel, as I was walking back to my hotel. The pain in my legs became so bad I didn't know if I could make it. Hobbling along, I wondered what was wrong with me and if I would be able to return home and teach my classes.

Back in the United States, I started seeing doctors who told me that I would need two hip replacements. I was devastated. I dropped most of my classes and suffered through the others. I contemplated what I would do when I could no longer teach, perform or direct my two dance companies. As I suffered from the thought of ending my career, I fell into a deep depression. I became more and more aware of what other women have endured throughout history and across the globe when confronted by unresolvable limitations. I swore that I wouldn't waste my potential.

Though totally doctor phobic and terrified to undergo surgery, there was no choice if I wanted to have a life. And there would be no guarantee of how much I could recover or if I'd ever be able to dance again, much less teach and perform with my dance company. As I was recuperating, I tried to imagine my life without dance, which was my all-encompassing passion. What would I do if I couldn't dance? And what would happen to the studio that I began 30 years ago?

My worry was less about the money I wouldn't be making and more about how I would be able to continue to resolve my two equally strong passions. You see, I'm a champion for beauty and a warrior against wasted potential. I'd been able to fulfill these two visions by teaching women to create beauty and, at the same time, inspire them to live up to their highest aspirations. My choreographies celebrate freedom and joy. I believe dance is a metaphor for life itself. Both should be approached with passion. I encourage my students to live out loud, to pursue all of their desires and shine on the larger stage of life. In my 30 years of teaching dance, I've seen so much woman-power being kept under the lids of being nice, subservient, and invisible. It was time to change that! Women and girls must cast off their limiting beliefs and allow themselves to be seen!

The less I danced, the more I felt that my life, like my jeans, was too tight. My world was getting smaller and darker. I needed to break out or I wouldn't be able to breathe. I wondered how I could bring my whole self to the world. How I could tap my fullest potential? How could I show other women that they need to take the risk to blossom, allow themselves to fly, and be the change that liberates the world, one woman at a time? How was I to regain my superpowers and become the hero of my life?

Again, I fervently asked Spirit. And again, the answer came in a vision. I was to create a physical manifestation of WomenRockProject.com by making Women Rock Project~Marin. Marin is the county in California where I live and about as big a paradise as you can find, with beautiful bay views, lush vineyards, and sheltered by the protection of Mount Tam. Women Rock Project~Marin would have a home in my dance studio and provide women with a safe and playful environment to discover their own beauty, power, and creativity. It would be dedicated to exploring our magnificent feminine life through workshops, classes, retreats, and journeys. Women Rock Project~Marin would arise from the ashes of my career in dance.

And so I began.

I usually jump in and start new things on my own, but I knew this idea was bigger than I could handle by myself. It had too many moving parts. And besides, my New Year's resolution was a very necessary two-fold gift to myself. I had vowed not to take on anything new that was too great an effort and would cause me undue stress.

The second resolution was to ask for help rather than being a lone wolf. I had built the studio with my husband, but I created everything in my dance world: the concerts, the choreographies and everything else needed by the studio. I knew that I could not continue on my own. I was taking on a great task by creating the first and only women's center in Marin County. I needed a mentor. I talked to a few different women who had models similar to what I wanted to create, but they weren't right for my vision.

As the Universe often does when things are meant to be, I received an email announcement for an event that was similar to what I imagined creating. Debra Giusti was hosting her monthly Women's Temple Night at her Temple on Pleasant Hill in Sonoma County. I was so impressed with her gathering that I approached her and asked if she would mentor me. She said that she had too much on her plate and just couldn't take on anymore, though she wished me well.

I was crushed. I knew intuitively that she was the right person to guide me. Apparently the Universe did, too. The next day she emailed me that she was very interested in my project and that Spirit had told her she should carve out time to help me. We talked and decided how we could work together. Basically, I would ask her what the next step was and she would tell me exactly what to do. Her experience, knowledge and wisdom promised to get my project off the ground in a quick and harmonious way. I ended up calling her "The Godmother of Women Rock Project~Marin."

We set a date for an initial gathering to test the waters and see who was interested. We called it "An Evening With Remarkable Women." I sent to my mailing list, attended women's events and gave invitations, and invited women who were doing interesting things in the community. I rented 50 chairs and waited for the RSVPs to come in.

Women Rock Project~Marin was off to an auspicious start. Fifty women showed up in my dance studio. All the chairs were filled in a big circle around the perimeter of the room. The women in Marin are so fashionable and interesting looking that the mirrors on the three sides of the room made an awesome kaleidoscope of colors and patterns.

I had created an agenda for the evening. I began by telling everyone how this vision came about; then, I introduced Debra. She spoke about the necessity at this time and place for women to come together and share our visions and commitment to saving the world. Eager faces nodded and often applauded as we poured out our heartfelt dedication to the rising of women around the world.

Next, we went around the circle and had everyone introduce themselves. They were instructed to say their name, where they're from and, in one sentence, tell us what they were passionate about. Have you ever tried to tell excited, intelligent women to restrict themselves to one sentence? It was, as they say, like "trying to herd cats." We had many laughs that warmed up the room and created a feeling of community right away.

It was gratifying to see the women immediately designing ways to collaborate with one another. I was thrilled that something I had created was so deeply appreciated and accepted. They were happy to be in a space that allowed them to connect with like-hearted individuals, growing the potential to make bigger changes in the world. This was the beginning of a new movement.

We scheduled our second gathering, "Another Evening With Remarkable Women," for early January and set the Launch Party for February. Then, Christmas morning, we got a call that our dance studio had flooded with the non-stop torrential rains in California. Long story short, we were out of commission for about a month as repairs were made.

You know the saying, "Man Plans, and God Laughs." I would have thought that the Goddess would have protected the studio so this project could move forward, but we never really know why things happen; The Goddess works in mysterious ways. When people asked when we would begin again, I kept saying, "After the flood…" I was beginning to feel like Noah.

We moved the second gathering to February and the Launch Party to March, on International Women's Day weekend. We felt that it was a divinely inspired date for the opening of a new women's center. With this new timeline, we felt like we were back on track.

Thirty-five women came to the gathering and again filled the circle around the studio. We began the intros. They were fascinating, as I knew they would be. I was excited to think about being able to bring this to the women's community at large. The evening ended with great anticipation for the Launch.

Everything was falling into divine order and the physical manifestation of Women Rock seemed well on its way when, once again, we were surprised by a new development. After 14 years of leasing this building for our successful business, our lease was up, the rent was to be doubled, and other stipulations were required. I was horrified that we could not continue under these conditions.

It turns out that the Universe was speaking to me again. It was telling me I had fallen off track; that the important thing was not the physical women's center. Rather, it was the bringing together of a community of kindred spirits and women-power to ignite the energy of others. As a result, I am following the original intention, organizing and promoting events *for* women, *by* women. The most recent event was completely sold out, to my delight, and I'm already hard at work on the next one.

It's always tempting to try to figure out why things happen. I've found that for anything to manifest, the time, place, and circumstances need to be right. I encourage you to find inspiration from others who created a vision, overcame obstacles to fulfill their mission, and live joyful, heroic lives. You, too, can become the hero of your own life, inspire others, and transform the world. The world is waiting for the gifts that only you possess.

Just remember:

Be Daring: Come Alive With The Fire & Passion Of Your True Calling
Be Dazzling: Radiate Healing Light & Transcendent Beauty
Be Divine: Become The Doorway To Ecstasy
Let Others Enter Through You
Dance For The World

IGNITE ACTION STEPS

The number one precept of all the ancient and contemporary mystery schools for living a conscious life is, "Know thyself." I've found that the quickest and most revealing way to learn is to ask questions. I believe we are always in conversation with the Universe. My question for myself is, "Am I listening?"

Your answers will begin to tell you who you really are and set you on the path to becoming the person you were born to be. Write and review your answers often, and you will begin to unearth the story of your life.

Complete the following statements.

My Mission — what is your personal and/or world vision for this lifetime?

I am Passionate About — what are you passionate about, either in your personal or business life, or some world cause?

I Think Big — give an example of how you think big in your life and/or in your business.

My Little Secret — share a secret that you use in your daily life that makes your life enjoyable.

A Funny Thing Happened — share a funny thing that happened recently that made you laugh. Your sense of humor can often save the day.

With a Little Help from My Friends — give an example of how your friends help you out — share something you would not be able to do alone, but with your friends, it is possible.

A Courageous Moment — share a moment when you were scared or unsure of what was happening in your life — and yet you chose to move forward anyway and faced your fears.

Divine Intervention — give an example of a situation or circumstance that was divinely inspired; where something big happened that you weren't expecting.

When you know who you are and your mission in life becomes clear, the next step is to love yourself. Then, you will become a light in the world.

Sherry Brier - USA
Women Rock Project
Founder/Dancer/Choreographer: Inner Rhythm Productions
www.SherryBrier.com

Ana Cukrov and Ivana Sošić Antunović

*"Live and lead consciously. Keep growing and connecting.
Let's weave the fabric of humanity together."*

Our intention is to remind you that you already are a true leader within. The need to lead is a moving force of the conscious person. We invite you to uncover your inner processes, becoming fully aware of how we all lead in our relationships. We enhance the quality of life and global evolution by continuously growing awareness in ourselves and in others. By keeping your awareness high and balanced in every aspect, your life satisfaction will expand. We hope to inspire you to connect and support each other — everyone's uniqueness counts.

A NEED TO LEAD

Dancing and strolling through life while connecting to ourselves and other people, we find the joy in sharing what we've learned and who we have become. Being twin sisters, different but very close, we had the privilege to grow side by side. That self-awareness process pushed us forward. Once we become mature enough to live authentically and openly speak about our truth, we felt blessed with peace and enormous pleasure. It derives from freedom and the power to inspire others. We became driven by a force so strong that we couldn't resist. We wondered, was it a need to lead?

This gradual unveiling of the leader within is precisely the experience we both have had in our lives. Working on this chapter together, we became aware of the whole process and we would like to share with you this gift of growing consciousness, so we bring it to you in the following dialogue.

Ivana: The other day I visited a local theatre to see the wonderful Andrew Lloyd Webber's musical "Sunset Boulevard." It truly was a masterpiece.

Ana: I love a good musical. Music and dance keep my soul warm, bring joy to my life and inspire me. When I sing and dance, I feel alive.

I: In the show, I noticed one particular dialogue. The lead character and his young sweetheart are passionate about writing a script together, but they both doubt it is possible. It reminded me of us, planning to do this chapter together.

A: It's a challenge, two authors expressing themselves in one story. But those musical characters achieved it. When you know and love someone, and share the same passion, it's easy.

I: We do love and encourage each other, sharing many of the same values.

A: But who are we to write on leadership? Just two twin sisters, hard-working mothers from the small country of Croatia, not having made a remarkable impact in the world. Can our simple testimonial be of use?

I: I believe yes. Being conscious of different aspects of your life is a way people lead, either leading themselves or each other. To get to know our physical self, emotions, cognitive processes, psychological background, our spirituality, intuition... our calling.

A: I believe that every person that ever lived is a leader.

I: It seems we can be on a different level of self-awareness. Someone can be really aware of their physique but unaware of their soul; or be very conscious about their emotions but not about intuition; or one can know his spirituality but ignore his body.

A: There's a great value in observing and accepting our strengths and weaknesses. It's empowering. Let's inspire others to live fully in each life area/phase.

I: Let's go back in time to remember and explore our personal growth path. Shall we start with the consciousness of our physical self? By that, I mean awareness of our body (posture, muscles, breath, health, exercise, etc.).

A: I remember when we started dancing as little girls and created a dance group. It was something we were passionate about and loved to do, and it raised our awareness and self-esteem. Sensing that, other girls joined us. We were awesome! Soon, teachers invited our group to perform at every school festivity. That is what leadership is.

I: Exactly. Showing our conscious selves in that flow gave courage and freedom for others to follow. We never questioned how good we were as dancers. So it was all around us. When you never doubt yourself, you glow and shine. Watching other girls trusting they are good enough and enjoying dancing warmed my heart.

A: I loved the fact that they trusted us as leaders. I loved the unitedness we felt. The best part of sharing our love of the beauty and harmony of the movement was transmitting our passion. It spreads and returns even stronger. And our developing skills led to self-confidence. Remember when you volunteered to dance with the principal at the prom? I was so proud of you! Some students hesitated, but were motivated by that and approached other teachers, themselves. That was leading by example.

I: We trained our muscles and our brains while dancing, each skill enhancing other skills in development, building like bricks one on top of the other. That's why we were also good at math, science, languages... In a way, we were leading ourselves in the intellectual sphere as well, and inspiring others to find the beauty in learning.

A: We loved to study and to play brain games. Getting good marks was highly rewarding and motivating. At the identity level, it was important to us that we enrolled in the best high school. We saw personal value predominantly through accomplishment.

I: Yes. Besides the physical and intellectual aspect, we needed to grow consciousness of other dimensions, like emotion, intuition and spirituality. Growing up with divorced parents, we naturally developed an interest in emotional wounds and searching for paths to overcome them.

A: That took us to the next level of self-consciousness: exploring our *psychological background.* Interest in that area motivated us both to study psychology. This choice of program probably derived from a strong need to understand and resolve some personal dilemmas. And we gained a lot of insight.

I: Learning about human nature and functioning inevitably created a lot of personal questions and broadened our understanding of ourselves. How can we even live free and fulfilled if we don't uncover our own baggage from our youth? Getting more and more in touch with the truth about past experiences was cleansing and awakening. I remember making my inner decision to never stop exploring and growing. I could feel the thrill of growing self-consciousness among both students and professors.

A: Some of them were true leaders: warm, accepting and encouraging — something that none of us was used to seeing in teachers back then. There were great teachers and mentors, but only some of them paid attention to our personalities and their relationship with us. Naturally, we were molded by the university professors that did.

I: We enjoyed these qualities and decided to be more accepting of others. In such an accepting atmosphere, it felt safe to explore our past and personality.

A: We also developed new skills like active listening, reflecting, giving and taking compliments, speaking up, accepting personal differences. These are tools that came in handy later, especially in family life and in business.

I: For me, every new working experience I had made me more aware of myself, my relationships with others and how we all affect each other. I discovered qualities I liked in me and also those I disliked. Sometimes I would get negative feedback from others, which was hard to accept. For some insights, I felt grateful and decided to change, but it was not always fast and easy. Some truths took longer to see.

A: I noticed a certain resistance in some areas, too. It made me feel angry when people criticized me. It was frustrating. Now, I see I was missing sufficient coping skills. Luckily, those came in later. Working with people in leading positions, I had different experiences — some were good bosses, some not at all. I experienced humiliation, not being recognized, and even mobbing. They turned out not to be true leaders nor self-aware enough. Although it was painful, those were important lessons. I learned how to be humble and, now, I'm grateful for that.

I: One more thing that helps in conscious leadership that we didn't mention so far is growing awareness of one's emotions. We now know how important it is to recognize your emotion, name it, choose how to properly express it, and control your reaction so you don't hurt other people.

A: We grow *emotional self-awareness* from early childhood, so it's up to the previous generation to show us how to recognize and regulate emotions. I realized the importance of that by becoming a mother. It was a double challenge, discovering my own strategies and weak points and teaching skills to children at the same time.

I: Me too. It's never easy to see my child get upset and guide them through it while staying calm at the same time. But these skills increase with practice —focusing on the feeling, allowing the emotion, naming it and letting it pass.

A: When my daughter was in the third grade, I started engaging with the school boards and collaborating in educational projects. Teaching her classmates about emotions had a significant impact in her class, improving both curriculum and human relationships in the school. But it had an even more profound impact on me as I grew into my strength as a leader, and it inspired other parents to step into leadership roles as well.

I: My work volunteering with diabetic children and their parents taught me so much. Walking side by side with parents in accepting a new diagnosis and coping with their fear of death helped me cope with my own experience as a mother of a diabetic. The most beautiful story was this teenage boy who, after having participated in the kids' support group, suddenly opened up so much that he was willing to stand up and talk about his experience. It propelled him to appreciate himself and helped his peers to see his wonderful uniqueness.

A: As I see it, humans have a need to gather not only for shared interests but also to experience the power of the group. We become more of who we are meant to be while connecting.

I: For me, forming and leading the Croatian National Twin Association was a huge challenge and honor. Hundreds of parents of twins have received support from people who understand what they are going through. Being a twin and a mother of two sets of twins, I felt it was a worthy cause to create.

A: I'm proud of you! Forming the twin association was your calling; mine was revitalizing the pastoral office in our diocese and conducting family Consultories. Helping individuals and families in crisis, lecturing and organizing national meetings made a long-term impact in the community. Seeing people gain from my professional competencies and knowledge is truly rewarding.

I: It is hard to see your calling without being fully aware of your whole identity. We couldn't possibly give love, share gifts so freely and joyfully, if we hadn't discovered another key aspect of life — spirituality. Being raised as atheists, religion was, for us, considered not only false but dangerous. Then, we met Jesus Christ and grew real faith. And it was the most beautiful encounter!

A: For me, too. Intimately knowing a person of immense power that loves me tenderly, above every human capability to comprehend, gives me both strength and insight. Opening to His love and grace, I become more and more ready to accept hardships and blessings. It gave a new meaning to everything I used to know.

I: Totally. I remember the moment I really felt God's presence. I literally sensed there is a higher consciousness and, at the same time, I felt showered with complete love, compassion, acceptance. It was total bliss. Somehow I knew with my whole self that everything I've heard about Him before is true. The Gospel is real! And suddenly, all the pieces fell into place. I felt aligned — my body, mind and soul were in harmony. Knowing from that moment on that my life was wanted by God, that I am truly loved, and that my existence has a meaning — gave my life a completely new turn. I learned we are all co-creators to this world and we are called to do it by supporting each others' growth in consciousness and love.

A: Unfortunately, most of us don't realize it. All the suffering that life inevitably serves to us has a meaning in growth. God is love; nothing cruel can come from Love. I know Him as a loving Father. We are not being punished, it is through hardship that we glow more brightly. Like gold being purified: the hotter the fire, the brighter the gold.

I: It is easier to accept all experiences if we see them as a step on the way; a step on the stairs to heaven. Our personal history is guiding us. It took a lot of inner work for me to learn to accept that. Seeing myself as not perfect but still loved helped me learn to accept others.

A: Letting go of the need to correct and force others to change is the crucial part. Following the lead of the Holy Spirit for me is the best part. I just sit and enjoy the ride.

I: It is connected to one's calling, THE unique purpose everyone has. The goal of personal growth is to become what you are meant to be and make your unique impact on the world. The secret ingredient of this process is the consciousness of it.

A: For me, life was about *joy* from day one. I always supported others so they could see how beautiful they already are. Looking back, I can trace it all the way. A friendless girl in school? I studied with her. Some lonely homeless guy? I would chat with him to lift his spirit. My colleague who wanted to make his girlfriend happy? I taught him how to dance. It was unconscious work, soul-responding, intuitively driven. While my actions became more decisive, the need was always to be happy and to make people happy.

I: I found out my soul's purpose is to bring light. As a preschool psychologist, I am truly committed to raising self-awareness in parents so they can be free in their relationship with their children. Free of their past, their fears, their struggles and their unconscious patterns. The more we put light into our darkness, the more free we become.

A: In my experience, children benefit most from conscious grownups. Still intuitive and accepting of themselves and others, children don't expect perfection. Until we teach them to judge and criticize, they are capable of both believing in themselves and supporting others. It's grownups who have to stop getting in their way.

I: I agree. A parent's role is of immeasurable importance in a child's life. Belonging and love, safety and autonomy, exploring and competence — recognizing and fulfilling children's needs is a parent's task and responsibility. A parent who is in tune with their child is more likely to foster a happy individual. If we are aware of the biases we bring to our parenting, we can prevent the negative impacts on our children. By offering parents a chance to develop positive parenting skills, we lead them toward being more conscious, growing alongside their children, and stepping into a fuller experience of their own lives.

A: As we keep learning and questioning one another, we enhance our lives. It empowers us to choose our leaders, models, and direction. We meet our guides as soon as we are ready. By gathering with those on the same line of vibration, we grow faster. By encouraging others, we personally gain — our capacities for compassion and serving expand, we grow humbleness, and we enhance our life satisfaction at the same time. Awareness allows us to be more effective, reach more people, give more back to humanity — reach fulfillment and meet our purpose simultaneously.

I: That is how, together, we build a beautiful net, a matrix; and, if all our individual threads in that fabric are interconnected, they are supporting the whole universe of souls. If I don't see my role in supporting togetherness, each thread lays on its own. But if I raise my awareness in all levels as a human being, uncover my unique purpose, and realize we are all One — then I can truly say that I am living my life.

A: We know your path is still yet to be discovered. Be gentle on yourself as you step into the greatest version of you. Awaken to your consciousness and embrace your leadership. Meet your need to lead. Let's strengthen the fabric of humanity together.

Ignite Action Steps

- **Pay attention** to the here and now. Be aware of what you are saying, feeling, doing.

- **Decide to live consciously**. Grow awareness daily, keep it high and balanced in all aspects (body, psyche, intuition, soul). Listen to your inner being.

- **Appreciate** all the leaders in your past and the lessons they brought. Cherish every experience and forgive what you need to forgive.

- **Remember** you have already affected many lives. Make a list and feel gratitude.

- **Envision** your goals and reconsider your role-models. Are the steps you are taking leading you towards the person you want to become?

- **Accept** your vulnerability. You don't have to be a perfect model to others… you're only human. You're good enough.

- **Connect** with others. Closeness warms your heart. Surround yourself with people that support your growth (at least 5).

- **Encourage** others to grow. Lead by example. Be gentle in reflecting to them what they don't yet see. Praise them and celebrate each step.

- **Recognize** your uniqueness. There's a special role meant exclusively for you. Seek and discover your calling. Live it bravely and proudly, having fun along the way.

Ivana: During the writing of this story, my mother-in-law passed away. Her name was Nada (meaning Hope). She was a passionate woman, who loved life in all of its fullness; she was intelligent and strong, brave and stubborn. A true leader personality, she was the heart and soul of every party, a people person. Although she had suffered a lot of hardship, she still managed to smile and inspire others. She dedicated her life to helping people as a professional nurse. She was most proud of her 5 grandchildren and she strongly lives in them still: her strong spirit, musicality, joyfulness, intelligence, leadership. I pray she rests in peace, and continues her impact on humanity through us.

Ana Cukrov and Ivana Sošić Antunović - Croatia
anacukrov@gmail.com, ivanasa22@gmail.com
Psychology prof.

EMILY C. ROSS

"YOU are the Hero of your own Story."

I share my story with you as a reminder that you're capable of so much more than mere survival. When you feel your lowest, weakest, most beaten down, that is precisely when the light inside you has the potential to be the brightest, Igniting in you a light to shine hope for yourself and others. May my story remind you that it is during adversity that we show ourselves what we're made of and what it truly means to be alive. When you thrive through trauma, it Ignites in others a desire to let their LIGHT shine.

KARUṆĀ

The Bayou Farm Adventure chapter is officially closed. I actually signed the sale a few weeks ago. It took a long time for it to sink in that it's not mine anymore; that I won't likely ever realize all those dreams I had attached so thoroughly to the most beautiful piece of land I will likely ever be able to call all mine. I have faith that, one day, this will hurt less. But, alas, that day remains elusive. I am grateful for all the ways God and his human angels on earth have shown up for us. I am enjoying the twists and turns Life has surprised me with. Yet there is something so unsettling about being ripped, mid-dream, from a Life you are enjoying so very much, then thrown into another that is nothing like the one you worked so hard to create. It does not matter how beautiful the new is, the sting from being torn involuntarily from the old remains a haunting reminder that none of this was a choice.

In the aftermath of a trauma, there tends to be a lot of waiting — waiting for help, waiting for agencies, waiting to be able to go back to work, waiting to feel normal… so my mind was left unattended for long bouts of time. Free to wander, my thoughts kept drifting back to a Trauma Training I had attended several years ago. This training was unique in that it was filled with Survivors rather than clinicians.

I should fit in there, right? If you know anything about psychology, you know they love research and scales. People love to quantify *crazy,* so we need to provide measures or scales of how far from *normal* someone is. I know therapist-readers are now searching their minds for a theory that does not have a scale. Trust me, every theory has some sort of scale attached to it. This was no different; their pet scale was fondly named The *ACE.* The *Adverse Childhood Experience* scale is a simplistic test that assigns a number from 1 to 10 for how traumatized a human is, then links it to horrifying outcomes such as rates of suicide, substance abuse and other mental health issues. I'm good at tests. I aced the ACE, impressing no one with my 10, the highest possible score, confirming the severity of trauma I'd been through, but no one in a room full of scores of 6s to 8s seemed phased.

SInce the trauma training was not led by a clinician, there were few, if any, euphemisms used to discuss the data. The facilitator saw my score, moved to the suicide statistics, and then announced to the class that, according to the graph, I should've been dead in my 20s. (I took the news rather well, since it was not the first time I had disappointed someone by not dying on time.) I did my best to feign apologetic for skewing the data by not complying with the "she-should-be-dead" stat while the rest of the class discussed *Rock Bottom* and how to dig up from there. Each member of the class was invited to describe, in horrifying detail, their personal rock bottom. When, to my horror, my turn rolled around, I was met with expectant glares. Everyone was eager to hear number 10's breaking point. Dare I say it? Do I tell My Truth? I almost apologetically declared "I have not reached rock bottom yet!" The shock was palpable.

How dare I — this perfect ACE score, outlier of suicide stats — not have a rock bottom? I searched my brain for some plausible explanation. All I am ever really left with is my personal truth, which is that I have been in an epic battle with the Universe ever since I can remember. We do this not-very-delicate dance of "how much can Emily take before she breaks?" Saying any experience is my *Rock Bottom* implies two things I will likely never admit to, the first of which is defeat. In my mind (and probably only in My mind) *Rock Bottom* is the end of the game; The Universe has won. It means I finally broke. I had enough. I gave *up,* or *in,* or however that saying goes. Any way you name it, I am not doing that. Ever! It is the proverbial *crying Uncle, I give,* or *ally ally, all come free.* I did not ask to play this game, but I am not going to lose at it either.

Second — it tempts the Universe by implying she has finished torturing me. I promise, she has not. No matter what the Universe has ever thrown at me, no matter how hard any obstacle has been, I know that there is worse... more... deeper pain... the Universe could impose at any time. And, if I am patient, she usually does. Sure, the flood was bad. But I don't think it is all the Universe has got and the fact that I am alive implies that she certainly is not done with me yet. So I will neither tempt her nor allow myself the pleasure of thinking that the worst is over now and I can carry on with an expectation of a simple, carefree, happily ever after.

Back at that trauma training where I'd been informed I was a few decades late, according to their suicide data, I was now further muddying their training by explaining that I will never admit to reaching *Rock Bottom.* No-one was pleased. After a few minutes of debate, I gave in, agreeing with them that I probably hadn't hit mine yet. I comforted them that I will eventually join them in that dreadful place one day.

A decade and several traumas later, Hurricane Harvey hit in our home in southeast Texas, stealing from me people, possessions and dreams. Through it all, I worked vigilantly to hold on to HOPE; to see the collateral beauty in all that was happening. My first public sharing, after seeing my home eight feet underwater, was a Facebook post:

"This update is really tough to write. The girls and I want to thank everyone who is reaching out to offer kind words about the house. Each time one of you says you see the pictures and cry yourself, it gives us permission to truly feel the depth of the grief, our personal torment. If we are to move forward, we must allow ourselves to feel the depth of the pain this is causing us.

Several things stand out now though and I promise material things lost are not among them. The neighbor who informed us of our house underwater did it in the kindest and most sensitive way possible and this truly softened the blow. We sat down together as a family, with the family who had taken us in, sharing a meal in which we all genuinely laughed. Most of our animals are also safe and we are very aware that not all families have been that fortunate. Most importantly to me, we know you are all watching us for how to handle this catastrophe. We will not let you down. We have not felt alone at all in this, the love and support has kept us going, changing us in a strongly positive way. "

I did not know it yet, but that declaration was the beginning of my Ignite Moment. It was the stirring in my soul that acknowledged that this natural disaster was likely going to change the entire trajectory of my Life... people were watching for how I responded to it. This was a test I could not fail...

In the days that followed, I determinedly focused on the positive — declaring it a miracle so many of our animals were safe — we were able to get five humans, five cats, three dogs, and six foster dogs all to safety in a Ford Mustang that had a donut for one tire and a second going flat. I focused on how God puts people in our path at precisely the right time. He guided us to make the very difficult, yet perfectly timed, decisions that kept almost all the souls, human and animal, we were responsible for safe. But the truth was that we lost a lot of Souls that dreadful day — not all of them were by a physical death. Not acknowledging that was creating caustic caverns through my spirit, morphing me into a person I did not want to become: cold, callous, jaded.

It seemed like a lifetime before officials lifted the mandatory evacuation for my street, allowing us to go in and assess the wreckage that was now our lives. During that vortex of time, it felt like the part in a movie where the crescendo had gone on too long. The audience knows that something amazingly great or terribly horrid is about to happen. They've been rooting for the good guys most of the movie but are so exhausted waiting for what is going to happen next, they don't even care anymore if it is happy or sad, as long as the crescendo ends and the scene finally changes. We needed a way to fill that time. I needed a way to occupy my mind, so that I didn't sit around, making mental lists of all I had lost. I couldn't just stare at my daughters — my 12 year old with everything she now owned stuffed under a chair in the living room of a friend's home. This was more than my soul could bear. We had to DO something.

Through generous friends, coworkers and compassionate strangers, we had been building up quite a storeroom of supplies. That's what first-wave helpers do. They send toiletries, clothes, water and food. We had so much; it seemed logical to share. I started reaching out to agencies, churches, assisted-living facilities to see who might need supplies, but most of the humans were on auto-pilot. No one knew anything. So, we packed up our friend's Expedition full of what could fit and headed into town. We would choose at random: an assisted-living facility, an impoverished neighborhood... Then we knocked on doors. "Do you need water? Do you have food? Are your pets fed? Need any toothpaste?"

People were excited to see us at first, relieved that they had finally been remembered. "What agency are you from?" one woman asked. When we responded, "None," they got scared and suspicious, "We don't have money for water. We can't give you anything in return. Why are you here?" I responded with my truth. My house is eight feet under water; the only thing that makes me feel better is to help other humans feel some Hope." I did not yet know that a word existed for this concept. All I knew was that every time I saw an elderly woman smile or a disabled man thank me for a case of water, every time I saw a spark of Hope return to another human's eyes, it helped my Soul heal a little bit more.

This experience is *Karuṇā*, a Sanskrit concept referring to the act of healing others and, in so doing, healing ourselves through the process.

I had been a therapist for 16 years when Hurricane Harvey completely altered the course of my Life, teaching me that real healing is in helping others to heal. This Ignited my soul and has become my passion, my purpose, the way I live my daily life: helping others as a way to heal myself. Harvey had not even technically hit, yet when the water in our yard flooded waist deep, one road already impassable by car, we were visited by emergency services shouting the simple statement, "It is time to go."

We had anticipated this moment, but try as we did, we weren't prepared for what it really meant. In those moments as I drove to be reunited with my daughters and our animals that had evacuated ahead of us, I made a promise to myself to keep my heart open to the collateral beauty. This is what saved me.

We could have sat around recounting those scary, difficult days. It is likely no one would judge us for grieving the many sentimental items we all lost. We could get comfortable feeling sad or lamenting the situation, but there is no healing in that. My Soul was Ignited to focus on the beauty of all the blessings around us. I did and do get sad, grieve and even get angry here and there.

I promise, gratitude is the key to healing. Gratitude for family, friends, co-workers, acquaintances and compassionate strangers who sent us hope and encouragement through words, gifts, resources, and by sharing their talents and time. For those who taught me through their actions, the meaning of Life is *Karuṇā*.

In all of this, I have learned that to heal, you need to help others, even when you are most raw. To catapult yourself into the healing process, you can start supporting others even before you feel ready. By sharing your pain with someone else, you allow them to also acknowledge their pain and you both may heal as a result.

IGNITE ACTION STEPS

* **Be willing to notice the collateral beauty**

The fact that I have been able to survive a fraction of what I have is because of my ability to see both the good and the difficult simultaneously. Memories of the Bayou Flood losses can and do come up. Then, and even now, those memories bring feelings forth that are wonderful and horrible, happy and sad, comforting and painful, all at once. People like to tell me I can only have one of those emotions at a time.

Do NOT let anyone tell you that you cannot hold multiple feelings simultaneously. Most people can relate to being angry with someone they Love. But it does not stop there. Since the flood, I have felt deep sadness and anger for the situations it led to while simultaneously feeling gratitude for others. Just because other people feel more comfortable when you voice positive emotions does not mean you should silence your voice regarding the tough ones. The moment you fail to give either emotion a voice, you are being untrue to a part of yourself that deserves expression. Give yourself permission to express that you are still grieving a loss, or sad because your cat died, or bored in a meeting, or frustrated at work… while also admiring the collateral beauty and feeling immense gratitude for all that is simultaneously going well in your life.

* **Shine Like a Diamond**

Diamonds get their brilliance from three things: reflection, refraction and dispersion. *Reflection* is the light that hits the diamond, immediately bounced back up, giving it an instantaneous shine. This is the light that others send to you through encouragement, hope and help. Its impact is instantaneous. It boosts your mood; it infuses you with hope, allowing you to also shine. But the transformation does not stop there. Only a portion of the light hitting a diamond is reflected.

The rest of the light travels through and is *refracted*, changing the direction of the light. When light passes from the person sharing their light with you, it goes beyond to people you do not even anticipate will be impacted by the original light you graciously accepted.

Dispersion is the final step. When Light enters a diamond (or a person's soul), it separates into all the spectral colors of the rainbow and then bounces back out into the world. This wonderful display of Light, referred to as Diamond Fire, is the transformation of having accepted another's light. When you assist other souls to Ignite from the Diamond Fire in you, the light is further dispersed with the potential to transform the lives around you forever. It is the proverbial ripple effect, confirmed by science.

Most humans need some sort of assistance from another person at some point in their lives; they need support of some kind: emotional, financial, housing, help getting a job... Truth is, a lot of us are conditioned to refuse help, as if it somehow makes us appear weak to admit we do not have it all together on our own. Through reading the works of Brene Brown, I have been able to see the concept of making myself vulnerable as being courageous. When people asked me how they could help after the flood, I told them what I needed honestly, from a place of humility, and with a spark of hope. What I learned was that by allowing people to help, we are offering them a gift; an opportunity to mean something to someone and a chance to step outside of themselves and do something kind for another human... a chance to shine like a Diamond.

- **Live Karuṇā. Every. Single. Day.**

Karuṇā is the act of helping another and, in so doing, healing a part of ourselves. When my biological Mother completed suicide, I worked four years on an intake-line for people contemplating suicide. When my house was eight feet under water, I was out rescuing animals and delivering water to people in need.

For years, my daughters and I had been going through a tough financial time; one day I received $100 cash in the mail. We headed to Dunkin Donuts. Sitting in the drive-through, my daughters were excited to engage in a tradition we hadn't enjoyed in a long time: donuts and the park. I caught a glimpse of a man with a dog looking through the trash barrel for food. I said, "Hello," and asked if I could buy him and his friend some breakfast. I explained, "I got a lucky break. I want to pay it forward." He accepted half the cash.

I was not doing any of these things to be kind; I was doing them to heal: heal others and heal myself. Your trauma need not be so severe and reaction so extreme to practice *Karuṇā* every day. Opportunities are always presenting themselves if you are watching.

Emily C. Ross - USA
Licensed Professional Counselor, Wellness Advocate
www.facebook.com/life.by.emspiration/

MEENA KUMARI ADNANI

"Step Into Your Own Power."

You are destined for GREATNESS and are so much more POWERFUL than you think. I hope my story inspires you to step into that POWER so that you can unlock the magic that resides deep inside of you.

THE POWER OF DREAMS

"I didn't educate my daughter to be a doormat."

My mom's words echoed loudly in my ears. It was past midnight. The lights were out and everyone was asleep at home. Even though I was extremely exhausted, her words pierced straight through my body and soul. I was in my 40s and her statement shook me. All this time, I wondered, was I waiting for the *permission* to be powerful?

You see, I was raised in a conservative Indian family. From the tender age of five, I was led to believe that, as an Indian girl, my only purpose was to get married. My whole life, I was supposed to serve two men: My dad until I was 17, then my husband. And that was it. I wasn't taught to dream. I wasn't supposed to have a vision or, God forbid, a career.

One Sunday evening when I was 12 years old, I was playing hopscotch outdoors with two of my sisters. In the 1970s, our only form of entertainment was either to play outside or to watch *Tom and Jerry* cartoons on our black and white television. As a child, I was very active. I loved playing outdoors more than I liked watching television. That particular day, the weather was perfect and the sun was just about setting. The sky looked like it was painted with a yellowish-orange tint and the air was filled with hope and tranquility. My sisters and I drew square boxes on the ground with a white chalk, then took turns jumping through each box on one foot. The person who could jump the quickest through each square, without stepping on the chalk-drawn lines, was the winner. Amidst all the fun and excitement we were having, I could hear my uncle's voice calling us to come inside.

Most Sundays, our family would get together and spend time bonding over a meal. It wasn't dinner time yet, but we were called to come indoors for some *adult conversation*.

"What do you want to be when you grow up?" my uncle asked. It was an ironic question, considering I wasn't supposed to be anything but married.

I was a full-time dreamer who happily lived in my dreams most of the time. My uncle's question was a bit confusing and I felt conflicted about whether or not I was supposed to answer. It transported me back into my own little virtual world, so I wasn't paying attention to the conversation that ensued between my sisters and my uncle. When my uncle nudged me, I came back to reality. With a twinkle in my eyes and a wide grin on my face, I answered, "I want to be a lawyer!"

Perhaps it was the Bollywood movies I watched while sitting with my mom and aunties that inspired me to choose the legal profession. I recall one particular movie where the heroine was a lawyer. She was wearing her black and white robe in court. Her long black hair, petite body and strong presence reminded me of a Greek goddess. Her charisma and confidence were oozing through the screen as she presented one of the most compelling arguments I had ever heard. She was beautiful.

The background music, the wide-angled shots, the power in her voice... it all added to the drama. I was mesmerized and inspired by her. I wanted to *be* her. It wasn't so much the legal profession itself, perhaps. It was the authority, the strength and the grace with which she carried herself. She was her own master — and I wanted to *be* her.

I played that scene again and again in my head. I knew that, someday, I would embody that same confidence, that same spirit, that same resilience…

"I want to be a lawyer," I responded enthusiastically. With sarcasm in his voice, my uncle chuckled and responded, "You mean you will get a Law degree and hang the certificate above the stove while you cook for your husband?!" His laugh was nonchalant and careless.

Was that supposed to be a joke? For a few seconds, I didn't know what to say or what to think. I was only 12. He was supposed to know more about life, about what is possible and what isn't. I didn't know whether to believe in the possibility of my dreams or to trust him on what life was going to be like for me.

After what seemed like an eternity (even though it was only a few minutes), I could feel my spirit rise up like the waves in the ocean during a high tide. I smiled and said nothing — at least nothing that could be heard by others. But the voice in my head was loud and audible. I responded to him in my head, embracing the spirit of the Greek Goddess. "Underestimate me! This will be fun. One day, I will prove it to you!"

From that moment on, I had only one goal in life: To pursue my dream of becoming a lawyer. Nothing and no one could keep me from that goal. For the next four years, I put my negotiation skills to the test. I worked continuously on my dad and convinced him to send me overseas so I could achieve my dream of becoming a lawyer and make him proud. Each year, he set a new condition for me: to achieve higher grades, to become one of the top ten students in my class, to be one of the top five students, and so forth. Every year, I fulfilled his condition.

Finally, when I was 16, it dawned on me that I needed to take matters into my own hands. I found an agency that helped overseas students get admissions to schools and universities in the UK and the USA. Without my Dad's knowledge or approval, I started the admission process to a boarding school in the UK. Once I was accepted, I told my Dad that I had made things "easier" for him. That he didn't have to do anything else — *except* pay for my school fees. After much deliberation and even more conditions, my Dad reluctantly agreed. I was a lawyer in the making! I went to the UK and studied hard. I overcame bullying, culture shock, critical illness and every obstacle that came my way. I was an Indian girl from a third world country who was in the process of making my dream a reality. There was very little I could not achieve. 15 years later, not only did I qualify as a Solicitor in England and Wales, I also became an Attorney in New York.

If I were a man, this would have been a monumental achievement. If I were an Indian man, I would have been the epitome of success. I would have received a long line of marriage proposals and been the most sought-after bachelor in town. As an Indian girl, being educated diminished my value. I defied cultural norms and social conditioning. Being *different* was by no means a good thing.

Over the years, I became more and more successful. I grew my portfolio and took on senior management roles for sales, marketing and business development.

But even though I climbed up the corporate ladder and worked in some of the most renowned companies in the world, the higher I climbed, the smaller I became in my cultural environment and social circles. I was everything an Indian girl shouldn't have been — independent, powerful, resilient. Yet, I didn't feel powerful. I did all that I could to shrink myself so that I could fit in.

In social gatherings, I did my best not to share my opinions. I didn't want the men to feel insecure, nor did I want them to feel less powerful around me. If my mere presence was a threat, my opinions and perspective made me stand out even more.

"I didn't educate my daughter to be a doormat."

I lay in bed that night contemplating the power behind my mother's words.

A few hours before my mother had said that, I was at a social event with my extended family. As is always the case in such get togethers, the men would huddle around the bar, drinking and nibbling on bite-sized snacks whilst discussing business, the economy, politics, and the latest business trends. The women would gather around the table on the other side of the room, also nibbling on snacks, discussing fashion trends, their kids and other people. Not quite fitting into either of the groups, I would float aimlessly between the two groups, back and forth, bored, asking myself, "Why am I here? What am I doing here? When is this going to end?"

A few hours into the evening, the ladies (who typically ate earlier than the men) would move to the dinner table, continue their chatter and enjoy their meal together. Once the women were done, it would be the men's turn to eat. Slightly or even heavily intoxicated, the men would make their way to the dinner table and the women would serve them.

As the men convened for dinner that night, I had a strong intuition to leave. Sensing my urge to depart, my sister whispered, "Please wait for another 30 minutes or so. I would like to stay and I don't have a ride home." I reluctantly agreed, even though I didn't think it was a good idea to wait. I stayed at the dinner table with my sister to accompany the men for dinner.

"So, tell me," one of my uncles asked, "Why does your dad consult a lawyer to draft his will? You are a lawyer, aren't you?"

I was slightly taken aback by that question. Having spent almost 20 years overseas, and given my *western* mindset, I didn't feel comfortable discussing my dad's personal affairs around a group of men, let alone a group of slightly intoxicated men.

"Yes, I am," I responded hesitantly, "but the laws differ from country to country and I am not qualified here in Indonesia."

I was hoping that he sensed my discomfort and would end the conversation. Instead, he continued, "You know what I think?" and before I could say anything else, he offered unsolicited advice on how my dad's will should be drafted. He then changed the conversation and cracked a joke about his wife. "We've been married for 30 years. It's way past the warranty period. Perhaps now it's time for me to return the product (his wife) so that the manufacturers (her father) can replace it with a new one (his wife's youngest sister). What do you think?" The men burst into laughter, approving of the joke, which brought a sense of camaraderie.

Unimpressed, while trying to stay calm, I responded, "I think the warranty period and product exchange works both ways." Ignoring my response, he proceeded to discuss my dad's will again.

"Can we have this conversation tomorrow?" I suggested.

"Why tomorrow? Why not now?" he insisted.

"Now is not a good time," I responded nervously, well aware that I was surrounded by a camp of hostile men.

"And why not?"

"Because…. You are drunk." His face turned red. I could see the veins on his face almost bursting. He stood up and slammed the table hard with both his hands.

"How dare you call me drunk? Who do you think you are? Just because you are educated?"

As a good Indian woman, I was expected to shut up. Never disagree, never speak up and never speak back. Within seconds, I had violated all those rules. I felt as if I had jumped from a very high cliff, heading for a free fall, going at a thousand miles per hour. Suddenly, something magical happened. My power dawned on me, as if I had just stepped into my superhero costume. It felt like someone had attached wings on my left and on my right. I had become invincible.

Agitated, yet confident, I stood up and said very slowly, "GROW THE HECK UP."

Turning to my sister, I said, "This is the reason I didn't want to stay." I grabbed my bag and left the dinner. My sister chose to leave with me. When I got home, I told my mother what had happened. Her assertive and unequivocal response was very clear: "I didn't educate my daughter to be a doormat."

Her words were like balm that soothed my soul. I felt relieved and assured.

That night, I made a commitment to myself. I will no longer shrink my power to make others feel good about themselves. If I, being educated and successful, played small, what hope would there be for other women in this world? By embracing my power, I gave voice and permission to millions of women around the world to do the same.

I am now a motivational speaker, a high-performance coach and a business mentor for women and women-led businesses. I inspire women to become conscious leaders in their own lives and I teach them to step into their power. It gives me great joy to see women grow to become the greatest version of themselves and to fulfil their highest potential. Pulitzer Prize winning historian Laurel Thatcher Ulrich once said, "Well-behaved women seldom make history." I never cared much for behaving well, nor should you. We can all become history makers, trailblazers, and inspire others to do the same for generations to come. You don't need to wait for anyone to give you permission to be powerful.

Oh, and about my uncles.... I am so grateful for them and cherish them deeply. They were the catalyst who catapulted my journey from Success to Significance.

Ignite Action Steps

Believe in *yourself*, not in other people's version of you. You are created with a purpose and for a purpose. As long as you don't give up, anything is possible. Here are some simple, yet powerful things, you can do that will transform your life. These easy steps create impactful results, so don't be fooled by their simplicity.

1. **Write your dreams on a piece of paper.** What are they? Be specific. If it is financial, be specific about the number and timeline. If it is a job, be clear about what it is. If it is to find a partner, write down all the qualities you seek in a partner. The more detailed you are, the better the results.

   By writing, we move our dreams from the virtual world into the real world. Our brain consists of the right and left hemispheres. When we think of our goals, we use only the right hemisphere, which is the *imagination center*. When we write it, we are tapping into the left hemisphere which is the logical part of the brain. Writing triggers the brain to command our entire body to make our dreams come true. This inspires us to take action. It helps us to identify opportunities and possibilities that we didn't see in the past.

2. **Visualize your dreams.** On a daily basis, visualize that your dream has already come true. How does it feel? What are you wearing? Who are you with? What are you doing? Connect with how it feels and keep that feeling throughout the day. Our feeling of bliss helps us raise our vibration and align us with our vision.

3. **Create a Plan.** Write this question down, "What must I do to fulfill my dream?" Spend some time thinking about it. If you do not know where to start, do some research. Look for role models and mentors. Learn from the people who have already done what you want to do. Write the specific action steps that you need to take to get you closer to your goal. Once you have written all of the action steps, split them into two categories: Short-term Plan and Long-term Plan. (See resources for further details.)

4. **Take Action.** Every day, take small baby steps. The magic is in taking action, so keep taking action! If you face challenges, remember that it doesn't mean you have failed. Tweak your plan and/or tweak your actions.

5. **Never Give Up.** If the Wright brothers had given up, we wouldn't be able to fly and travel around the world. If Steve Jobs had given up, we wouldn't have MacBook laptops or iPads today. There is no such thing as failure, only lessons. As the old saying goes, "Try, try, try until you succeed."

Meena Kumari Adnani - Indonesia
High Performance Coach
Business Mentor and Motivational Speaker
www.strongandshine.com

NANCY L. MCFARLAND

*"Becoming our greatest self is ever-evolving in each
story we live and how we choose to tell it."*

**As you read my story, I want you to recognize yourself, your humanity and
see it in others. I want you to know the power and grace of your tears, giggles, rage and love; to know your values; to realize your vision and live your
legacy. I want you to know that your life is *Your Greatest Evolving Project.***

MY EVOLVING LIFE STORY

At 37 years old, I used a burgundy bucket along with a cheap, light green,
32oz plastic cup filled with tinted green water to bathe most days. Both were
such common household items you could easily buy them on the sides of dusty
roads, out of rusty carts people pulled around town, or public markets as well
as cheap stores.

The 1,000 liter water tank positioned just outside our flat was filled with
freshwater monthly. My first husband, Armand fetched fresh water for us. The
water in the tank started turning green within days. It was hot in Pointe-Noire, the
second-largest city in the Republic of Congo. All sorts of bacteria knew standing
water as their paradise. I washed my dishes, mopped my floors and flushed my
toilet with this water every single day, until it was dark green and gone.

During the three years that I lived there with him, water flowed through
the pipes and electricity ran through the wires no more than 15 days in total.
I squatted in the shower many days, crying in despair. It felt like I lived in a

body with no blood running through it. The sand was plentiful, soft and dirty. I had to walk in it to go everywhere. The most obscure places were adorned with reeking garbage as well as haphazard parts and pieces and fragments of mundane life, from machinery to hair combs to rocking chairs. I hated it.

Not infrequently, I reminded my husband that I was a 'good deal' for a bride; he knew it. I was free — as in *gratis*. I'd told him from the beginning that our union was socially illegal; it was not considered an equitable match. We'd laugh about it. Had I been Congolese, I would have been worth endless sheep, beer, JM Weston shoes and whiskey. Our masonic tie was our greatest bond, as we were both members of the order of Le Droit Humain (a group of people making a change in the world). We met during my PhD studies at the University of Cape Town. I headed there right after completing a master's degree in International Public Health from the University of Sydney in Australia. I'd leave with him for Congo right before my dissertation was done. He'd been a legal resident in South Africa for 12 years. He was a hardworking sales rep with integrity about many things who worked in an exclusive French store.

He'd told me numerous times, "I'd hit you if you were Congolese." My American status didn't prevent him from yelling; regularly and sadistically putting me down. I remember one day, he was so furious and I begged to know why. It would be many, many hours later that he would confess to tormenting me so that I'd never ask him another unnecessary question again. He never hit me.

To ensure he would have no further claim on me as his wife, I stayed until I had secured my divorce. My aunt had told me, "Divorce is to be earned," so I optimized myself as a wife in that span of my life and checked off the consciousness boxes before cutting the ties. I became no less than the best wife I knew to be. Divorce was especially brutal in the Congo; no referral line or support group available. I didn't speak Lingala and my French skills were superbly average. Whatever pity and justice the locals offered during the process, I accepted graciously.

Before I met him, I had lived in Turkey, Australia and South Africa by myself. Being comfortable alone was a powerful edge I'd developed out of necessity. I was quite proud of my unyielding volition to get things done, like moving myself around the world. Exceedingly lacking, however, was my capacity to trust and embrace vulnerability in something like a life partner. I suppose that's why he'd often look at me, exasperated, and yell, "You're just like a man!" He resented my strength and independence.

In retrospect, I realize Armand was never a total stranger to me; he was actually very familiar. I was quite comfortable in emotionally unsafe environments where I was told how to feel and exist, then shamed and blamed when I didn't conform. I learned in it childhood. All my romantic relationships had been doomed. Those men that truly adored and loved me... I couldn't accept what I didn't believe about myself. However, what I learned from Armand was that I didn't deserve abuse either. His abuse was so much like my adopted mother.

Despite the circuitous and tumultuous journey that led me to the Congo, flashes of someone greater than the self I knew lit up inside of me. I was evolving. I was consciously recognizing my value and the values I held about my life. A tiny part of me began to see myself as 'a person who has commanding authority or influence.' Hence, my Conscious Leadership began, and it started with me.

Like so many, I was not wanted. My birthmother, a beautiful 16-year-old white girl with long, blond hair and blue eyes, conceived me on the island of Terceira in the Azores, off the coast of Portugal. My father, a 21-year-old black United States Airman, had just left the Black Panther Party and college to escape probable jail time.

In those days, abortion was only legal if one was deemed insane; psychological tests deemed Mom not so. She hated that she disappointed her parents. Being young, desperate, devastated and feeling lost, Mom ingested a large quantity of quinine. It didn't kill me. Neither did having my uncle jump up and down on me when I was in the womb. Her parents took her to an adjacent state to the Florence Crittenton Home for unwed mothers until I was born. Being half white was not good enough for me to be kept and my birth-father had no better option. "Bitch" was the first name I was called, but I was legally named "Jennifer Jenise," the names of two black girls who had been Mom's friends when she lived in the Azores. She chose to spend a little time with me after I was born. She fed me and changed my diapers for a couple of days before she let me go, and she made sure I would have the yellow and white blanket bordered in purple that she'd crocheted for me.

It does not seem that I will ever know where I was for the first 18 months of my life, but I do know they called me Rebecca until my 42-year-old black, adopted mother, who was in mourning of her husband, took custody of me. She named me Nancy.

I would become a statistic, raised by a single mother who was an elementary school teacher. Little girls without two parents are glaring targets for some people; like the educated, close family friend who molested me for years. He groomed me to seduce truck drivers using the CB radio on a dresser in the bedroom he shared with his wife. I felt the most powerful when I successfully lured foolish truck drivers to made-up meeting spots. I would sit on the bed and wield my 7-year-old power just as I was taught by him, and it was the only power I really remember. He found it amusing.

The more my mother "prettied me up" in frilly pink dresses, the more I hated her for not protecting me, particularly after she knew I was being molested and did nothing. I told her what he was doing to me one Saturday morning at the kitchen table. All she said was, "Just don't go back over there." I was about 8 years old. I felt a part of my soul leave my body right then and there. The love–hate relationship with my adopted mother only grew over the years after that.

More parts felt like they were leaving me all the time like when she lashed out because I was not being the sweet, pretty girl who obeyed her even when she was abusive towards me. She would often pick up the receiver of the yellow rotary telephone affixed to the wall next to the kitchen door, pretending to call the authorities to tell them to come and take me away. As a child, I did not know it was pretend. I hated her; and I hated that I needed her.

I was 14 years old the day my mother was about to marry her second husband. I freaked out and begged her not to go through with it. My gut knew it was going to end badly. I made a scene pleading and crying; it was useless. She would never be able to admit that her husband, the minister of three rural churches, was also molesting her daughter, and she did nothing other than tell him not to do it again. Not one of my educated, religious relatives helped me. No one protected me or offered me respite from the nightmare I was living in that house, always being told to act right and be good, as if nothing was wrong. I was scared to leave my room but was forced to go to church every Sunday and act like life was fine. I was 15 when my mother refused to take me to the doctor despite witnessing me cry in horror for weeks as the excruciating sensation of blistering, broken glass passed through me every single time I urinated. I only figured out that it was a urinary tract infection years later. I was a virgin, but my mother wasn't willing to compromise the perceived high decency of her household. I suffered alone.

I do not know how I survived, considering the vicious bullying on the school bus and the hell I endured inside my house and family, but I graduated from high school. I screamed endlessly to be heard, I drank the cheapest alcohol, attended college parties and drove to seemingly far away places on the weekends to escape. I have always felt a powerful impulse to find out how life could be different, opening myself up to the next book, thought, movie, prayer, practice, or opinion that could even remotely offer a bit of inner reconciliation.

The walls of my room were covered in poems that assured me that life was not meant to be as it was.

The love–hate relationship I had with my adopted mother endured, fueled by my fury until only recently. I was enraged that she could never admit she was wrong, that she deeply hurt me and allowed my innocence to be ripped away. She never did apologize. She just could not. And finding and connecting with my birth-families didn't fill up my endless half-empty glass. Neither did living abroad.

I quickly learned that you take yourself wherever you go. No matter how exotic the city was in whatever country I was in, I was still Nancy. The one who wasn't wanted, didn't matter and wasn't good enough. Nevertheless, I grew to realize that Nancy, the American, *meant* something everywhere else in the world except at home. I allowed myself to enjoy just being that. Even being half black didn't matter when I was Nancy the American. One of the greatest lessons of my life has been realizing that human nature is completely consistent everywhere. Everywhere I went, skin color and hair texture, the region of birth, accent, political affiliation and even founding father lineage can be used to determine your worth/value in any given society.

The day came that I defined "my line" with my adopted family. I had to decide between my health or them, and I finally chose myself. My healing sped up, as I no longer split my energy. It was all for me. In my surrender, I no longer cared about that one more thing I could do to make them see that I mattered. It did not matter what they thought of me. It was then that I entered a new world, right inside of myself, that I had not truly known, even after traversing the globe.

It was upon the completion of my Master of Social Work degree when I returned to the US and obtained a position at an acute county psychiatric hospital as a social worker that my Ignite moment would take place. My patients were suffering. They were in the throes of extreme psychosis, they used gruesome means to try and end their lives and many ended the lives of others. For so many, devastating traumas simply halted their lives. It was a volatile, dangerous place, and I felt right at home. I also felt able to understand the pains of my patients.

I now understand that conscious leadership is cultured and developed over time as parts of a life are incrementally optimized into Greatness — as values become known, visions are realized and impact is lived. I had always been Evolving. There were two main parts to the culmination of the moment: first, my second husband and second, my office mate Melanie.

Yes, I did choose another unavailable man, one who really wanted to be available. But he was also Jeckyl and Hyde, so nice, so not nice, and then so not there, withdrawn and plagued by his own dreadful trauma. It was excruciatingly painful, never knowing which side of him would prevail. It was, again, familiar. The years we spent in this desperate dance… It was the only dance we knew. I finally learned to spin out of it as I completely leaned into Contrast's lead. With every breath, I'd ask myself, "What is this about for me?" — wanting to be free of repeating my patterns. It required me to surrender into myself, to turn away from all of them and to trust the whisper of the unquestionable liberty that was beckoning me back to my core.

Then, there was Melanie with her big, open, loving heart. She recognized my value when I could not see my own. After countless sessions with patients, I would share with Melanie how I was excited, humbled and in awe about the great shifts they were making. She echoed the voice of so many, cheering that I had some great gift, but I still did not understand what it was. "Nancy," she would say, "You are so accepting, so non-judgmental; you see what is truly happening. You are safe, allowing people to show-up and let go. You offer mind-altering reframes of their pain that resonates with who they want to be." She remained sweetly relentless. Regardless of the reason that they were there, I held the space for their humanity and all the ways it showed up. It took some time to realize that just being me — mattered. It made a difference for not only my patients but my friends, family and often strangers.

I know my clients can only go as far as I can, so I strive to optimize the gifts of my own story and ever-evolving life so that they can go as deep as necessary and rise to heights well beyond who they believe they can become. Speaking to the most hurting parts of them allows their pain to feel relief. I also remind those most hurting parts of their great value; this inspires and ignites them. Even their tiny, brief glimpses of self-worth heals them. This is my Conscious Leadership.

At 90 years old now, happily singing her favorite song *"Precious Lord"* countless times a day, my adopted mother lives with advanced dementia. Her safety and care are my priority. I am still connected to both birth parents and their families with all the interesting twists and turns; I am grateful to know them. To be so very happy is what my heart holds for the two men I married and loved the best I knew how. Dead for years now, I extend belief in soulful reconciliation for the men that molested me. My story is that everyone did the best they could, and I was meant to be here.

I've shared pieces of my story with you and now I feel wholly relieved, satisfied and complete. I sensed My Beginning lovingly holding out its hands for me, which let go so I could remember myself. I now embrace my values, realize my vision and live my impact as much as I can every single day because Conscious Leadership is achieved through incremental optimization. I know the power and grace of my tears, giggles, rage and love. I am proud of my life.

Your story is still evolving. It desires to be told and to know it matters. Tell your story so that you are proud of your life and the way you live it. What IS the story you want to tell? Commit to it and love it completely. Enjoy its delicious delights.

IGNITE ACTION STEPS

• **Make it your mission** to find out what truly matters to you and let yourself be at the top of your list.

• **Desire to know how to use your life in its Greatest form.** Allow this desire to speak into you, into your thoughts; then listen to how to use your fingers, breath, thoughts, feet and intelligence to elevate your household, social circle, neighborhood, company and your world. This is your consciousness.

• **Live as authentically powerful and present as possible in your life.** Know your thoughts/feelings/body/spirit 'and how they affect your actions, reactions and choices. Know that they affect Your story and how you tell it, and Life itself. This is *you* in your Conscious Leadership.

Nancy L. McFarland - USA
Social Worker & Transformational Coach
www.projectevolvinglife.com

Ana Sofia Orozco

"That place of true self is the only space where
meaningful leadership can happen."

Leaders have the power to write history and to take our world to a better place. I believe leadership can be meaningful only if leaders operate from the wisdom of the true self, the power of a true purpose, and acknowledge that we are part of a bigger reality. I wish for this book and my story to open up space for leaders to join this conversation, understanding the responsibility that comes with their influence over others. I wish to inspire them to strive for higher levels of consciousness.

Leaders, Tune into Self, Love, and Purpose

When we are children, we are more genuinely tuned into our true selves and values. Our particular circumstances, society's expectations and culture induce us to change these values and form new beliefs, letting our ego take charge. Our ego does this to protect us because we need to survive, adapt, fit in, and be loved.

Unfortunately, our ego does not care who we really are, what we need or what we really want. It mainly wants to ensure that we are accepted. Even if society's values do not serve us, our ego might lead us to misguided action for us to fit in. Conscious Leaders hold the power to make a difference — but to do so, they need to be present in their true selves and maintain a connection with genuine universal values. Conscious Leadership can only happen when we distinguish our true values from those adopted from our environment, and when we make decisions from this place. Wonderfully and beautifully, I experience this *place* as being the source of Love, the most essential value for a meaningful life.

Finding the True Self

I was about 18 years old when I realized there was nothing more real in my life than my sense of self. I had lived in the same city since I was born and I had gone to the same school for 14 years. I had friends from when I was a baby. My country, my family, my social circle, my school, my neighborhood, determined my identity before I graduated high school. After graduation, I decided to leave my country, go see the world, learn about other cultures and speak another language. Something in me wanted to just set sail and go explore beyond the horizon.

We had goodbye parties, my family helped me pack my bags, and one very special day, I took a plane by myself and headed to Europe. I was so excited that I don't even recall feeling scared.

It was the first time I was leaving by myself. I vacillated between the convenience of a smaller village in France or the challenges of a bigger city. Following wise advice, I headed to the alluring City of Lights. Shortly after arriving in Paris, I decided to embark on an adventure with new friends and drove to Italy by car. I was not aware that my student visa only allowed one entry into France until registration in a school was completed. Returning back to Paris from my unplanned trip, immigration officers at Charles de Gaulle airport denied my access to the country. I was to be deported!

Given I was Colombian, I was scared! I was sent to an office that dealt with serious illegal issues. The moment I entered, I started explaining my situation in my broken French to the officer in charge. A middle-aged, slim, short, anxious man with dark hair was crushing out his cigarette. He looked at me and started yelling for me to stay away. I was shocked. I sat nervously on a bench with my bags and waited. There was a mix of intimidating people around. I felt confused and weak. No one knew me there. I did not speak the language. I felt helpless.

Hours later, that dreadful officer came out of his bureau, asked me to follow him and pointed at a door. He opened it and shouted, "Get out!" Walking through the door, I was blinded by car lights and deafening traffic noise. It was dark and disorienting. I had been kicked out of the building and back into Paris! He had snuck me back into the country illegally, with no visa, as if I had never left. I walked for a while until I decided to take a taxi to the apartment I had rented near the school. I felt confused and fragile. It was a feeling that stayed with me for many months. I registered at the university, obtained my student resident card, studied, made new friends, and discovered Paris. None of these things cured me of that sense of fragility and I felt no real identity. I had not learned to be me from within. I had spent 18 years being what my external environment dictated back home and now I was lost in this new place.

I loved Paris. I rejoiced in trying to speak a new language and listening to songs in French. I enjoyed meeting people from all over the world. I over-indulged in French pastries. I adored learning French history and I became intrigued by reading the Realists and the *poètes maudits (cursed poets)*. I delighted myself looking at the most amazing art. I felt free and empowered, being able to take the *Métro* or a bus to go anywhere I wished. But I did not feel *whole*. I felt dismembered, in pieces. I remember a time when I was walking in a subway station and thinking, "I am just one more person heading somewhere," with people rushing by in all directions.

One day, writing a letter and trying to figure it all out, I thought, "Everything I have is Me!" This was the beginning of a true connection with myself. Lonely, but empowering. This profound feeling of a *true self* is my anchor. Whenever the seas get rough in my life and I feel lost, I can throw down the anchor and come to this safe place of wisdom, calm and truth: Me. I breathe and spend time in this space. My mind and ego sometimes try to get in the way; but, as I have learned, you know when you are in the space of the *true self* because IT FEELS GOOD TO BE YOU.

The Balance between Ego and True Self

One day, while having a conversation with a close friend in a leadership role, we started talking about how we get disconnected from our *true selves*. He shared, "I try to work on becoming a better leader. I try to find a way to keep up with my professional challenges and also enjoy my personal life, but I have a hard time. It's as if my successful career and my personal fulfillment could not happen simultaneously. I'm not willing to accept this."

I could see how his introspection was a huge step in a quest for a meaning-ful life. This dialogue became a big opportunity for me to look for a way to start a conversation with people about consciousness and what it means in our lives. I knew I wanted to collaborate with leaders to overcome this dilemma. It made me understand the extent to which we are impacted by our need to find a balance between expectations, duty and self-realization. In other words, a balance between ego and *true self.*

One's professional successes and personal contentment should be able to coexist. This is possible when we find the way to being *whole*; when we learn to integrate our body, mind, and emotions; and when we embrace their intrinsic power. This process does not happen arbitrarily. It requires as much effort as a professional career.

People do not invest much in developing a more consolidated and stronger being, which is the main reason why there are so many individuals with empty, meaningless lives. It is very unfortunate. *We are naturally wired to being whole and living in fulfillment.* The first step to fix this is to become aware, to identify the voice of our ego, and to connect back to our real selves. Learned paradigms and prejudices are the main obstacles, but the soul is wiser than we know. If we learn to push our ego aside, allowing the soul to lead, we connect to our *true self* and our sense of purpose. *Regaining the connection to one's self and one's heart is where our true power lies.*

The Power of Empathy and Purpose

Powerful leaders influence others, infusing them with their passion. The intensity of this passion is what moves people. When passion comes from ego-centered goals, it lacks the noble influence of an authentic purpose and does not bring fulfillment nor generate sincere motivation. *If we can tune into ourselves and identify what we genuinely feel passionate about, we can tap into our biggest opportunity for real power and strength.* This passion is the power that makes meaningful leaders.

Sometimes, there are moments in our lives when we get lost in enthusiasm and joy while doing something. Time disappears. We work hard and don't even notice it. We feel satisfied and energized. We even might be impressed by our own capability and talent. Identifying these moments can help us understand where our true power lies.

One beautiful summer in Colombia, a few friends and family invited me to join them in an expedition to Gorgona, a beautiful island in the Pacific known for exuberant green flora and captivating fauna. Humpback whales come to mate and breed in its waters yearly. To get there, we had to fly to the little coastal village of Guapi and then take a boat. My stay in Guapi was one of the most exotic experiences of my life. It seemed the perfect place to inspire a *magic realism* story.

Once our plane landed, we were greeted by children who jumped into the plane, put our suitcases into carts and ran all the way to our hostel to drop them off. After meeting our very peculiar guide, we were taken for an exotic dinner of chipi chipis at a local restaurant and then headed back to go to bed.

The following day, I was invited to watch a basketball game in the village. I did not know that this afternoon I was about to discover the power and passion of a true purpose. While the public cheered and shouted, one of the strongest players made a move and hurt one of his opponents quite badly. Blood started coming out violently from the man's face. I ran to help. He had a very big star-shaped wound. He seemed a little dizzy and no one knew what to do. There was no hospital in Guapi, so a few locals and I walked the patient to a small urgent care post attended by an inexperienced medical student.

When we arrived, a very nervous young man came out. We followed him inside and helped the patient lie down on an old stretcher. Blood was every-where. The student doctor left to find a stitching needle. After a few long minutes, he finally found one and started stitching straight away — without anesthesia! It was dark. I was handed a piece of wood with a lightbulb nailed to it. The young doctor looked at me, his eyes nervously begging for support. I knew it was going to be challenging but I felt absolutely devoted to helping. The patient seemed to be in a trance. I could see that he could take no more pain. I massaged his shoulders with one hand and held the lightbulb with the other. I helped him breathe. The wound looked bad, but the bleeding had stopped.

Suddenly, a loud cry startled us. A mom ran through the door, a little girl in her arms, kicking and screaming, with a stick protruding out of her lower jaw. The doctor looked desperate. The injured man had to immediately stand up and free the stretcher so the little girl could use it. The girl was biting and thrashing, so the doctor decided to tie her down and he left to find some rope. It all felt very primitive. I was astonished. I held the girl gently and started speaking to her in a soft voice, looking into her eyes with compassion. She stopped screaming and looked back at me. I will not forget those beautiful dark eyes. I assured her I was going to help. I hugged her and told her I understood she was afraid. I asked her to trust me and she gave in to me totally. When the doctor returned with the rope, he realized it was not necessary anymore.

I did not feel the hours that passed. This was a transformational afternoon for me. I profoundly experienced the beauty of *Love* and *Empathy,* and I also connected with some kind of higher purpose and passion. I was impressed with my strength and determination. I could sense how being of service to others was a powerful source of realization for me.

Our trip to Gorgona was memorable. We saw the whales, dove, met inter-esting people and adventured on the island. A few days after the trip, I was back in college. Even though I had profoundly felt a living purpose, I did not elaborate around it and kept living my ordinary life. I was studying Business Administration and it felt very empty to me. I knew I needed something more, so I registered myself to study philosophy and ended up in the Comparative Literature department. Who knows what unconscious beliefs and values guided me to make those decisions?

I am sure that my weak sense of identity at the time prevented me from seeing a clear path. I was not yet ready to listen to valuable messages about my purpose. I was striving to match what I understood as society's expectations.

I earned my degrees in Business and Comparative Literature, and soon started working as a successful business consultant. I was not very happy. Still confused, I decided to get an MBA to see if another title would change that. It did not. I felt accomplished but unfulfilled. I knew inside that I needed my job to involve connecting with people at a deeper level.

Many years passed in doubting whether I would have the chance to feel satisfied with my career. Sometimes I was mad at myself because I had known my real passion and I had not chosen to pursue it. I probably should have gone into the medical field or studied psychology, but how could I have seen the truth if I was not present in myself? I was still lost and disconnected. I had learned to connect with my *true self*, but I was not able to maintain this connection consistently. I had not yet learned to let the wisdom of the *true self* rule my life. I was living as most of us do; trying to accomplish what we believed might create a decent life; acting upon external values and not our own.

With time, trying to find a way to my true purpose, I became a professional coach. Today, I call myself a social entrepreneur, a transformational coach who helps organizations, teams, families and individuals transform their lives by motivating the development of consciousness. I feel in ecstasy when I can inspire people to strive for a meaningful life. As I said before, *we are wired to be fulfilled and life is our biggest gift*. And with it, our ability to Love and be Loved.

In the same way that I had, in the past, helped a man deal with pain and a little girl feel better by showing compassion, I nowadays help people find more meaning and joy in their lives. I motivate and facilitate self-awareness, and I try to promote Empathy and Compassion whenever possible. I have learned to do it outside the medical field.

It took a lot of work in the consciousness field to learn that the sidesteps in life are not really a failure. Even today, I have to tell myself to embrace life as a learning process. *The pleasure of building the puzzle is the process.* We do not really own our lives unless we find that connection with our *true selves*. We need to know ourselves well, identify our ego, and recognize the unconscious beliefs that confuse us and stop us from seeing who we really are. This is a very relevant challenge for leaders.

Many leaders have powerful and passionate egos that inspire decisions with specific consequences, but decisions that come from ego are unreliable. Meaningful leaders must learn to recognize their ego. They need to be able to talk to it and push it aside to make decisions from a place of inner truth. They must know the ego does not have a legitimate and authentic identity. I invite leaders to strive for higher levels of consciousness so that their actions are benevolently inspired. A conscious purpose transcends individuality. It serves Humanity and helps create a better future for the generations to come. Leaders, let's go within. Let's allow Love to lead our way. Let's find the wisdom and passion of a true purpose.

IGNITE ACTION STEPS

To tune into your true self. 1. Find time to be with yourself and connect with your core being. Try to identify your ego. 2. Find a way of pulling yourself away from your usual environment. Go someplace where you are unknown or do something that might be bizarre within your usual group of people. Observe how you feel. Reflect upon this experience. Analyze your connection with yourself. Remember, it feels good to be you.

Live more in tune with your authentic purpose. Sit down in a quiet place and try to go back to moments when you have felt an absolute passion for what you do. Try to recreate the situation and identify the true source of that joy. Talk to yourself about this and make a plan that allows you to have more moments like this in your life.

Study and practice. Consciousness can be developed and trained. Invest energy and effort in this area and you will see how you can live a more fulfilled life. This is especially relevant to leaders because they are modeled by others. Meaningful leaders usually have to become activists in some way to be able to generate positive change in the world. They have to challenge and defy what does not work; improve it and generate positive transformation. With more consciousness, we can create a beautiful future.

Ana Sofia Orozco - Colombia
Transformational Coach
www.planandthrive.com

DANA SHALIT

"It's not I'll be happy when, it's I'll be happy then..."

My wish is that by reading my story, you remember not only who YOU are, but who WE all are. That you learn to witness yourself and, in turn, have the courage to witness others — so that, together, we move forward as one conscious body spreading love and understanding to everyone in the world.

MY JOURNEY FROM BE TO DO

I'm in the middle of the Massaii Mara, Kenya, standing in a circle, watching dust rise off the dry earth. In the middle of that circle stands a Canadian prima ballerina. She is standing erectly on the points of her toes. We are a united group: volunteers, non-governmental organization (NGO) workers, community members, mamas and kids. With one full swoop, we watch as she lifts her leg slowly above her shin, her knee, her waist and — there it is — lifted high above her head so that her legs are one straight line vertical to the ground. The Mamas gasp in awe, looking around for agreement. *Have you ever seen anything like this,* their awe-struck gazes imply. *Are you seeing what I'm seeing,* their eyes question.

As Director of an NGO, no matter where I've travelled off the beaten path, that look is always the same. That look is one of understanding that the limits that we had before that moment are no longer there. Possibility has expanded, and we are inspired by what is possible.

We saw it again and again. The moment where the 16-year-old Massaii warrior held a brush, joined the group, and painted on a mural for the first time. Or when a small boy in Haiti used the pink crayon to colour in Dora the Explorer in a colouring book. Do you see what I'm seeing? Do you see what I *see?!*

Why Art? That's the main question I get when I share that I run an Arts-based charitable foundation aimed at using creativity and expression to break cycles of poverty. In a world where there is so much need, why concentrate on Art?

I often explain, "Art is a global language. It brings us into the present moment. It helps us connect as we share our unique human experience."

We can give people food, water and shelter; but the will to live comes from human expression. It is only then that we feel truly actualized.

Dr. Abraham Maslow explained it in his 1943 theory showcasing the hierarchy of human needs. Physiological, safety, love/belonging, esteem, all leading to self-actualization. The human soul wants to self-actualize. We are here to create.

We hesitate to create and to live out our full potential for different reasons.

In some of the impoverished areas I have visited around the world, there is often a very real fear for physical safety. It's one of the basic needs, as Dr. Abraham Maslow explained; and therefore, living out our potential is thwarted.

In our society, we all want to be seen, but we hesitate to show ourselves fully. We turn away from judgment. We people-please. We never start due to fear of failure. We idealize celebrities, we wish to be famous *when we grow up…* all in an effort to be approved of, understood and acknowledged.

Our obsession with people-pleasing begins early in our development. We want approval from our parents, our teachers, our coaches, our bosses and, of course, our partners. So we put on a mask to show our best selves because we are scared to show our true selves. The good, the bad, and definitely… the ugly.

I have learned that the *shadow is* "the parts of us that we wish were just not there."

We all want to be witnessed, but we don't allow ourselves to fully witness all of our "self:" the guilt, the shame, the not enoughness, the unloveable in us.

It took me years to undo the shame I bestowed upon myself as I attempted to be perceived as perfect. The guilt followed me around through every failure and success; always keeping me just short of happiness and waiting for that moment where I finally felt seen, understood and good enough to stop and finally breathe.

It followed me through an intense event-production career that would be worthy of the most Instagram-able moments — fashion shows, festivals and partnerships with some of the world's coolest brands. Then, through a career change into the social marketing industry where I skyrocketed to the top of the company, receiving accolades, recognition and prestigious awards.

But on the inside, I still felt flawed, not heard and misunderstood. In the same way as I have been lonelier in a relationship than I have been outside of one, the more I succeeded, the more lost I became. The more I received accolades, the louder the voice became: *"If they only knew the real me."*

When real loss entered my life, depression took over. I had lost three family members in a few short months, closed down a part of my business, and had some close relationships end. For the first time, the identity that I had clung to that defined every success was no longer there. Who was I, if not my family, my relationships and my work? If I can't rely on those externals to bring joy into my life, then what can I rely on? Even though I knew happiness was an inside job, I struggled with finding that spark in me.

When the darkness started to affect my ability to function, I connected with an energy healer. I shared with her that this didn't make sense. I have only things to be grateful for. A thriving business, a great income, winters by the beach, recognition, awards, and giving back. But inside what I felt was sadness and self-loathing.

My healer stayed with me for a while and when my breathing calmed she explained,

"In a society obsessed with doing,
we have completely forgotten how to be."

Interesting. "So how do you BE?"

"You engage your senses... see, smell, touch,
taste and hear all that is around you."

Be in your body. Feel your emotions. Witness your thinking.

Her words sank into my heart. I had learned through the years that the only way to achieve was through *doing,* and that the more I achieved, the happier I would be. Yet here I was, swollen with achievement, chasing the next big thing... miserable, disconnected and depressed. I knew in that moment that if I wanted to elevate my doing, I had to elevate who I was being. If I wanted to find my purpose, I had to get to the bottom of why I was creating in the first place.

In today's world of growth and transformation, we think the solution is "positive thinking." We even meditate to make thoughts go away. That was me. But even my meditation was something else I HAD to do.

For once, I was being instructed to "stop the doing." Maybe the solution was not to do more, but to *be* more and to allow myself to *see* myself fully… then I could confidently and powerfully express that to the world.

It was time to take a deep dive into that part of me that "I wished was not there" because as I had heard before, what we can't be with — won't let us be. What I've also learned is that what we resist in others is what we resist in ourselves.

We feel like we should be doing something so that we *are* happy *one day*. We are taught from preschool to go to school so that we could get that job so that we could work for thirty years and then eventually reach those golden years. We rely on outside sources to feel witnessed and heard so that we can be happy. But happiness is determined by how we feel *now*.

It's not I'll be happy when, it's I'll be happy then…

I always had big dreams. Since immigrating to Canada at the beginning of the 90's, I always knew that I was meant to help people. It was time to strip down the layers of the onion and understand why my emotions were taking the best of me and causing paralysis. So I continued my quest for knowledge.

At that time, I was scheduled to do a 10-day silent meditation course called Vipassana. I had registered for it almost a year before, not knowing that I would be grieving my loved ones and in the midst of one of the darkest times of my life. I was nervous but decided to move ahead with my commitment. Ten days of no talking, reading, writing, or exercising. Ten hours of meditation per day and me alone with all of my very crazy and dark thoughts.

On day one, I was excited and ready. By the morning of day two, I was ready to make a run for it, down the hill, leaving all of my belongings behind. The thoughts in my mind were harsh. I was irritated by everything and already feeling some physical pain after only a few hours of meditation. Surely I can't make it the full ten days! But I resolved to stay and something magical started to happen. As the pain got deeper and harder, I had no choice but to sit and wait. To sit and *be with* my body and thoughts. And as I stayed with the sensation and it reached its pinnacle, it was as if I felt a *POP* and bliss would radiate through my body.

I would experience these sensations again and again. Extreme physical and emotional pain followed by bliss. The less I resisted, the faster the bliss would come; therein lay my biggest realization about my thinking: *This, too, shall pass. This, too, shall pass.*

Just like the clouds in the sky, the only sure thing was that this, too, shall pass. The course had provided me with great awareness around my thinking and then classified depression. Although we sometimes walk through a tunnel of grief and pain that seems to have no doors, there will, in fact, be a light at the end of the tunnel.

With this new awareness of my thinking, I was now able to explore my full being without the self-judgment that was present before.

For this next act of elevation, I relied on my love of personal growth books. I had been recommended a book whose title intrigued me: *The Dark Side of the Lightchasers* by Debbie Ford.

Although the book was filled with insight on so much of our resistance to self, there were a few exercises that truly helped me transform. I seemed to still be in a spiral of self-judgment. Feelings of guilt and shame still emanated from my pores.

The book is a deep dive into our shadow selves. I went head to head with the parts of me I wished were not there and realized that all the things that I resisted in others were parts that I resisted in me. Moreso, I learned that each part of me that I resisted had something to offer me and helped me become a holistic expression of universal truth. In the book, Ford suggested taking time to sit with what she called your *sub-personalities,* the parts of you that you wish were not there and tend to judge in others.

I did as instructed. I noticed a personal aversion to others who judged harshly and acted selfishly. So I sat in meditation with *Selfish Sally* to hear what she has to offer. She shared her urge to ensure that I was filled up first before filling up the cup of others. Her only goal was to ensure that my oxygen mask was securely fastened before I fastened that of another. I learned from *Judge Judy* that she was there to remind me of my preferences toward what I wanted to do, how I wanted to act and who I wanted to be. She was a reminder of the part of me that wanted to separate from others, close up, and stay better than and safe. And she would now serve as a reminder to open up and express love whenever I judged again or went up against someone else's judgment.

There were many sub-personalities — Guilty Gita, Loud Lisa, Introverted Irene — and every one of them had something to teach me. As I continued to become aware of and accept all of me, the fog started to rise and empathy grew for everyone else. How can I judge another when I see that same light and darkness in me? Every time I saw my resistance towards others who were loud, judgy, or selfish, I would now remember this reclaimed part of myself and smile at them with compassion.

As my self-acceptance grew, I was finally inspired to *do*. For this part of my journey, I was inspired by an incredible woman named Mama Gena. I attended her School of Womanly Arts in New York City where I learned all about *doing* from a place of joy and pleasure. I learned from her that we all want to be witnessed and cherished, but that we have completely forgotten how to witness and cherish ourselves. It is not up to others to create our internal happiness but up to ourselves.

It would mean that I would have to summon Selfish Sally and let her lead the way, and I was ready. I created a joy menu and every day, I was committed to checking something off. I danced, I walked in nature without my phone, and I fed my body with decadent and nutritious food. Every day, I did one act of self-care and committed to small acts of joy.

As I elevated my courage to love myself, feelings of joy and bliss started to whirl through my inner state yet again. One day at a time, I started to emerge from the darkness. My journey was one of self-love and rediscovery of true happiness. It was a realization that nothing "out there" could create true happiness, and that it was up to me to witness and cherish myself. As I noticed my thinking and how it was affecting my being, I could eventually take my doing to new highs.

If you find yourself in darkness, I hope you remember that this, too, shall pass. You are perfect, whole and complete, just as we all are. I encourage you to witness your thinking, embrace your darkness and find your joy, one day at a time. And, the next time you witness another amidst their darkness or within their light and creativity, remember that the same universal force is in you.

Have the courage to fully see yourself so that you can wholly see another.

IGNITE ACTION STEPS

Find a baby picture of yourself. If you don't have access to one, find one in a magazine or online. Stare at it and take a few deep breaths. Slowly let yourself start going back through your life to the time you were the baby in this picture.

What would you have been like? What did you look like? What noises did you make? How did you cry? How did you laugh? Allow yourself to start imagining the raw, perfect, confident, ray of light that you were... and still are.

At what point did that change? At what point did we start to emphasize our own imposed imperfection versus our inherent perfection?

Sit with your baby picture for a few minutes or for as long as you like. Examine yourself and let yourself enjoy your immaturity. Allow yourself to remember who you were before your body changed and your mind developed... pure, source energy created by a morphing of biology into a speck that eventually transformed into who you are today.

Going forward, when you see another picture, remember your young self and stand in awe of their same perfect imperfections. We are all that same speck.

Dana Shalit - Canada
Transformation Coach & Philanthropist (TBC)
www.danashalit.com

CHRISTINA M. GHOSE

"Grace shows up when growth and grit are at play!"

May deep resonance be activated in you, dear fellow seeker — that which inspires fierce action to unleash latent potential. May you know that, from whichever dark space you might be in, whatever cards you might be dealing with, you are one choice towards your highest and best version. Make it count!

STAKE YOUR CLAIM

Growing up in a city in India, studying in a convent school, coming from a middle class family, life was tough and yet filled with fun memories. Our needs were basic and so were our dreams. We lived within our means and were conditioned to do so. Having said that, it was good to be the norm and to be a "good" norm. Being brave was deemed foolish, being inspired was called wishful, being ambitious was termed selfish, being curious and questioning was seen as disobedience. Those were the conditions of society in the 70s and 80s. That was the mold I came from.

My life went on and I worked to please and to ensure my reputation was not tarnished. This was not a conscious effort as much as an unconscious wiring. I did the right thing, I said the right things and I behaved the right way. I was a good daughter, the family pride, a great student and a nice friend to have. I had extracurricular abilities in dancing, singing, debating and leading large groups. To the onlooker, this was a perfect portrait picture.

Thankfully, very early on in life, I was wired to be competitive and had a need to excel. These were, I thought at that point, good qualities to have, because to society and my community, it meant I was what we called a "rank" student, something to be proud of. However, it also meant that I was cut in the mold of being a goody-two-shoes; somebody who always did the "right" thing.

Growing up, life was filled with hardships and limited financial means. Witnessing that ongoing struggle up close, I acquired qualities of tenacity and resilience, both of which would take me far in life and help me make a success of myself. I went on to finish my post graduate diploma in Business and seemed ready to take on life.

I coasted into life with a will to do well and rise above my lot, and with skill sets I believed would help me get there. I got myself a glamourous sales job and quickly realised that it was not for me because of the long hours, skewed value system and, most importantly, the fact that it kept me away from the things and people that I loved. I dabbled in a few other roles, still finding my thing. These years were filled with a rush of newfound financial independence, novel experiences and new friendships.

I married early and, at 27 and a half, had my son. Life seemed like a whirlwind with one milestone arriving after another. It was exciting, so much change, so dynamic. However, as I look back now, it seems like all that I succeeded at was surface-level and I seemed to have gotten lost in all these new identities and roles I played. I had not paused to realise who I really was and how I truly felt.

At 33, I stood at the end of one chapter of my life and hopefully at the beginning of a new phase. I became a single mother. My son was 6 years at that time. I lived in the city that I was born in — Bangalore, the IT hub of India.

Professionally, I was a partner in a business venture in the real estate industry. I was led into this industry, and it was not my thing. I was the leader of my team, the face of the Venture, the start-up which held the idea of something novel, relevant and telling of a future to come.

While freedom and independence beckoned me with wide open arms, fear rose from my belly and consumed me, leaving me nauseous. I was overwhelmed by multiple questions. How was I going to come through on my own? How was I going to parent right? How was I going to not allow the scars from the past to tarnish the future of my young one? What if I screwed up? How was I going to make this business work? How would I keep the business profitable and continue to let it provide for the livelihood of my 30-plus team members? It was the dark night of my soul. However, as I took a breath and let it all sink in, a voice inside of me said – *one moment at a time, one step at a time!*

At that point, I asked the Force, the Universe, the angels that held me safe for so long — "What was the role I played in the not-so-successful past chapter? How can I move into the next phase armed with the lessons from this?"

I knew that I had to avoid repeating old nonfunctional patterns. That I had to make some hard hitting changes and work on returning myself to me. And that was, I believe, my first epiphany towards becoming a conscious human.

Unbeknownst to me, the Universe had begun to rally to peel the layers of the onion that needed to be uncovered. It began to bring to me people who could support me, connections to cherish and rely on. Opportunities to grow and learn. Tools to evolve and transform.

Thinking of how I had felt stuck in all areas of my life, motivational expert, T. Harv Eker's words rang loudly in my ears: "*How you do anything is how you do everything.*" Years later, I also understood that when one area of your life begins to shift, the other areas, by consequence, must move also.

Back then, I threw myself into the three areas of my life where, even though they mattered the most, how I showed up was suboptimal — my own **identity**, my **parenting** style and my **relationships** (connections) beyond that of my marriage. I knew I had to reconnect with myself before I connected outward to anybody or anything that life might offer. And the Force nudged me in that direction, tackling one area at a time.

My insights were as follows:

Learning:

I was a good student right through my growing years; a leader and a popular, successful one. However, since my post-graduation, I had stopped formally learning. Life was just a bunch of experiences — much like that of attending many workshops; however, not pausing or taking the time to reflect upon them and integrate them. 11 years hence, I knew I had to learn, unlearn, grow and shift gears; however, this time, not for a mere degree. I knew that the theory from education was not enough to take me through this next phase. I needed to learn and integrate life lessons. And this time around, it was not a time-bound conventional educational course. It had to be ongoing learning and upskilling. I enrolled into becoming a *Student of Life*. To discover fully, deeply and meaningfully my own identity. I began to design my own curriculum, which resonated within me.

I first began to search for how I could reconstruct my personal life. How I could heal my wounds and show up as a parent — whole. Not that I was broken; however, I was certainly not whole. I knew my style could no longer be conventional nor conservative. I had to break through.

I quickly began to think about how I could show up as an effective Leader and not a fractured one. How could I steer the ship without causing a Titanic rerun, given that I was in an industry that was largely male-driven and in a country that had a strong inclination to look at the male contingent for anything successful? The challenge, for me, was enticing and highly seductive.

Parenting:

Prior to this chapter of my life, my parenting style was highly task-oriented, clinical and very matter of fact. As I began to soften through the healing, I began to heal my own growing-up wounds. I began to feel the love and also the joy of parenting. I rolled up my sleeves and dove deep in.

William Wordsworth said, "The Child is father of the Man," thus beginning my journey from "parenting down" to evolving as a parent. The platform of parenting brought forward many limiting belief systems, fears and anxieties that I was carrying and imposing on my child. A big one was my childhood memory of being told not to pursue my own passion or my own vocation. My love for dogs and my desire to be a veterinarian was not good enough for society in terms of the inadequate money and status that it had. My other passion of dancing was also sadly vetoed.

At the point where I stood, I knew that the paradigm of parenting had shifted. Being an avid and eager learner, I met the student in my son as an equal. I learnt how to Ignite my child's dreams. I also knew that I had to become a role model that he could look up to; so, moment by moment, day by day, step by step we grew to have a deep connection.

I began to take on and learn new skill sets. I trained to become a licensed counsellor and therapist. I pursued joy in dancing. I kept myself in a state of learning, working on my own dark sides every now and then. I was constantly tweaking and testing, reflecting and integrating.

I also chose that my son and I take on the platform of "Travel" to explore, learn and bond. We began to embark on many journeys together and travelled the world. We made new connections and renewed old ones, learnt history, expanded our mindsets and created a big bank of memories to cherish and hold while we journey on and eventually take different paths.

Relationships:

When a key relationship gets displaced from your life, you begin to question the basis of what makes a lasting relationship. Marriage to me, then, was not companionship as much as ownership. It was a safety net, the known, the comfortable. It was stereotypical and cliche. And now that I stood at the end of a defunct marriage, I had to step into the unknown and unfamiliar. I was vulnerable in all my relationships.

I could choose to play the victim. The void of this was in my face and, as much as we can go shopping and searching for others to fulfil the emptiness, I learnt very quickly that I needed to fill my own cup so that I could share from a space of being full rather than draw from being empty.

With work, my old approach was highly transactional. I quickly chose to make these connections count and go deeper. I connected to friends. I invested in my team members, who were slowly and surely becoming a close inner circle. And when that happened, I fell in love with my work, whether it be meeting new clients, closing deals or expanding the business.

Each equation became an investment of "deep connection." Interesting opportunities began to arrive that created deep experiences with my connections. It seemed as if grace was at play and I felt truly blessed. Thankfully, with every phase, when I saw connections getting stronger, I saw the link with myself deepening and expanding. *The external became a reflection of the internal.*

Not all was hunky-dory. Like every business, our company hit multiple recession periods where fear, anxiety and uncertainty prevailed. However, each time, I looked within to see how I could reinvent myself and how I could reimagine the mundane... we reached out to experts who could facilitate us breaking through to the next level, each time strengthening our start-up into an entity that was sought after to be acquired. By this time, a big learning that sank in deep and hard was the need to collaborate; to synergise and join forces to make magic happen.

We are people's people. We thrive in connections. We co-elevate as we join forces. When I started off into this new phase, I was filled with questions of being alone, with feelings of doubt and worries of being inadequate. However, life had come full circle to show me that I was always held and I just needed to trust.

The Business was eventually acquired; however, the relationships that mattered remained. This, to me, was another moment of epiphany because, ultimately, the Business was only a platform to create something far more everlasting — deep and meaningful connections.

In learning all these things, it took courage to dive deep into my essence. I had to trust my life would be taken care of. It starts with us doing the self work and then becomes a ripple effect. Anything we touch can turn into gold. Like the Alchemist, you have it within you to transform yourself in nonreversible ways. It is this deep change that allows you to develop yourself to consciously live your authenticity.

IGNITE ACTION STEPS

The Axis is from within. Always start there.

1. Step back and evaluate:
There is a need to take stock of our own lives, of our growth, and our selves regularly. We must pause to integrate, to reflect, to take stock and then choose to realign. This is best done as a conscious, calendared practice. A good way to do this is to seek feedback from both your inner and outer circles — more like a 360-degree appraisal of one's self.

2. Build and Develop:
Enroll into becoming a Student of Life. Learn something new, upskill an existing strength, challenge your status quo on a subject and then build from that space. Given that the world (and our lives) is so dynamic, that content is so easy to access, we have no excuses for not upgrading our own software (thinking) lest we become redundant and obsolete.

3. Create new networks:
While it is a human tendency to stay within what we have known, there is immense growth and expansion in stepping out of our comfort zone and making new connections. The old belief system of "it is difficult to make friends after a particular age" is redundant, given that the world is now an open platform to make new connections. How deep we go with these connections is our choice to make.

4. Lean into your resistance:
Inside anything we resist is a call to our greatness, and it takes a courageous stance to break through. In that act of bravery, phenomenal growth occurs

that shifts one's being-ness. Grow that muscle which has the brave gene. It will take you places — literally and figuratively.

5. Turn transacting into connecting:
Bringing the emotion and connection into every equation leaves it stronger, more steadfast and more everlasting. Business and Work leave us very scientific and highly logical; however, when the spirit is called into the mix, alchemy happens. It pays immensely to shift the lens from transacting to connecting.

This list of action items may seem long and intimidating, so be kind to yourself— break them down and do them one step at a time, living one moment at a time.

Christina M. Ghose - India
Entrepreneur, Consultant, Coach,
Therapist, Volunteer, Philanthrophist
www.christinamghose.com

HANNA MEIRELLES

*"Your most influential state happens when you are not
consciously aware of how you are TRYING to influence."*

**My wish is for you to feel confident bringing your awareness to the table
in all your leadership interactions with people worldwide. May your curiosity awaken your sensitivity and may you realize you already have all the
resources to deal with whatever comes your way.**

THE INTERCULTURAL CONSCIOUS LEADER

One of my most experienced employees once said, "Hanna, please don't
touch me."

I was astonished and wondered what she meant. I had been leading a team
of 21 people in a corporate environment in a country foreign to me for about a
year at that time. I thought I was making a huge effort in my everyday actions
to not demonstrate my Latin habits of not only talking with my hands, but also
hugging people or holding their hands, or greeting them warmly by giving
them kisses on their cheeks.

As she saw the shock on my face, she offered more details: "Sometimes when
you arrive in the office, while you greet everybody and say 'good morning,'
you have this habit of placing your hands gently on our shoulders as you pass
by. I don't like that. I am a very private and reserved person. The only person
whom I allow to touch me is my partner."

Until then, I had thought I had mastered cultural sensitivity, especially because I had lived abroad for seven years and in four different countries. I had also travelled to and worked in almost 40 others with people from various nationalities. That was my life, *my theme*, the thing I worked with. It was the concept I was teaching to other people; what to do and what not to do. The value I was most passionate about as a leader was how to be culturally sensitive and respect the diversity around us.

My employee's request was a big eye opener. First of all, it told me I knew very little about the world. Secondly, it made me realize that there are things we do unconsciously. That even when we think we are doing it *right*, we might be breaking someone else's rules; we may be intruding in someone else's space.

That was the beginning of something totally new to me. I asked myself, "how many times have I stepped into someone's surroundings without asking? How often have I unknowingly offended someone by something I did?"

I knew I couldn't change the past, so I immediately started to rephrase my questions. What can I do to not end up repeating the same mistakes? How can I still be myself and respect others at the same time?

It was very difficult for me not to be a *classical* Brazilian. By that, I mean smiley, a hugger, touchy, expansive, extroverted and friendly. Of course, that was just my perception of my own culture and, by principle, I should have never generalized it. Culture for me is what a group of people do instinctively when they get together. It's infused by the values, beliefs, behaviors, rituals and symbols from that group. They live it without thinking about it.

With such a clear example of me automatically reproducing my own habits staring me in my face, I wanted to go beyond and understand where else I was acting unconsciously.

That awakening was a process. It didn't happen overnight.

That same year, *strange* things started happening to me. I ended up in the hospital six times. Once with an excruciating pain in my leg that began in the middle of a 14-hour flight that the doctors thought might be thrombosis. The next time, it was heart palpitations that they worried would result in a heart attack. On another occasion, I fainted in my bathroom for no apparent reason. The scariest moment for me was when I felt an odd pain in my chest and the doctors did 12 different exams that were aiming to identify if I had cancer. Thankfully, none of their medical suspicions were confirmed. Instead, all of the symptoms led to the same diagnosis: high stress levels. I was totally burnt out; working so hard that I couldn't really experience the luxury in my life. I disliked my job and many people around me. I became more introverted as a result.

The Universe was trying to tell me something that I would discover only further on in my journey: "You can only grow professionally to the extent that you grow personally." It sent me so many messages, but I didn't listen. Then, in a graceful move, it gave me a chance to review my own values and attitudes. One single moment in time forced me to jump into change, making me step out of the avoidance cycle I had put myself into.

That moment was on a Sunday night. I, along with my sister and two other friends from Europe, had just finished a wonderful evening in my favorite dance studio in Brisbane, Australia. It was where I went three times a week to dive into the thing I love the most in my life: DANCING! We left the studio, crossed the street to enter a 24-hour shop, and bought some bottles of milk and juice for the next day's breakfast. That would be our last time together as the three of them would go back to their respective countries the following day.

Leaving the store, we walked about 20 meters to find a taxi to go home. On the way to the taxi queue, my life changed forever. As usual at that time in my life, I was totally unaware. Unaware of my thoughts. Unaware of my physical surroundings. Unaware of where my life was headed. It was late and it was dark. All the other shops and restaurants were closed. We were walking down the pathway (which I knew very well as I had walked there often), talking happily about the evening. As I looked to my right-hand side, I was distracted by a shop window. The next thing I knew, I was bleeding and in pain on the sidewalk.

I had overlooked an electricity box in the middle of the pathway, tripped on it and fell down three meters in front of it. Since I was holding glass bottles, I didn't have the instinctual reaction of protecting myself with my arms and hands, so I landed with my face straight in the concrete. I saw so much blood and the physical pain was horrendous. That distraction cost me a broken jaw in three places and two months without speaking or eating solid foods.

Looking back, I can now say, thank goodness it happened. It was exactly what I needed, when I needed it! In those two months, I grew on a personal level more than I had in 20 years. Being in silence allowed me to listen to what my body had been trying to communicate to me for a long time: that I was disconnected. Disconnected from my purpose and disconnected from the life I was meant to live. Before breaking my jaw, I was totally and deeply unconscious of what was going on with me. I was aching inside. Aching for meaning. Aching for connection: with others, with myself, with my work, and with what really mattered.

I realized I wanted to truly belong again. I also noticed that, until then, all my efforts were making me *fit in* with a culture that was not mine. Instead of *belonging* to a group, I was thinking and acting just like the people around me: complaining, blaming, justifying, judging... without even being aware of it. Living that reality, I couldn't even ask myself the question "As a leader, am I allowed to complain, blame, judge and justify? Is it all right to have those behaviors?"

During those two months, I had enough time and space to realize I was behaving like a victim instead of a leader. I thought the world was happening *to* me and not *for* me. The worst thing was that I was blaming the culture I was immersed in as being responsible for everything that had happened to me. I gave up my accountability. I left my autonomy in the closet. I was unaware that I had a choice. I could clearly have chosen another way. Another path. I could have chosen to change that reality. Instead, I was judging a culture and the people in it. I was making assumptions, which is exactly the opposite of what an intercultural leader should do.

That broken jaw was the sign *and* the opportunity I needed to change my entire life approach on being an intercultural leader. I learnt principles that became part of my new values' system, all originating from that incident; or, as we call it, from that Ignite Moment:

1. A conscious intercultural leadership is about being present.

I noted how my beliefs and behaviors were influencing other people. During a team-building exercise in a ropes' course, an employee looked over at me and saw that I was terrified to climb a tree. She, too, became afraid. When she saw that, in spite of my fear, I did it anyway, she immediately found her own courage. After her climb, she realized she hadn't been truly afraid until she saw that *I* was afraid. My fear had been unconsciously transferred to her. I had no idea.

Leaders are the example. We inspire and influence people just by our presence. Sometimes by just walking into a room. Most times just being there, in the moment, not only physically but also spiritually and mindfully, we notice what's going on in that situation and become aware of the emotions and feelings around it. We are then conscious of our own attitudes and thoughts, which helps us see what no one else is seeing. When we look beyond the things that are in front of us we create the capacity to speak about what others wouldn't speak about.

2. Intercultural leadership is about standing up for something and speaking your truth with authenticity and compassion.

Everyone has a message to share. I needed to stay in silence for two months to realize that. What if I would never have my voice again? What if I was deprived forever of one of the greatest gifts I have ever received? How foolish was I for not being grateful for my ability to speak!? Now, I wanted my voice back! I had so many things to say. I wanted to express how much I believed in freedom of choice, how much I believed that, for humanity, inclusion and integration is the only way. Being whole as a species will help us find solutions for the huge problems we face on our planet today.

Once, I heard one of my students explain that *diversity* is to invite everyone to your party and *inclusion* is to make them all dance together. I wanted not only to invite all the people to the party, but I wanted most to hold their hands on the dance floor and create a powerful awareness that *tolerance* is not enough. By definition, tolerance is the ability or willingness to tolerate opinions or behaviors that we don't necessarily agree with. I feel we need to go to a higher level than tolerance. Once you are aware that differences exist, the next step is to deeply understand what is there so you can consciously choose to accept it or not. When you do accept that message, speak up. Stand up for your belief and you will realize you are not alone in your message.

3. Intercultural leadership is about creating a great environment where people can thrive.

I realized I wanted to replace the people around me with more positive and uplifting companions. Leaders surround themselves with and create for their teams and families a supportive and enjoyable environment where there is no space for practicing victim behaviors, such as complaining about something or blaming someone. A leader takes full responsibility for their own life and makes hard choices; such as, breaking up with a toxic friendship or ending an abusive relationship. A leader also takes on the responsibility to educate others about intercultural differences and the beauty of diversity in the workplace, always aiming at adding up, never intending separation. Always seeking respect for each other, never allowing discrimination in any form. A leader strives for equality and promotes acceptance. For example, a male leader steps up and supports the female leaders. A white leader steps up and supports the black leaders. A heterosexual leader steps up and supports homosexual leaders. An older and very experienced leader stands up for the younger generation. He or she is not afraid of losing his or her job, status or position. When people feel threatened or uncomfortable from any of those ideas, they have to do their inner work first. Clearly, there is something still in their subconscious that they haven't dealt with and *this* is standing in their way of being totally authentic and free to help others to thrive.

4. Intercultural leadership is not about working hard and burning out. It is about stating your mission clearly and attracting great people who want to join you on your journey.

Do you know what your purpose in this life is? During my forced silence period, I had a lot of time to think about that! In fact, I remembered I had a mission. I had worked on it many years before, as I was very fortunate to discover my mission when I was 18 years old. I had lived according to my mission for quite some time; but during my introspection, I realized I had abandoned my purpose in order to feed my own ego with trips, luxury items, titles, positions, all those false powers that made me feel inauthentic. When I was almost burnt out, I said to myself, "There's got to be another way." Working so hard in something that was not even remotely giving me joy could have been a sign for me, but I was totally unconscious of it and kept going until I felt lost, lonely, in a foreign land, unable to connect with my own employees. Being out of touch with my purpose made me push them away, but when I realized I was lost, a miracle happened and a friend gave me the greatest gift that someone could give: an opportunity to educate myself. She gave me a ticket to a wonderful personal development training program that changed me fundamentally. Most importantly, it allowed me to reconnect myself to my own mission in a sensitive, understanding, accepting and action-oriented way.

5. Intercultural leadership is about tapping into spaces where nobody else would, taking risks and innovating.

It's what happens when someone calls you and offers you an assignment in a country that others don't even know where it is on the map; where serious epidemics exist and wars are happening. Not even knowing anything about that place yourself, you immediately say, "Yes! I am in!"

If you are already a globetrotter or want to travel and interact with people from all over the world, I recommend you become an intercultural conscious leader. In this way, you can experience performing your different leadership roles and create a positive impact on the individuals you love, in the society you live in and on the planet you care about.

Grabbing these opportunities to lead consciously is something that I do to enjoy life. It is a choice you can make, too; not just for the sake of the adventure, but for the chance to contribute while living an innovative lifestyle. Sometimes you may risk your reputation, question your own values, and change your mindset along the way, but the journey is always worthy when you help transform other people's lives.

Ignite Action Steps

I have some suggested actions for you as you embark on this journey, to help you become more aware of your surroundings and so you can consciously influence on a global scale.

- **Speak their language.** Wherever you go, if you don't speak the local language yet, learn at least a bit of it. Including the local idiom, their body language, habits, acronyms, ways of speaking and behaving. Forget that idea that everybody just needs to speak English. Although this is true for the business world, you will be seen as a thoughtful leader if you learn the local culture, and more people will be willing to connect with you.

- **Ask for help.** Show people you want to learn from them. Be humble as a leader and say, "I am not from here; please be my coach and tell me when I do something wrong."

- **Find yourself in that other culture.** Sometimes, we think we need to act as other people in a culture do. We don't. Seek out the things in that culture which you like to do. In that environment, you will be able to thrive and connect with people who have something in common with you.

When you consciously blend cultural knowledge with respect and understanding, you become a global citizen and an influential leader. Be sensitive and enjoy the ride!

Hanna Meirelles - Brazil
Brazilian Citizen of the World
Global Trainer and Development Facilitator,
Leadership Specialist and Founder of Life Level 10
www.hannameirelles.com

JAMIE TAKAHASHI

*"First, lead yourself with love, focused intention and purpose;
then, you will inspire others to lead themselves."*

**We are all leaders regardless of where we come from. Leadership is culti-
vated and expressed in a multitude of ways. By awakening to our personal
truth, we can consciously connect with others to become a catalyst for
positive change and growth. In sharing my story, my hope is that you
discover your leader within.**

THROUGH CHAOS TO MINDFULNESS

I am an unlikely leader. I do not have the formal education or other usual
qualifications for leadership. I was not born into a family structure that modeled
consciousness nor leadership. My upbringing was unconventional and unstable.

As the product of an unplanned teenage pregnancy meant I would grow up
alongside my mother who was 17 years old when she had me. My grandfather
was an alcoholic, unable to properly care for his teenage daughter. My grandmother had passed away from cancer the year before my birth. Mom would
not end up with my biological father and would marry twice, with boyfriends
in between. The saving grace is that I knew I was deeply loved and wanted.
Aside from being told this repeatedly, I simply had to look into my mother's
eyes to feel this truth. I learned early on that love is present in all people and
all situations; it may just be clouded over.

Born in San Francisco in the '50s, my mom and her social circle were influenced by the hippie movement. Sex, drugs and rock and roll were a way of life. My caregivers were, for the most part, figuring out their adulting. Listening to music, smoking pot and drinking beer were the usual pastimes. Jimi Hendrix, Janis Joplin, Black Sabbath and Led Zeppelin were the albums typically in heavy rotation. I was eight years old at one get-together when my mom showed me a tiny, acid-laced piece of paper with the picture of Mickey Mouse Fantasia. She emphatically told me not to touch it (which, of course, I didn't). That was my first time seeing LSD. Drug use would be a regular presence throughout my upbringing.

I had a lot of autonomy growing up. Being an only child meant I became adept at entertaining myself. My early elementary school years were spent at the creek catching lizards and tadpoles, and I loved reading, getting lost in books, daydreaming and listening to music.

Neither my mom nor stepdad completed high school, which equated to unstable, low-paying jobs. We moved a lot, often living with different family members in small apartments and, at one point, a motel. This regular uprooting meant I had attended nine different schools by the time I reached tenth grade and I barely completed one year of high school with full credits.

By the time I reached my teenage years, several things were apparent:

1. I loved the social aspect of school. I learned how to connect with others and made friends easily.
2. I hated sitting at a desk and being told what to do and how to do it.
3. Being poor sucked! As did food stamps and being the recipient of donated items.
4. If I was to get out of poverty, it would be on me. Any future success was in my hands.

During a brief stint selling cocaine, I began witnessing some of the painful truths of drugs and alcohol, including friends being raped, kidnapping and murder. I knew then that this was not the life I wanted. The harsh and painful reality of experiencing loved ones go through these things is unbelievably difficult. Witnessing how we can lead — as well as be led — down dangerous and detrimental paths showed me that we all have the potential to be powerful influencers. The question is, how will we channel our personal power and influence?

At 14½, I started my first legitimate job as a food server in a retirement community. The pay was $3.50 hour. While it wasn't a lot, it was honest money.

My employment lasted less than a year as we moved... again. I craved stability and normalcy. Exactly what that was, I didn't know; I just knew I didn't have it.

One thing I did know from a young age was that I wanted to be a hairstylist. After the move and sophomore year, I received my high school equivalency diploma at 16 years old and started cosmetology school. I was the youngest student, which suited me well as I often gravitated toward older friends. To earn money, I worked at a beauty supply 15 to 20 hours a week. Coupled with another 40 hours a week for school, I was busy.

My home life became more unpredictable with drug and alcohol abusers frequenting our place and I knew I had to get out, so at 17, I moved in with my boyfriend. While that situation came with its own challenges, at least I had more control over the chaos. With some stability and focus, I completed school the following year and was working fulltime as a hairstylist.

Over the next few years, learning to lead myself into becoming a responsible adult was a bumpy road. Self discipline wasn't easy. Our apartment was the party house for our friends, which wasn't conducive to a healthy lifestyle. Exercise was nonexistent and my daily intake of fast food, soda, alcohol, cigarettes and sleep deprivation did not add to my wellbeing.

Right after my 20th birthday, Mom died unexpectedly from cirrhosis and a heart condition. She was 37 years young. Losing the person who gave me life, the person who I knew loved me unconditionally, was devastating. This scared me straight into sobriety and put me on a path of self-inquiry. Who was I, really? I questioned everything. I dove into psychology, philosophy and spirituality in search of meaning and answers.

As I learned new ways of living and thinking, I had to let go of unhealthy habits and relationships. I discovered that when I set an intention to change, took actionable steps and started living into that vision, the Universe answered the call and support manifested.

Later that same year, I was invited to attend class at a kung-fu studio. Saying "Yes" to that invitation changed the course of my life. I immediately fell in love with the art, physicality, discipline and philosophy of kung-fu. I learned how to properly fuel and rest my body and gain some control over my emotions, and the community and practice provided me with the structure and stability I needed and craved.

My first formal introduction to meditation was in kung-fu class. Diving deeper into Buddhism and Taoism opened my heart and mind, and I would later go on to study Chan Buddhism with a monk from China. Learning to rest in the space between thoughts and detach from the constant dialogue in my head was a gift. It changed the way I interacted with myself and others, both personally and professionally. By becoming more present, I could hold space for others with an intention of openness and kindness.

I worked full-time doing hair and attended kung-fu class five days a week. I took and assisted in teaching private lessons, and assisted in leading kids' classes. I started competing in tournaments regularly for both forms and fighting, which challenged me greatly. What I realized was that with the intense schedule I kept, I had more physical and mental energy. Doing what I loved and was passionate about fueled my Being, as opposed to depleting it.

In 1994, I was invited to compete in The Beijing Wushu and Kung-Fu Invitationals, by the recommendation of my teacher. It was my dream come true. I didn't have the financial resources to cover the cost of the trip, but I had a vision and determination. I knew the Universe would provide.

Upon sharing my invitation and my dilemma with a client while cutting hair, he graciously offered to help me solicit sponsorships by drafting a letter to go along with newspaper articles I had been featured in. This was a skill set which he was perfectly suited for. It was amazing how the right person showed up at the right time to fulfill the need I couldn't do on my own. We are wired for community and service to one another and often these synchronicities make for inspiring encounters.

With my travel costs covered, I secured my place on the team. Our coach, originally from Hong Kong and having come to the USA in the '60s, was a Grand Master of Seven Star Praying Mantis Kung-Fu. He was accomplished, respected and well known in the martial arts community. He was also incredibly tough and stern, and I was intimidated by him.

Our two-week trip consisted of a three-day tournament and some tourism. We visited The Great Wall, Tiananmen Square and The Forbidden City, among other sites. Our travels also took us to Shanghai, Hangzhou and Qingdao, as well as on visits to kung-fu schools.

At 22 years old, I had never been out of the country. China was the one place I had dreamed of visiting and I often found myself filled with gratitude and disbelief that I was actually there. It was a contrast to my life in California; from the food to the customs, landscape and crowds, it was new and I completely absorbed it. I stood out, with my blonde hair and fair skin, and people would frequently stare and invade my personal space. Many of the areas that we visited had seen few foreigners back in 1994 and they were as curious about me as I was about them.

The tournament was held at the site of the proposed Olympic Grounds in

Beijing. Each team would have set practice times in the facilities to prepare. There were competitors from all over the world. During our warmups, I heard the Grand Master who had been coaching me tell my teacher I wasn't good enough to be there and ask why was I on the team. His words were harsh and judgmental. I was crushed.

I immediately ran out of the practice area and into the hall toward the bathroom, holding back my tears. The toilets were holes in the ground without plumbing and one could smell the area long before you reached it. I entered one of the stalls and broke down sobbing. The stench coming from the ground only added insult to injury. While using my T-shirt as a mask (and in spite of copious amounts of snot), the smell was horrible and it only added to my self-pity. The emotional overwhelm had taken a toll. I didn't want to be there. I wanted to run away, to quit, to never see my coach again. Surely, he knew best who was fit to compete, and it wasn't me. I was the only female competitor on our team and I felt utterly alone.

Often, I have negated my capabilities, buying into another's opinion of me. This was one of those times. When I could no longer take the smell nor see through my swollen eyes, I realized I had to get myself out of both that bathroom and my mindset. I had a responsibility to the sponsors, my team and myself.

I made my way back to my teacher and my teammates who, of course, were encouraging. Fortunately, I would have a night to sleep and to pull myself together for the competition.

Walking into the large hall the next morning, I was sick with intimidation and fear. For the opening ceremonies, Chinese women in beautiful traditional silk dresses were holding signs for the teams to line up by. Hundreds of martial artists were there from around the world, all with the same goal: To win their division and take home a medal.

When it was my turn to take the floor, I looked at the judges on each corner. I knew I wasn't the best, nor the worst. All I needed to do was keep my mind focused on the moment and let my body do the motions that were wired into my muscle memory. I reached for the familiar stillness that had served me well many times before. During both the sets for weapons and for empty hand forms, my routine was clean and flowed well. Relieved I hadn't messed up, we all waited until the others finished their routines. Then, I could see where I landed in the scores and standings.

The gold medal in traditional broadsword and silver in open hands for an intermediate female was mine. Overwhelmed with shock, gratitude, and relief, I was in disbelief. My coach hugged me. Given his cultural background, generation and temperament, I knew his gesture was genuine and generous. What I saw in his eyes has stayed with me all these years. I could see deep kindness, joy and relief. He was proud; his goal was accomplished. While I demonstrated my ability to my peers, he also was demonstrating his in a parallel situation with the other coaches. The win was a win for all.

I have learned that leadership is a dance where at times we are the leader and at other times, the one being led. How we guide others and accept guidance sets a trajectory for outcomes. Knowing why we are leading and what we intend to accomplish is essential. Clarity is key in achieving our goals. In my 30 years of being a hairstylist, I've led myself as an independent contractor and then transitioned into salon owner and salon director. Whether I'm providing guidance to our 30-plus team members, to clients, to my children, or to my friends, my goal is always to communicate from awareness. I love being in leadership. I love the growth that occurs. Is it always easy? No... of course not! The path of evolution is often painful, messy and meandering. But I do believe that we all have a deep desire to bring forth our best self. When you interact with others, try to genuinely connect from a place of non-judgment and unconditional love. Whether you are leading one person or a thousand, your role in becoming a conscious leader is to ignite others to become the best and brightest versions of themselves.

Ignite Action Steps

Knowing, loving and caring for yourself is the greatest gift you can give to others. Every interaction is shaped from that primary relationship. Becoming conscious of our thoughts, intentions and actions, we can more skillfully impact the world.

- **Meditation and mindfulness are powerful tools and practices.** Regardless of one's faith tradition, there are a multitude of disciplines and techniques to choose from. Podcasts, online learning courses, books, workshops and classes are available to help you. Guidance and instruction are important when beginning. Free and donation-based classes can be found at spiritual centers, yoga studios and even hospitals.

  When I began my meditation practice, I sat for 10 minutes and simply counted my breaths 1 through 10. My practice eventually evolved over time. Now, I sit for 20-30 minutes every night before going to sleep. It's part of my nightly routine, like showering and brushing my teeth. We give a lot of priority to our externals. Your interior life is equally important. Start by sitting for 10 minutes at night and/or morning in silence. You can count your inhalation as 1, exhalation as 2 and so on until you reach 10. If you lose count or get lost in thought, simply start over. The goal is not silence nor to judge the mind and its thoughts. The aim in learning to observe our inner dialogue is for us to, over time, become skillful in navigating our perceptions and communications.

- **Meditation practices can also be expressed in movement.** Currently, my passion is Tai Chi and Qigong, and I attend both group classes and private lessons. As a form of exercise, it fosters greater balance, strength and flexibility. It also has the components of mindfulness movement. What I deeply appreciate about these exercises is that they can be practiced at any age and fitness level, and are often taught outdoors. Being in the fresh air and listening to the sounds of nature is very restorative to the mind and body.

- **The balance of rest and movement for the body and mind** is not be underestimated. Sleeping at least 7 hours a night and giving yourself permission to nap, daydream, spend time in nature, or simply watch the clouds provides a break from a world so filled with stimulation.

Loving and leading ourselves and others is an ongoing journey. Remember that the goal is progress, not perfection. Accepting whatever arises and cooperating with that guides us toward living in the moment. In that space, you can become the brightest version of yourself.

Jamie Takahashi - USA
Director – Writer – Speaker
jamietakahashi.com

DAMIAN CULHANE

*"To truly make a difference and serve others with your
unique gifts and talents, you must have the courage to overcome your ingrained fears and win the battle of the soul."*

**I invite you to rise up and reach beyond your fear; to connect with what
your heart wants and create a legacy beyond your unconscious ego. My
desire is that you are inspired as a Conscious Leader to triumph over your
self-imposed limitations, defeat the boundaries of your beliefs and create
a life you love.**

YOU MUST REACH BEYOND YOUR LIMITATIONS

It was a winter morning. The journey to London's specialist hospital felt
eternally long and I felt ill-prepared for what lay ahead. On the hospital ward,
I sensed awkwardness in the staff bustling around us, softening the moment
and distracting from the impending news. We were there to receive lab results.
I felt sick, my mouth dry, my whole body tense, similar to when the doctor
had taken the muscle biopsy several weeks before. The specialist, in her early
fifties and slightly aloof, dressed to match her age and disposition, engaged
in a few moments of polite and gracious chat before coldly announcing the
news my family had been dreading: "There was no dystrophin present in the
muscles." The announcement was like an ambush, poised in silent preparation
for its strike as it exploded rudely into our world. Just like that, the fatal dis-
ease established its impenetrable stronghold. The destructive muscle wasting

condition was relentless and unwaveringly determined to take a life: The life of my six-year-old son Ben.

I comforted my sobbing wife, tears rolling down my cheeks as I soothed and reassured her. Ben's diagnosis of Duchenne Muscular Dystrophy (DMD) was a hammer-blow to our hearts. The brutal enemy was upon us. The challenges Ben would face were unknown, unexpected, uninvited and unwanted. DMD was an utterly agonizing and unwelcome guest.

On the way home, we visited my Mum who had been looking after our eldest son, Conor. He was joyfully playing with his cousin Joe, both now joined by Ben. My Mum moved away from the boys and as I told her the outcome, her eyes filled with tears; she was distraught. During her physiotherapy career, she had treated many patients with DMD. She knew what to expect. I hugged her for a moment, already acclimatizing to my new role of soothing others – a role reluctantly thrust upon me.

Overcoming the emotional trauma of a child being diagnosed with a life-limiting condition takes a significant depth of character. My shallow life experiences up to that point revolved around trying to persuade people to buy goods and services. None of what I had done was particularly meaningful, but I had been using my skills and talents in a productive way. I had experienced moderate success in my career but had struggled lifelong with binge eating and junk food.

Like most parents of a disabled child, I was determined to confront the monster full on and deflect my sadness, launching into solution mode. I had to focus on being positive, a natural disposition that now intensified and escalated into a hard protective shell. I made contact with a charity who guided me through the current scientific research. At that time, it didn't take very long to read the full dossier of research. It was a small list. I attended the annual conference to receive scientific study updates and meet other DMD parents on the same loathsome journey. Back home, my loved ones, still reeling from shock, were coming to terms with the new reality of Ben's diagnosis while DMD relentlessly and silently continued the slow erosion of Ben's body and our hope.

On the surface I was thinking positively, but I was crumbling inside. I concealed my fears, frustrations and sadness under my brave coping mask. I would lie awake at night, the overwhelm gripping me. Why was this happening to Ben? I longed to swap places with him. DMD was unaffected by my thoughts or emotions; it ignored my endeavors. It was winning. To soothe my suffering, I sought comfort in the addiction I knew: junk food. Nothing else existed outside of those secret binges.

DMD is brutal, unrelenting and never wanes, retreats or surrenders. It just pushes on. Its unstoppable bluntness is a cold and sobering reality. But it also has a polarity – gently awakening people to new possibilities. Just when you feel exhausted from the struggle to cope, a tiny glimmer of hope emerges. I got involved in a campaign to lobby for more funding into scientific research. Encouraged by the responses and the momentum the campaign had achieved, I shared the campaign with family and friends. I felt I was achieving something. I was so grateful for the support of others and, for the first time, I had an awareness of the depth of human kindness. There were new comrades willing to join in the battle. I was NOT alone.

A family friend suggested we organize a 300 kilometer cycling event to raise funds for a power wheelchair for Ben; another suggested a fundraising tea party. The local press picked up on the story, providing great coverage along with an article featuring the tea party. During the tea party, a man walked in, very unassuming and unknown by the other attendees. He approached me to confirm I was Ben's Dad. As he handed me a folded napkin, he said four words, "This is for Ben." After he left, I opened it to see a cheque; my jaw dropped. I walked over to the friend who had organized the event and she gasped at the generous total. We were both amazed, touched by the kindness of a complete stranger.

The bike route offered some challenging conditions and we trained hard as a team. I felt awkward being responsible to get a large group of enthusiastic cyclists safely across the UK. I was nicknamed 'Captain Clipboard' for my part in the event and we bonded well. In spite of getting lost and random mechanical issues, we made it from the West Coast to the East Coast of England with tears and laughter. My own mixed emotions arrived with me on the beach, watching the riders safely reach the final destination. Relief flooded me; I turned to the friend next to me, placing my head on his shoulder, and started crying. I was so grateful for the depth of human kindness I had just witnessed and shared.

The next leg of my journey as I continued on my personal quest to fight the dreaded DMD was becoming a Trustee of the charity I had contacted when Ben was first diagnosed. There were a few moments that required strong and conscious leadership, but it was largely a collective effort by everyone. Two years later, I was invited to participate in a 1,600 kilometer ride from the most southerly point of England to the northern tip of mainland Scotland. I started preparation and training months before departure. During one of the early training rides, my nutrition and fitness were out of balance. I had been drinking alcohol and up late the previous night. When we stopped for a break, I indulged in a lemon drizzle cake. For the remainder of that ride, I found myself trailing behind. I was embarrassed, apologizing to my fellow riders for falling so far back. I knew I was riding for an important cause and I was determined to never experience that again. I resolved to change my behaviour and habits immediately.

It was a difficult and challenging period. I was constantly meeting the needs of my family, training for long distances, running my business, learning about maximizing my nutrition and visiting my seriously ill Dad in hospital. I juggled the competing demands, relieving the stress by cycling. On a personal front, my wife and I had been growing apart for some time. The changes in my eating had become an obsession for me. I was determined to be fit and ready for the big event, and was preoccupied with avoiding old habits. Nearer to the event, I was fit and lean, ready and committed to the ride. I had made a promise to myself that went beyond the bike ride. I'd shifted the unresolvable tension of serving others first to focusing on what *I* needed. This was new, putting myself first.

Changing nutrition habits was minor. Adapting and shifting to stand up for myself in relationships – that was prickly. Holding my ground in my new self-imposed leadership meant I was becoming more aware; more resolute in what I needed.

On the morning of the event, we gathered early at the starting point in Land's End. There was horizontal rain and strong headwinds. The organizers were asking us to be patient whilst they evaluated the safety for all. There was a mixed group of abilities, about twenty cyclists in total. After a short delay, it was a 'go'. We set off with great spirit and enthusiasm, soon tested by the severe conditions. By no means the strongest rider, I steadied into a good rhythm and settled in for the first leg. I was easily able to match the pace in the lead group. At the first stop, it was obvious that the delay between the front of the group and the back was widening. We had two to three days of relentless hills on our way out of Cornwall. I saw the look of exhaustion on the faces of the rear riders and I decided at that moment that I would position myself at the back, for support. I knew how they were feeling.

There was a mother of a young lad with DMD, and a grandfather too. We were all there for the same reason – to do something to help our loved ones. We made steady progress and it was nice to get to know them. I settled into my new position of leading from behind – offering emotional and mental support while 'pulling' them up the hills. At the end of each day, they thanked me, grateful for the support.

On day three, we were heading away from the hills. The pace was fine and the weather improving. During the afternoon break, I received the dreaded news: My father had died. I shared my pain with some friends on the ride and just started crying – finding the familiar shoulder from the beach to rest my head as I sobbed. My immediate thought was that I must call my step-mother and sister to see if they were okay. They were together, both had been prepared for the outcome. I asked, "Do you need me to come and help with any arrangements?" There was a resounding and reassuring 'no.' We all agreed that Dad would want me to continue my sponsored bike ride and complete my goal. I did it for both him and Ben!

I went to visit my dad at the Chapel of Rest as soon as I returned home. When I saw him on that final occasion, I realized he was on a new journey. It occurred to me that he had created a life he loved and his passing would be no different. He had spent his life traveling, reading, learning and enjoying the experiences life offered. I learned so much witnessing this and I was ready to follow that lead.

Whenever you raise your game, inner and outer tension arise while you create a life you love. I was determined to ignore unsupportive comments. To stand up for who I was becoming, not fall back to what I had left behind. I needed to stick to my new identity. At times I felt lost; confused and uncertain; caught between the old me and the new, still not powerful enough to overcome my ego resisting and flaring up. I was suffering like a helpless victim around certain people, powerless in their shadow. At times, I would separate myself from them, enjoying my new freedom to be who I wanted to be.

With my new perception, I saw that parents in the DMD Community handle the continuum of acceptance differently. At some stage, ALL parents become desperate to do something as their child's quality of life slowly deteriorates. High levels of stress and depression in the community often erode family ties.

An idea to help heal DMD suffering first came to me in a meditation. It took me a while to process what that meant. I developed a grand vision as to how the program would work. But when I introduced the idea to DMD parents, it fell flat. I felt deflated. My idea was to empower others and help heal their suffering. The challenge: Parents were not ready for the message. Burdened by the weight of sorrow and grief, so many parents detached from their own personal dreams. Not knowing where to start, my vision was overwhelming. I felt sad that I was not able to do more for the community. I wanted to help, yet I was alienating myself and abandoning my vision. My ego was in full unconscious sabotage mode.

It became obvious that those in the DMD community were at different stages of processing the change caused by the diagnosis. Some people were actively seeking how to be positive whilst others were in stages of shock, denial, anger, frustration or even despair. I had experienced these stages myself. To build engagement with the community would require a different approach. I was so frustrated, knowing that I could help this group of people but having limited resources and no prior knowledge of how to reach a larger audience. It was obvious that I would need to give them added value. Creating a series of webinars, I knew the title had to be "Healing DMD Suffering." I gathered feedback, observed themes and developed a structure. I put together a unique program for the benefit of the parents. To maximise impact, the content included experts with informative knowledge and expertise. I knew the cause was much greater than me and that to honour the community would require transformational content.

When a person adopts change, their mindset can swiftly adapt to a new way of thinking and manifest a new life. They flow in the river of life between the banks of pleasure and pain. Getting stuck on one of the banks is the issue. Life is about how we transform and alchemize our thinking. There is a Buddhist saying, "Pain is part of life. It does not have to rule your life." Thanks to my own awakened journey and what I learned, I have formed a vision of building a bridge for others to follow. This requires courage and determination. I have to lead myself first, to beat a path so others can flourish. I reached beyond my own fear and sadness to rise up and allow my light to shine, and I'm inspiring others to do the same. No one should be defined by **DIS**-ease. My desire is for you to win the battle for your soul and create a life you love, a life worth living.

IGNITE ACTION STEPS

For anyone who has a desire to rise up above their unconscious ego, the action steps below will be a guiding light. The ego has an inconspicuous driving force, alienating you from what your heart desires. It aims to keep you safe and to survive. To truly master your 'self' and become a mentally powerful and strong person, you must have a greater awareness of 'self' and connect with your purpose to create what you love. Pay attention to the whispers of your soul. Listen and be aware – your 'self' has unknown potential, wisdom and capability to create everything that you dream about. To move your ego, reach beyond the mountain of your self-imposed limitations and go deep within.

Whatever challenges you experience in your life, no matter how difficult, to be a Conscious Leader, you must connect with your purpose. Your journey is what ensures you will cope with the bigger cause. You were born to create and share your unique gifts and talents to benefit humanity. You have a responsibility to transcend and make a difference. Here's a recipe for success in becoming a Conscious Leader:

- **Connect with your Purpose:** Know what you can do to serve humanity and make a difference in the world. Map out your true purpose (see resources).

- **Stakeholder Map:** Know who all your connections are; the people in the community, and beyond, who you wish to impact.

- **Add Value to Stakeholders:** This seems pretty obvious, but make sure you understand and have empathy with your stakeholder. What can you do to make their lives better?

- **Allow others to contribute:** Be authentic in your praise for the people who contribute to your success. Notice the depth of human kindness inside the hearts of individuals you have the pleasure to work with. Enjoy the ride.

- **Focus:** Regularly remind yourself of your vision. Have accountability buddies or a structure where you can be challenged by a trusted peer or coach.

- **Lead from your heart:** Always connect with what your heart wants in any given situation. When I wanted to give up and scrap the idea of the webinar series, I meditated and reflected on my highest desire. What did my heart and soul want? The answer was simple: To heal emotional suffering.

Damian Culhane - United Kingdom
CMgr, FCMI, FISM, MIOD, MEMCC
Teacher. Coach. Speaker.
www.damianculhane.co.uk

AMY O'MEARA

"Never allow your patterns of the past to be the author of your future."

We all have a past: A story we tell, emotions we carry forward, and behaviors we learned. These have an effect on all of our future relationships. My hope is that you understand we have a choice in how our story affects our future. We can allow our subconscious fears to be the narrator of our story that plays out in our future life; or, we can choose to stand in our truth and heal through the development of our inner self. When we allow the past to be a catalyst for change, then we have the power to rewrite our future, not define it.

GET A DOCTORATE OF YOUOLOGY

I could tell you about the thousands of sad moments in my life that have been filled with: crippling anxiety, never feeling safe or accepted, always worrying, self-sabotaging, meltdowns wearing on everyone around me, feeling as if nobody loves me, everyone leaves me, I have no friends, I'm not enough, whiney-ass, oh poor me, I'm a victim, blah, blah, blah bullshit that plagued thirty-five years of my life.

Or, we could skip all the self-created drama, victimhood, and learned behavior from childhood trauma – because let's face it…it ALWAYS leads back to our childhood and one or both of our parents screwing us up in some way (which was probably passed on from their parents) – and get to the good story. The epiphany. The moment we all pray for, from whatever source we believe in.

That breakdown moment that changes everything.

I wish I could tell you in that ONE life-changing moment that it was just *one* moment, but here's the truth: It was a melting-pot of all those epiphanic moments stirred one last time in the black cauldron of human failure. It all came together in one final meltdown to end all meltdowns for good, forcing me to recognize the hardcore truth.

IT WAS ME that was the problem, NOT everyone else.

In that moment, I was lying on the kitchen floor in a puddle of my own tears, sobbing after yet another horrific fight, ultimately ending my relationship for good. (I should have let go a long time before, but that's another story.) With my hand vice-gripped to the phone and paper towel wads surrounding me like sorrow-stained snowballs (tissues were never enough for my hurricane meltdowns), I lay in my own self hatred. Why I always chose the cold kitchen floor for meltdowns was beyond me! I knew this place all too well. I had fallen to pieces on floors more times than I cared to admit. Who am I kidding... only a very select few ever knew this side of me – the victim. Uggh...even typing those words now, *the victim,* makes me ill.

It was in this final, epic, emotional unspiraling, life-altering moment that all the dots connected for me. Every critical word ever uttered by every fight and breakup in every relationship I had ever had (marriage included) came crashing down upon me. It was a tidal wave of a hardcore truth that I had denied for so long. It washed over me until I drowned in it. It was the one truth that I was unwilling to EVER face. One truth repeated. One lesson I apparently refused to learn but the Universe vowed to repeat until I relented.

I was playing the victim role in every relationship – I loved the drama because that is what I had learned love was.

I choked on that thought. It settled upon me like a death sentence. I was forever stuck as a prisoner of my subconscious mind. While this seems like one hell of a truth to choke on, it was also the moment I realized this awakening would set me free.

It was in this altered state where I felt I had no love left to give that I surrendered.

I lay there on the cold marble floor just staring but not really seeing; an altered reality, per se. It was as if I had finally cried all the tears I could possibly cry. As the last tear streaked down my face, my shallow breathing slowed and steadied.

With a deep surrendered breath... I just *knew*.

I had finally acknowledged with all my Being that the Universe was tired of teaching me this lesson and gave me this one last chance. With perfect clarity and no fear, my subconscious quieted and allowed me to see the lesson.

> *The past is not my future.*
> *This is not how my story needs to end.*
> *I have the power to rewrite it.*

I lay there. Time didn't exist. Neither did the world around me. It was just me and this solo culminated epiphany that would from this point unknowingly alter my life forever.

> *The past is NOT my future.*
> *This is NOT my story*
> *and I WILL rewrite it.*

It was from this one thought that I began to question everything. After what felt like hours of this idea repeating, I slowly came back to the present. Picking up my weak body from the floor, I was able to sit up in curiosity and look at my life. Hadn't I been here before? After all, I had sold my life for a new one after my last tragic breakup so that I could live and travel abroad. Bound and determined to find '*My Life Meant*' – what I was meant to do. Hadn't I already been here once before? What made this time different? What changed? Was it all one big giant lesson? Every relationship, every story I told, every damn thing I believed about myself was called into question. With that final thought, I pulled myself up from the floor. Why me? I wondered.

I'm NOT talking about that "WHY ME?!?!?!" we all shout out when yet another terrible life event parks on our doorstep. You know, the one where you are cursing the gods because you believe life is happening TO YOU. No, this *why me* was different. It was the kind that would lead me to take a long, hard look inward (a place I had avoided for years, blaming the world around me).

This *why me* was the first time I asked why did I bring this into my life? Why do I keep experiencing this over and over? Why does this keep happening? The why's were endless; but now, I was super curious to track down the answers. This time, the pain I was experiencing was going to become my catalyst for change. No one was going to help me unless I started helping myself! This meant being ready to look within and start healing all the fear, self-doubt and victimhood. I am no victim! I am a successful educator and it's about damn time I educate myself about... well...MYSELF!!

So it began, this quest like no other. Yes, the pain of yet another breakup would wash over me in tsunami-like waves, but I was finally tuned in to *me*. I listened to what my subconscious was saying – good or bad – and journaled it. Then, as it passed, I would dive into the meaning behind it; the psychology, the behaviors, and the valuable lessons.

I made observations of the mirrored behavior of others; basically, how did people react when I displayed a certain emotion or reaction? I studied my triggers, my beliefs and my emotions. All of it. Some of it was real, but most of it was shit my subconscious mind was making up from fear-based thinking and anxiety. What a revelation! I became my own research project and I was determined to get a doctorate in the Understanding of Me.

Socrates had to be on to something with his saying, "Know thyself!" Which, of course, led me to take an even deeper dive into philosophy where I discovered what Socrates had actually said was, "My friend... care for your psyche... know thyself, for once we know ourselves, we may learn how to care for ourselves." YES!!! Eureka!! That's what all that self-care hoopla I was learning about was for. The gratitude, forgiveness and the meditation I learned all had a greater role to play in my healing journey. It was no longer a bunch of new-age bullshit, as I had been led to believe in the past.

Over the next two years, I committed to myself. No dating, no relationships, nothing. But not in the way that I thought I would never have a relationship again like the age old, "I swear off men." No, not at all. I was on a mission to find me and know me. A mission to show up better in life and in relationships. I stopped fixing everything around me (and everyone else's issues) and followed the advice of that Ol' Greek Dude Socrates. I vowed to become the master of *me* and how to care for *me*. It wasn't selfish. It was necessary.

So... what does one finally learn when they dive into themselves? I could write a book about that, but let me sum it up for you. What I realized after all that research, after every course, every book, the personal coaching and more... it came down to this: I needed to find my relationship patterns, where they came from and own the truths I learned from them. Then and only then would I know myself. I would own my truth. After all, the karmic lessons were there all along; I just wasn't listening or paying attention. So, each time, the universe (with its twisted sense of humor) decided to teach me a harder and more painful lesson.

Which brings me to: Why must we always learn the difficult shit the hard way? Why does it take a breakdown moment to change? There were those *whys* again. Well, when I dove deep into personal research about a year later, I discovered something during a life-changing seminar in Tallinn, Estonia. The facilitator, Amrit Sandhu, shared about the Buddist philosophy of awakenings. At the time, I was like, "What's an awakening??"

It turned out that, in life, we can experience growth (or basically truths) in two ways: Satori or Kensho. In a Satori moment, we have a sudden awakening experience where we become aware of the truth as it is, and it immediately shifts our perception. We have an insight. An 'aha' moment (which, ironically, I was having at the time). Or we have Kensho moments where we learn from our mistakes, suffering, and pain through a gradual process. Either way, you grow and awaken to your truth.

AND — awaken I did. I realized this series of life-long failed relationships were all Kensho moments meant to teach me. They no longer needed to be the pains of my past and the story I was repeatedly living. I could study them, find the lessons in them and use them to grow. I could find out exactly what I was doing, so I could discover where I needed to improve my emotional intelligence. I no longer needed to be a victim of my past. I could use it to rewrite my future. I sat there in that Satori-moment – stunned. I felt like I learned the secret to life. I mean not *actually* the secret to life. This was the secret to *my* life. In that moment, I also realized that life wasn't happening TO me – it was happening FOR me.

What a fundamental shift in my world-view. It was the shift that made me ask, *"Why was I never taught to know myself, care for myself, or better yet, how to deal with myself in relationships?"*

These major questions led me to where I am today and what I do. The irony of experiencing all those failed relationships that guided me to that life-altering final meltdown is what made me an expert in 'what-not-to-do.' Being committed to myself taught me who I am. In addition, diving deep into psychology, philosophy, personal growth and development brought me to what I am today: a life and relationship coach. All those miserable marble floor moments have made me qualified! I dug even deeper and wrote a book about it! — *Letters to a J.E.R.K. — The No-Bullsh*t Guide To Relationships and Living A Life Meant* — so that I can lead other women towards their own self-love revolution.

I want to share that you can be spared some of the pain. It is not necessary. I invite you to learn from mine. I've lived it. You don't have to. Our past pain does not need to be the excuse or the story we tell ourselves as to why our life sucks or feels unfulfilled. Life really *is* a choice. We can choose to deal with and heal our past as we begin to rewrite the story of our future. We can live like a '*J.E.R.K. – Just Experiencing Repeated Karma.*' Or, choose the '*N.E.R.D. life*

- *Now Experiencing Repeated Dharma.* I choose CONSCIOUSLY the latter, a dharmic life. A commitment to growing myself and living with intentions.

I enjoy now knowing who I am and being able to consciously lead others to knowing themselves. I seek healthy and positive connections. The most important thing I have learned is that when I didn't know myself, people would cross my boundaries. Why? Because I never had them to begin with. Knowing YOU and owning YOUR TRUTH changes how you consciously show up in all your relationships. I am not saying it prevents failure, but it sure as hell makes you 100 percent aware of how you are presenting yourself to the world. When your values are in alignment, you are able to stand in your truth and express it. The way to find and maintain healthy relationships is to be your best and work toward the highest version of yourself. This is the true Conscious Leader. Other people will follow your lead. You'll fall in love with the real you...getting your Masters of YOUology.

IGNITE ACTION STEPS

Creating non-negotiables allows you to define boundaries in any relationship. By creating non-negotiables with yourself, you'll continue to set new relationship patterns to support the structure of your best life. When you truly begin to funnel all of your energy, effort and focus on making your life fulfilling, the results will surprise you.

Create a list that you hold yourself accountable for. Your non-negotiables list should be a living document that helps you know and understand yourself. It's part of rewriting your future relationships.

Directions: Choose a way you want to create your agreement. As you go through the list, answer each part in as much detail as possible and go as deep as you can. Come back to this as you reflect on it over a few days, a week, a month. Finalize it and then set the intention to practice living by it. Review it at least yearly. Remember, you are about to make life changes – this is a living document. It will take time to transform and live by it. Allow yourself the room to fail, forgive, and move forward.

Creating the Non-Negotiables

Please note, non-negotiables are *for you* and *about you*. This is different than an expectation of someone else to be a certain way.

- **I will no longer allow...** (Make a list of what you will no longer allow into your life.)

- **List your emotional triggers** so that you fully are aware of them. (These can be things like when you are criticized, not feeling valued or appreciated, feeling belittled and worthless, feeling controlled by someone, etc.)

- **Who will you filter or remove from your life,** including people on social media channels. (This can be hard, but it is so worth it. Try it for a week, a month, a year, etc., and then review what a difference it made.)

- **How will you set limits or say no?** This can be about work, love, or things that drain or affect you physically, emotionally, or spiritually. (This may take a bit of time to answer.)

Well, there you have it! Your non-negotiables. It's all written down, which means you have taken a huge step forward by setting clear intentions as to what your boundaries or non-negotiables are.

When you are done, I recommend going for a walk or doing some light exercise to release positive endorphins. Self-care is important, so take good care of yourself! The last step is the most important, as this is how you will begin to rewrite your story: By growing your emotional intelligence around saying 'no,' having clear boundaries and being able to communicate them. We were never taught this in school, yet it's the most important subject you *never* learned.

By growing your emotional intelligence consciously, you can become the best version of yourself.

Amy O'Meara - USA
Life & Relationship Coach / CEO Life Meant International
www.lifemeant.com

Beth Medved Waller

"It's always working out, even when it isn't."

My wish for everyone is that you come to know the profound truth that everything in life is always working out, even when it isn't. Perhaps, like the old me, you have a busy and blessed life but feel empty inside, or you're living on autopilot and longing for change. I hope my story inspires you to discover your "soundtrack" for becoming a conscious leader of your life (and your thoughts). In doing so, you too can create a passionate journey in which you prove that when "what matters is your heart," anything is possible.

Running Away from the American Dream

We all have those fleeting moments when we are aware that what is happening will become a snapshot in time that we preserve in a treasured photo album in our memory banks. Unlike so many experiences on any given day, we unconsciously press record and capture them as memories we'll long recall. Well, most of my monumental moments happen to transpire with a soundtrack.

One of those remarkable experiences occurred on December 31, 2014. I stood in the archway of my dining room watching *"Dick Clark's New Year's Rockin' Eve."* As I gazed past my children and friends frolicking in our family room, I found myself transfixed on the television as Fergie sang, *"Big Girls Don't Cry."*

It was as if time froze as I listened to her lyrics, *"The path I'm walking I must go alone... It's personal, myself and I, we've got some straightenin' out to do...* " I suddenly became a third-party observer of an evening I knew would never be duplicated. I understood with a certainty impossible to describe that everything in my life was about to change. But instead of apprehension, I felt at peace for the first time in years. It was as if my heart, which had been paralyzed by a fear of uncertainty and change, was suddenly throbbing with hope and an inexplicable resolve.

There I stood, on the dawning of 2015, a woman who had spent a decade secretly struggling in a picture-perfect (though unhappy) marriage and speed-collecting accolades and awards too numerous to even care about. I was so busy "living the dream" that the only way I could survive week after week was with my mother's help balancing personal chores, childcare, grocery shopping, and even the family cooking. Quality time spent with my loved ones was almost non-existent. I cried myself to sleep many nights as I tucked myself in after logging my hours spent working, volunteering and exercising (so I could look back and feel some sort of justification that I was at least "putting in my hours" despite the never-ending list of things still left to do).

I was exhausted as I strove to be the "perfect mom" by attending every event, sports game and field trip. I carefully followed the advice of child-rearing books and documented the well-crafted childhood memories I created in journals for the children. My vicious schedule was replete with custom birthday parties, frequent gatherings at our home, bedtime reading with prayers every night and annual family vacations. I'd blink and yet another year had passed.

I was passionate about traveling (even logging a brief stint as a flight attendant on my resume after college), yet my getaways were virtually non-existent (unless I count the once-a-month 20-minute drive to Costco and those beloved annual summer vacations to my college town). I remember feeling like I needed a holiday after a vacation just to catch up from my exhaustion of working in the middle of the night to stay on top of my responsibilities while away. I recall having to sneak into the bathroom on trips so my family wouldn't catch me on my phone checking work messages. I longed for an employer who would grant me just one full day off to relax, but as the owner of my own business, I had become my own malevolent slavedriver. My favorite indulgence on those sacred days away was 30 minutes of "me time." I would lace up my running shoes, eager to jog and listen to the "theme songs" carefully selected for my run. The order and the songs varied over the years, but on each of my playlists, (from the cassette days to the mp3 to the iPod to the Android), one song was always at the top of the list: Edwin McCain's *"What Matters"* has always spoken to my heart more than any other song I have heard before or since.

An Edwin song first piqued my interest in 1996, during college in Charleston, South Carolina. It was one of those moments I knew I'd remember in the future. It emerged as a profound experience because I was driving on a random day and it seemed like such an insignificant moment to capture in my memory. As I heard the song entitled *"Solitude,"* I felt a strong, sudden urge to pull my car over so I could discover the name of the artist who was singing. At that moment, an "Edwin fan" was born. It was unimaginable, at such a young age, the series of events that moment would manifest nearly twenty years later.

I believe music is the ultimate universal language that transcends time, space and diversity. In my humble opinion, there are only two distinct types of people in this world. Regardless of age, gender, race, economic status or any other demographic separation, there are people who like music for the beat and tempo, and there are people who like music for the lyrics and words. I am, without question, a lyrics girl, almost to a fault, because I couldn't care less about listening to a song that doesn't have a message fitting for the soundtrack of my life.

When Edwin released the album *Misguided Roses* in 1997, he buried the song *"What Matters,"* lavished with lyrics that would make it my instant favorite. It conveyed a sentiment that felt as though it had been written expressly for me. He sang of giving up on passion, living day to day and keeping dreams locked down inside. His encouraging lyrics professed, *"It ain't about the money, it ain't about the time... or the things you think you left behind... What matters is your heart."*

I felt an uncanny comfort playing *"What Matters"* to remind me that, one day, I'd not awaken wishing I tried, as the lyrics encouraged. In hindsight as I look back on those years, I was trying *too* hard to reach some level of accomplishment that always had me longing for more. I had amassed, by anyone's definition, the American Dream — complete with the boy, girl, dog, church-going family, positions of leadership in my community and blessings too numerous to count. I was debt- and mortgage-free (with large retirement accounts and college funds for the children), had a pontoon boat that we enjoyed taking out a handful of times each year, and I had a bright financial future with a thriving real estate team.

But I was wasting away inside. What looked like perfect to everyone else wasn't right for me. Month after month, I'd sit on my therapist's couch and weep while uttering the same frustrating question, "Why am I so miserable when my life is so perfect?" As time passed, my self-loathing increased as I punished myself for not feeling happiness or fulfilment, even when I knew beyond a shadow of a doubt that I had more blessings than most. I felt like a fraud, living a life that didn't belong to me. But even on my most stressful day with responsibilities spinning out of control, playing *"What Matters"* brought an absolute assurance that, one day, things would be different.

Perhaps that's why, on that unforgettable New Year's Eve, the Fergie song spoke to me the way that it did. Music has always been able to get through to my heart. To me, songs are waves of light streaming like a beacon from a lighthouse in the distant sky, beckoning me to an unknown shore. Had I known what was in store for me on that momentous New Year's Eve — the ups and downs, the twists and turns, the wins and losses, and the things I'd leave behind — I would do it all over again (mistakes and all) because, as Fergie sang that night, I needed to *"be with myself and center, clarity, peace, serenity."* The more I embraced a heart-centered life and an authentic path of my own, the more I was able to watch what seemed like magic unfold around me.

Just three weeks after that poignant New Year's Eve, I booked an evening out with my best friends from high school and college. All three of us are busy mothers and we hadn't made time to get together for ages. When they said they could come with me to an Edwin McCain concert scheduled for the next month, I quickly logged online and booked our tickets.

Much to my dismay, about a week later, I received a phone call saying that the ticketing company couldn't secure tickets and to call them for a refund. I was so disheartened that I couldn't bring myself to return their call nor to tell my friends our evening was canceled. Weeks went by, and an unforgettable moment occurred when I was about to walk in to pick up my kids from my parents' house. After a stressful day, I found myself in need of spiritual affirmation, and I pleaded for a sign that the major changes I was contemplating in my life would lead me in the right direction. Within seconds, my phone rang. "We're calling to tell you that we're overnighting tickets for the Edwin McCain concert. You've been upgraded to front row center."

I don't know how or why that upgrade happened, but getting that phone call was an unforgettable "Ignite" moment. To this day, recalling that miraculous sign still brings tears to my eyes. But those tears are nothing compared to the sobbing I did when, on the night of the concert as I sat in the front row, my friend slipped Edwin a note (which I now have on my wall) asking him to play *"What Matters."* She knew that with everything going on in my life, I needed to hear my favorite song.

It's impossible to describe what happened in my heart as I heard the lyrics being sung *specifically for ME*. I sobbed like I have never sobbed before or since. I was awestruck. The artists who wrote and performed the song that had been such an inspiration to me were playing it live, just feet away from me — FOR me. It was that experience that validated the profound truth that the *"ask and you shall receive"* and *"anything is possible"* verses can truly be realized. As the song finished and I wiped my eyes, I made a vow to stop *"choking on a lifetime of never taking a chance,"* as the song lyrics encouraged.

Since that monumental winter of 2015, I've been on a journey to discover my passion and purpose in life. It's a transformation fueled by taking chances, discovering new ways to make a difference and unlocking one dream after another. What's the secret to my newfound lease on life the past five years? It's this: through the sweet sounds of music, I found my way back to myself. Instead of living life on autopilot, I became a conscious leader of MY OWN life and MY OWN thoughts. That singular decision caused me to look within and start following the direction of my soul. I made time for self-discovery that led me to an enlightened understanding that my heart and my mindset are what matters. Being a conscious leader of my own thoughts (realizing that everything is always working out, even when it isn't) and my own life (sometimes appearing quite selfish with my decisions) has led me to make even more of an impact as a leader of my community and the world. And, though my teens won't admit it now, their "crazy dreamer woo mom" is teaching them life lessons I didn't understand until I was nearly 40.

I discovered that in trading my abundant American dream for my heart's dream of nonprofit passion projects, I was blessed with even greater prosperity in *all* areas of my life. I've closed a thriving real estate brokerage to have more time for my mission. I created a 501(C)(3) nonprofit named WHAT MATTERS (after Edwin's song, of course) and have formed initiatives from scholarships and interest-free loans... to a community meeting space and nonprofit center... to video interviews to promote causes and events. I'm now a thriving co-parent instead of an incompatible spouse and my travel has metamorphosed into frequent flights across the globe, including ten mission trips in less than two years. My passion for providing support to children in Africa (including the construction of a Ugandan primary school named after my hometown) is another long story with a soundtrack of its own.

Now, I live with my heart as my guide; and there's even a song to prove it. I wrote the lyrics for a song of my own while at a recording studio in the ghettos of Kampala, Uganda. The song *"What Matters is Your Heart"* is my nonprofit's theme song and is also the basis of the first of my global nonprofit fundraising endeavors centered around music.

Sometimes, when I'm feeling especially blessed, I find that my gratitude is best experienced by playing a song from my life's ever-growing playlist. I always seem to know which nostalgic lyrics my heart yearns to hear. This time, it's Fergie's *"Big Girls Don't Cry"* and tears are streaming down my cheeks as I listen. Ironically, this big girl *does* cry. In fact, I cry so much that I've given my tears a name, "OPA tears." *Opa* is the Greek word that means *happy*. I cry because instead of living with stress and self-judgment, I let gratitude, generosity and connection to the unseen world around me direct my days, filling them with ease and grace. I cry because I've been transformed into a conscious leader, not just someone trying to accomplish things on my own while playing big in a small way.

I invite YOU to OPA cry with me. Become a conscious leader of *your own* life so that you can best be a leader in your family, in your community, and in your world. I'm an everyday girl from a small town in Virginia who, through music, heard the song of my heart. What is YOUR heart trying to tell you? Make a decision *TODAY* to start listening and watch your life transform as you see proof that anything is possible and that it's always working out, even when it isn't. As my own lyrics declare, "What matters is your heart...let it lead the way."

IGNITE ACTION STEPS

To become a conscious leader, it takes conscientious daily effort to separate your mind from conscious thought. In doing so, you allow your heart to hear guidance and communicate with your mind through your unconscious and superconscious thought. An easy method to do this is through music and dancing. This 5-minute daily practice of a unique form of meditation, combine visualization, prayer and dancing for inspiration, exercise and mood-enhancing energization. Regardless of religion or belief system, this active meditation (I call it *Medicizing*) is most effective when adapted to individual preferences.

The "Prayer Dance"

1. **Grab a pen and a journal/notebook** (to document your "Prayer Dance" inspirations) and **select a song that elevates your mood** (with lyrics that inspire you and a rhythm that is danceable). It could be a song that brings back happy memories, shares empowering words or otherwise lifts your spirits. The length of the tune is insignificant and it's fine to rewind it if you aren't finished with these steps by the time it ends. Similarly, it's permissible to pause the music to write down a reminder note of a thought that comes to mind during the process.

2. **Press play and start jumping/dancing** as simply or elaborately as you feel comfortable (I squeeze in my stomach and buttocks for added exercise, and close my eyes for less distraction). As you do so, breathe deeply as you call in the unseen universal forces who are ready to co-collaborate with your life to help you bring your dreams and goals into reality. Solicit assistance and guidance for the hours and days ahead.

- Picture your departed loved ones, your spiritual guides, saints of all religions, your past and future selves. Exude loving thoughts to them and visualize their love enveloping you as you draw it in by waving your arms inward.

- Picture your loved ones on Earth and those who need prayers, think of relationships that could be healed or released through the power of forgiveness. As you're imagining, wave your arms outward to radiate love and energy towards them.

- Ask for forgiveness and special assistance you desire in any area of your life. Mentally ask for guidance and support in those areas while waving hands inward to integrate the universal forces ready to assist you.

- Conclude the experience in a state of gratitude. Picture love and light empowering you. Make a commitment to be open to heart-centered guidance. Understand that, even if your day does not go as expected, everything that happens is part of a greater plan of divine timing. Embrace the concept: "It's always working out, even when it isn't" and vow to remember that fact throughout the day when frustration or disappointment strike.

3. **After the song ends,** immediately text, email, call or write a note to three people who come to your mind AT THAT MOMENT (don't forget that it's also fine to pause during the dance briefly to send a quick message or jot down a thought) — the key is to take immediate action after you've felt an urge to reach out to someone or have been inspired with an idea.

4. **Repeat.** Watch the magic unfold around you as you use this tool to help become a conscious leader of your own life and inspire others to do the same.

Beth Medved Waller – USA
Founder & Director, WHAT MATTERS
www.whatmattersw2.com

VICKI GRAHAM

"My inner voice is the voice to behold;
from there, all my solutions are revealed!"

My wish for you, the reader, is that after reading my story, you come to a realization that all the answers you need to heal yourself and create a life of joy already exist within your own soul. All the solutions and steps are waiting to be revealed. All you need to do is quiet your mind, ask, and then listen to your inner voice. The rest unfolds organically.

YOUR INNER VOICE IS THE SAGE GUIDING YOU

We are all connected to – and are an extension of – The One Mind, God, Universal Energy or Source. I first connected to Source Energy through my invisible friend, Rose. It wasn't until later in my life that I realized that Rose had been my inner voice all along. I will formally introduce you to Rose later in my story.

We don't need to go outside of ourselves in search of our answers or our purpose. Usually, this is what we do when we are spending too much time in our forebrain (our conscious mind) searching for solutions. We listen to the stories our mind tells us about our situation and draw CONCLUSIONS mainly based on ILLUSIONS. This part of our brain operates from our perceived beliefs about our connection to our external environments and how we can SURVIVE in them, not necessarily THRIVE.

This 5% conscious brain tends to direct actions of choice from a place of fear, doubt and judgement. When we seek out this part of our mind instead of the voice within, the 95% subconscious mind, we tend to search for our answers from others, feeling inadequate or, even worse, incapable of resolving our own challenges.

This sometimes leads us down a path of dependency on what appears to be an authority wiser than our own. This is not to say that there are not times when it is beneficial to learn from the experience of others. In the end, though, we need to make decisions and choices based on what resonates within us… what is in harmony with and coherent with our own highest good. Only *you* know that ultimately. There is no one who knows what is better for you than you!

The beginning of my journey and the relationship with my inner voice.

One of my most treasured memories as a little girl was during the years from about four to five. My dad would shout out to me, "Are you ready to go on our excursion?" I was always excited to hear that invitation because it was one of the few times I had my dad all to myself. We would not really be traveling very far — it was just a few miles down the road to the local drugstore to get my mother's prescriptions — but it seemed like a huge outing to me. We would get into his spanking new 1957 Buick sedan and off we'd go. He took so much pride in having the latest, shiniest new car to show off. This was also *my* time to show off a little. I would sit close to this man who was brimming with pride, sit up on my knees, put my head on his shoulder and pretend I was his girlfriend. In my mind, I thought everyone else watching would think so too, especially when he left me in the car to get my mom's medications. I would adjust the rearview mirror and pretend to put on my lipstick, making sure everyone could see me.

Even though I was only five years old, I was convinced I looked old enough to everyone else to be his girlfriend. Those were my moments of bliss, being his little girl; until a couple of years later when I became aware that the medications we were picking up for my mother were the culprit that worsened her unavailability and I came to realize what an illusion that trip with my dad really was. My mother suffered with severe depression and allergies. Most days, she slept a good part of the day, surfacing only when she really had to. As a kid, I didn't realize that being left on my own and sequestered to my room for hours until she emerged was abnormal. What I did know was how it felt dark, lonely and scary at times. I was left on my own to figure things out.

One morning, as I was sitting in my room feeling lonely and uncomfortable,

I heard a voice. That was the first time I was connected to my inner voice. Of course, during the couple of years that followed, I wasn't aware that what I was connecting to was my own innate intelligence. I only knew that voice was what would become my imaginary friend Rose.

Rose turned out to be one of my closest friends, at least when I felt lonely in the house or needed someone to talk to. Sometimes, she would suggest we have a tea party and entertain ourselves, since we were going to be there for hours and it wasn't very nice outside.

Sometimes the environment was a bit unstable, with my mother prone to erupting at any moment, so Rose would direct me to sneak out of my bedroom window and hide in my favorite bush, which made a very cozy fortress. Rose and I would color or play cards, staying put until it felt safe. There were other times when I was hungry or bored. In those moments, she would advise me to sneak off to the neighbor's house. My childhood friend Jim would let me in, his mother would feed me, and we would play until, eventually, his mom would send me home.

This was the start of my becoming very independent, which continued for the rest of my life. Rose eventually disappeared. I knew if I wanted to learn to cook, to keep a house, raise children, develop a skill or sustain myself, I had to figure it out on my own. I learned to rely on my gut and inner voice to direct me. I followed instinctively, still not realizing that I was connecting to a universal consciousness that all began with Rose.

Even though I was raised atheist, I always knew there was some force bigger than me and I was determined to find it. The search started by becoming a Hippy in the '70s. I tried to find a higher consciousness through experiments with weed and LSD. Then, I marched the Washington Green and protested against the Vietnam War. I was the one clearly seen by all as the Flower Child, spreading love and fighting for peace. I became very involved in Transcendental Meditation and eventually joined a religion that promised a world in the future where everyone would live in paradise and all people from every walk of life would live harmoniously among nature and in peace.

As my search continued, I became aware that the voice within was growing stronger. I relied on it more and more as I was disillusioned by the world around me. Then came the moment when I truly recognized I was an Intuitive, knowing or understanding something (without reasoning or proof) before that something exists or before it's about to happen. Quantum physics has revealed to us the science behind this phenomenon. Simply stated, I believe we are all Intuitives and have the ability to connect with that consciousness, that inner voice that is the 95% subconscious part of us that can find solutions to any challenge or personal issue we have. I made the decision to intentionally use that force. I go into more detail in a book I published called *I Can Breathe Again, My Inner Physician has Revealed the Secret to Heal Myself*, where I share how a person can understand and use it.

I started using my intuitiveness in my twenties and my Ignite moment came as I watched my family environment deteriorate. My parents divorced. The drama with my mother intensified with her attempts to take her life and trying to hold on to unhealthy relationships. It got to a point that the drama was embarrassing and it felt inappropriate to expose my kids to that kind of atmosphere, so we visited less frequently. In the throes of one extremely dramatic occasion, I had an 'aha' moment and associated all the medications my mother was taking with the decline of her coping mechanisms and quality of life.

It was then that I made a vow never to follow or allow a dependency on pharmaceuticals to control me or my immediate family. This intention started with the vow to take care of myself first, seek healthier solutions, as detached as I could from traditional allopathic methods. Eventually, this led me down a path to what became my higher purpose in life – to serve others in a conscious way. That vow led to a series of events and an education that has altered the course of my life. It also led me to share this information with others.

It seemed what followed — a long history of many of my own health challenges, allergies, continuous bronchitis, kidney infections, hypothyroid, fibroids and more — was a setup to discover my own solutions to heal. I never could use traditional allopathic medications as I would react intensely to them, so I had no choice but to seek out other methods. No coincidence there! I realized many years later that by establishing that vow so fervently, my soul was going to make sure I kept it, and I did. What a blessing that turned out to be. For every health condition I developed, it plunged me deeper into research to find an alternative treatment. In each case, my inner voice would reveal the person, the education, the place, the treatment or the tool to seek out my answer.

I was introduced to the art of muscle testing when my children also developed sensitivity to medication and vaccines. In the realm of energy transference, I believed my children, to some extent were passed on cellular memories of my beliefs, both good and bad. When they got sick, they reacted to traditional treatment poorly and needed help. I learned how to use the tool of muscle testing as a way to tap into my innate intelligence and theirs to find the cause and the solution.

This tool trained my skeptical brain to become more confident and listen to the answers my inner voice would reveal. It will take another book to tell the endless stories of success I have experienced. I still am in awe, even after 40-plus years of my professional practice, with the accuracy of what gets discovered through this modality. So many times what was revealed and the course of action to follow were not the traditionally approved protocol. With each occasion of illness came an opportunity to learn more tools for healing.

As time went on, I expanded my practice into healing, teaching and certifying others. It was a privilege to use my tools for clients. They also were healed by using non-invasive alternative modalities. It became very important to me to teach them not to depend on me to 'fix' them, but to recognize my intention as being the Sage on the side; to expose them to tools to heal themselves and to help them to listen to their own inner voice.

Sometimes, when you listen to your inner voice, the solution or answer may be very different than what you thought. If you release the judgment of your conscious mind, you will discover that it truly is the voice to behold. I think back on one of my own examples. I was experiencing many challenges all at once. I was going through menopause, suffering a very debilitating outbreak of Lyme, developed Hashimoto's, and was in a head-on collision in St. John, United States Virgin Islands (my fault; I was driving on the wrong side of the road).

As always, it seems I had to experience conditions so I could discover how to become the mediator of the solutions to help others. In this case, after the accident, my inner voice kept trying to grab my attention to reveal I had developed a thyroid tumor. During the collision, the impact of the steering wheel hitting my throat exacerbated the tumor. I knew something was wrong, so I went to get a few tests on my thyroid. As usual, all the tests came back normal.

I had learned many years earlier, from a very progressive doctor, that many blood tests are inaccurate, especially thyroid screening. They will show negative results even though a condition exists. The reason is that when they draw blood, it is taken from a vein which carries dirty blood back to our organs to be cleansed. But it is within the arteries the real information resides. The arteries carry our good blood to the rest of the body to nourish and rejuvenate our cells. They also may, conversely, be carrying too many toxins or missing valuable nutrients and hormones that our body needs. It is this arterial blood that can tell the stories of illness.

I insisted on having a sonogram of my thyroid. Sure enough, a tumor, possibly cancerous, was seen. When I received the results, I was petrified. The doctor was demanding and tried to convince me there was no other way to treat the tumor than to remove it. He insisted I needed to have surgery immediately to remove my thyroid and voice box, which the tumor was attached to. He declined to treat me further if I refused to follow his advice. Off I went in search of an alternative healing program.

Once I got beyond my own fear, did my own testing, listened to my own voice and dipped into my own toolbox of remedies, the top choice my inner physician suggested to use to heal my tumor was sound healing. This was very unconventional at the time. I found an endocrinologist in my area and informed him that I was looking for a doctor to support me and monitor my progress using this method of treatment. His response to me was, "That's your throat chakra. What's going on there?" Clearly, I had found my match. He was the right guy for the job.

My inner voice directed me to resonate with the tone of G for 45 minutes twice a day. I tried alternative ways to accomplish that — tuning forks, other CDs, pitch pipes... but it was too difficult to sustain the tone for that long. This led me to hire a recording studio to help me create a CD that isolated the twelve tones of the seven chakras into three-minute tracks. This new CD afforded me the opportunity to repeat that isolated tone for that length of time. I also did some cleansing, supplementation and reflexology; but I primarily used the sound healing. To my astonishment (and my doctor's), my very large thyroid tumor disappeared in one month. Again, through the trust and faith in that voice, I was able to heal myself. I produced the CD *The Sound of Balance, Vibrational Healing* so others could benefit as well.

When you learn to listen to your own voice, trust it and activate it, then you are on the road to empower yourself and build confidence. You will no longer be at the mercy of others' limiting beliefs about your body's ability to heal itself. Then, as you have practiced this for yourself, you will become a leader who can help others do the same thing. My other favorite affirmation I created for myself, which I repeat often, is this:

"Because I love and take care of myself first, all others benefit."

The beginning of your own healing starts with listening to your gut — your inner voice — and trusting that it will guide you to your own healthy solutions. That is the absolute truth. When you take the time to take care of yourself first, you then become the *'Conscious Leader'* who now can help others empower themselves. Be the example you want others to follow.

IGNITE ACTION STEPS

The following steps have served me well in developing a relationship with my inner voice. It is easy to become a victim of our own busyness, doubt, lack of self-responsibility, care and love. Instead of just rescuing others, we must buy out the time in our day to focus on our own healing. Go for it and reap the benefits!

1. Take a few moments first thing in the morning to **ask your inner voice,** "What three things do I need to do today to take care of myself?"

2. **Activate one of them right away.** That begins your day with self-responsibility, love and care.

3. **Engage in 10-20 minutes of deep breathing.** This allows you to move into your day in a more grounded and relaxed state. Doing this allows an environment where your inner voice can be heard.

4. **Meditate every day.** Meditation is the means to turn your attention, awareness and mental process to being under your voluntary control. This is how we train ourselves to hear our inner voice and connect to the one mind of consciousness. Sit in stillness. Find a quiet place to turn inward and listen.

5. **To build confidence in the ability to hear this inner voice and trust it,** I highly recommend learning the art of muscle testing. This tool is an outward material demonstration of what you already know within, but now you can see the results. We tend to believe more fully in what is tangible.

Eventually, you will hear yourself say, "I knew that," and trust that you really did!

Vicki Graham - USA
Integrative Holistic Therapist, Medical and Spiritual Intuit,
Energy and Body Worker, Reflexology and Kinesiology Instructor –
Life Coach – Best-Selling Author
www.harmonyhealth.net

ANAY PATEL

To have a truly fulfilling life, we must be able to blur the lines between work and play, understanding that all of it IS the essence of life.

My goal is for you to truly understand that your potential is with YOU. No matter your circumstances or your past, you have the ability to shift your reality once you truly embrace who you are. By the end of this chapter, you will have strategies to take away for both work and play to help you enjoy a conscious flow in your life.

DISCOVERING MY POWER

I have always wondered why people define work and play as opposites. I think of the two as one. For me, combining them is the grand philosophy I live by. 'Work' is, by default, a charged word. Even just reading it, you're thinking to yourself about your deliverables, the emails from a not-so-happy client, or your boss asking you to do something on an 'urgent' basis. I'm here to tell you that the work I've created for myself, I've never seen as 'work.' They say if you do something you love, you'll never work a day in your life. Work turned into 'play' for me when I started freelancing at the age of 16 and I'm still reveling in that playground. However, the journey to that milestone was (in the traditional sense) work. *Hard* work.

School was my introduction to 'work.' I struggled with my studies, not starting reading until I was roughly seven years old, much later than my peers. My personal view of school as 'work' was created while bearing witness to conversations between my mum and my teachers, which usually resulted in the answer "It's possible he's a late bloomer," though the attitude the teachers had towards me was that I was lazy. A common error I used to make was spelling my surname "Petal" as opposed to "Patel," but that was out of laziness... or so it was decided.

I would never know, not until I was much older, how those conversations had an impact on me. Being labelled in this way by my teachers made me feel different compared to my classmates. It was an extremely uncomfortable feeling that I had to surrender to; I had peers who were extremely bright and I felt illiterate by comparison, with thoughts of "not being enough" going through my head daily. I feel with all the benefits of education, the institution of school is ultimately there to define you to their requirements, not to your own and therefore, not enabling you or your individuality. I constantly questioned, "Was I like everybody else?" It was clear to me that I was not.

Around age eight, through my mum's persistence and paying for a private test, I was diagnosed with dyslexia and dyspraxia. At the time, I was too young to really comprehend what those words meant, let alone spell them. Despite mum's efforts, the school was reluctant to act upon this knowledge so, my path to 'play' remained out of reach until high school.

I remember the day when I completed primary school. Signing the other kids' shirts, I was overjoyed and celebrating. Anay 'Lazy' Petal's shift in primary school was done. Then, I entered a new work environment — high school — and a completely different set of challenges lay ahead. Though the routine was different, the feeling was all too familiar. Days felt like weeks, as I was never engaged in most subjects and struggled for even average grades. I chose a high-achieving friendship group. Upon reflection, I thought they could help me. They did, just not in the capacity I expected.

Bored with class activities, I was always waiting for the bell to ring, looking to escape, but I didn't have anywhere or anyone to escape to. I wasn't comfortable or content with one group of friends. I didn't fit in with most of the kids in my class. One time, I was placed to sit opposite a girl who I thought was pretty. I was nervous and, at the same time, thrilled. She unknowingly would have a radical effect on me. Before the end of class, she gave me an unflattering nickname, which seemed harmless. I didn't take much notice. However, when that nickname started to catch on with everyone else in my year, what little confidence I may have had was completely gone. I became hyper-conscious about my looks and worried about how my peers saw me.

It got to a point where I needed to make sure I looked decent just to put the trash outside, thinking people would see and judge me based on what I looked like or what I was wearing. That feeling where I felt everyone was staring at me would stay with me for years to come.

High school was the same as primary school when it came to me passing exams. In my final years of high school, I was preparing for my General Certificate of Secondary Education (GCSE), which decided the Sixth form or college for the next stage of my education. This was an important milestone as it was the first time I started to think about what I wanted to do as a profession. I knew my dad had a desire for me to go into medicine; however, I knew straight away that it was not for me. I remember the heated debates we would have and feeling like my opinion didn't count.

One of the subjects which I had taken an interest in at school was Information Technology (IT). The teacher had a big impact on me; she encouraged me and believed in me, even at times, I didn't deserve her kindness. Her teaching style, combined with my fascination with websites, quickly made IT my favorite subject. It was in her class that I realized this was the avenue I wanted to take when I was older. I still remember when I told my Dad about my choice. His response to my decision was to argue that IT wasn't a good industry for my future. I could tell he was disappointed.

When I believe in something, I fight to get my view across. Even then, I was convinced I was suited for IT and, this time, I stuck up for myself, though it was hard to deal with my parents who did not fully accept my choice. Though these incidents seem isolated, they each started affecting me internally in ways I wasn't able to predict.

Despite my family's disappointment and even though it went against my dad's wishes, I chose IT. I had to believe in the process. College was a great period as I had more independence. I openly accepted this freedom, spending time with a disruptive crowd who influenced me and pulled me into activities that were not helping me succeed.

I lived in a flat with my mom, who was a single parent, and I needed to make my own money to be able to go out with friends and enjoy myself. Through a friend, I found employment and started an internship in East London, Shoreditch. At that job, I learned how to build websites and the mechanics behind it all. I also learned to give speeches to a much older peer group, an experience which, although I was nervous and shaking, built my self-confidence. The feeling when people came up to me after my talk was finished was addicting. Though I didn't realize it at the time, I wanted to have that feeling back one day.

My life was going well, but I wanted more. I decided to take the skills learned in my internship and do freelance websites. My first client was a family friend; I remember asking him to trust me. I was able to confidently pitch that I'm the best person for the job. When it came to the cost, I picked a number from random at the top of my head: a whopping £350! Big bucks for me in those days, especially compared to my part-time weekend job where I was making £240 a month. As soon as he signed up, I was so motivated. My imagination ran wild on the bus journeys to and from the client's house, thinking about sports cars and fancy houses; a life I had never been exposed to, yet fantasized about having. It only took me two weeks to deliver that first project, which surprised even me. There was so much I had to learn.

One moment that will never leave me was when that first client paid money into my bank account. I was at work at my part-time job when a light bulb went off for me: I had just made more money in fewer hours working for myself doing something enjoyable.

That was when I mentally committed to having my own company and being my own boss. I didn't know at the time what that would look like for me; I only knew it was something I desired. From that point on, I went about picking up more web design projects and spent more time improving my craft. There was, however, a tradeoff; instead of spending time with my friends, I put those hours into my work. Others didn't fully understand my commitment to working on my future.

As the end of college approached, I knew higher education was going to be even more hard work. I didn't want to continue; I felt lost and conflicted and I was looking for another alternative. I knew if I found one, I would pursue that. I remember thinking "I wish I could just start my company now;" however, I knew the reality was that my parents would never let me. I was left with only one option, the option I tried so hard to avoid but couldn't anymore: university. All I kept thinking and saying to my parents was, "When I finish this, I'm going to do my own thing." Though at the time they agreed somewhat, I'm sure they didn't really think it was a serious statement.

I decided university would be a fresh start and so I created distance from most of the friends I was hanging around with at the time. In the upcoming chapter of my life, I wanted to be defined as a social butterfly and I did what most people did, which was a *lot* of socializing. Within my first year, I was going out four nights a week. My vision of running my own business slowly crept further and further to the back of my mind. I was living the life I wanted: Invited out all the time, drinking, partying... for a long time, I didn't know any better and I was happy. I was told the first year of university never counted towards final grades, which allowed me to justify my consistent partying and not paying attention to classes. Before I knew it, exams had come around and those familiar insecurities around 'not being enough,' being dumb and not being capable rose to the surface.

The pass rate to get into the next year was around 40 per cent and I didn't try for anything above that; I thought 40 per cent was all I was capable of. I did pass my first year, but not by much. I didn't think a great deal about it at the time – I really treasured the joy and relaxation of knowing I had done *just enough* to make it through another year. After a summer of working, I started my second year. This time, things were different from the start. Things were about to change.

I was living away from home for the first time, which meant I needed to make more money to survive. I couldn't sustain the lifestyle I'd been enjoying for another year. I moved into a new house shared with four other people. All of them were hard-working, striving towards their dreams. When I first sat in my room, it was small — smaller than the room in my flat back home — and a very tight squeeze with not much space to move around. I sat there and thought about my situation and what I was doing. How I'd acted in my first year of university. How I had reached this place in my life and forgotten about my dreams and ambitions.

That was my Ignite Moment. I went *all in* on me and my future. Within a month, I had prioritized working two — and sometimes three — jobs and buckling down at university. Once I stopped socializing as much, very few of the friends I'd accumulated in my first year stayed in touch. It shocked me and showed me there wasn't much of a relationship there to begin with.

Going from knowing lots of people and being invited out daily to having less than a handful of people around me called for an adjustment. I didn't know how to feel because it was my decision. I was making a hard but necessary choice: I wanted more out of my life. Upon reflection, having the old "friends" drop out of the picture was a real gift. It allowed me to show myself that I could be a confident person that I could have my own group of peers. I learned that I was full of potential.

I connected with a deep desire to be in business and started learning about marketing, sales and the pillars of what it takes to build a successful company. To make my business fantasies a reality, the starting point was improving me. Aspects of my past like not having the confidence or lacking emotional intelligence didn't serve me, so I had to let go of my conditioned self and get serious about who and what I wanted to be.

The best part was that while I was putting in more work and commitment than I had ever done previously, I was loving every moment. Struggling with things that did not turn out as expected did not deter me. I was intentionally building the future I desired.

An in-depth reading of positive psychology opened me up to a whole new way of thinking: simple concepts could profoundly impact people's lives. It's possible to have a stress-free life to live in a constant state of flow. When I was doing my own business, I dropped into these states. Not wanting to be like most of society, I examined the influences of my past environments, becoming aware of my limiting beliefs. Paying close attention to who and what I was letting into my life was a big first step in finding my own flow and taking control of my time and energy.

Initiating intentional connection with people, even meeting up with strangers, helped build up my self-confidence. In my first year, I was still projecting fear on a subconscious level, leading to inauthentic relationships without much meaning. This time, I clearly knew the types of people I wanted to connect with and the kinds of conversations I wanted to manifest. Having futurist debates and exploring ideas enhanced my well-being even more. From this point onward, the lines between work and play were blurring into one.

As I kept seeing parts of my life change and had amazing opportunities, such as traveling to other countries (for "work"), visiting NASA's Goddard Space Flight Center for a private tour, speaking at multiple events, building relationships globally. I went deeper into personal growth and lived more of my life on the premise of a *growth mindset,* which boiled everything down to simply this: We are all capable of achieving what we want with the right habits installed. As I became aware, I started building emotional intelligence. I applied strategies to tough situations and handled difficult clients while reducing stress and taking my power back. I started building a foundation and enjoying the process. It wasn't a 100 per cent foolproof plan, but every time I did fail, I would try again.

I now aim to consciously lead my life and put my struggles into context. I am an example of how everyone has things they need to endure. I hope that those experiences won't define you. In sharing a few of my vulnerable moments in life, I'm here to tell you that no matter how hard you may have had it, *you are enough.* Don't let anyone decide what's important for you. We only have one life, so I say make it the best one you could ever imagine and live confidently... consciously.

IGNITE ACTION STEPS

To start blurring your own lines between work and play, take some time to read and take action on the following three steps:

- **Audit your life:** Think about your life and where you are. Start slowly going back to your earliest memories and write down any significant emotional events from your past to the present day. Please don't rush this step. Once you've completed this, take a break and come back and review what you have written. Look for any patterns or beliefs you might have gained as a child and ask, "Does that way of thinking serve me today?"

- **Affirmation:** This was my fast-track way of creating confidence in my life. Pick one or two phrases that start with "I am…" For example, "I am loved."

- **Critical Questions:** One of the things I've tried to master is asking great questions that have the potential to shift your perspective. Here are two questions for you to think about:

  - What do you want to be remembered for?
  - How can your work turn into more play?

Anay Patel - United Kingdom
Social Entrepreneur & Founder of YugenWay
www.yugenway.com

MAGGIE REIGH

"Go beyond your role; Connect Soul to Soul"

We are all One. We are here to help each other. Our greatest teachers are our most disturbing adversaries. They rattle us to the core and have the potential to shake out the beliefs that keep us separate and small. This story illustrates the depth of our eternal connection and the power of forgiveness to set us free. I hope that you are inspired to see your relationships from your Soul's Eye View, and to break through your protective personality's conditioning so that you can experience the Freedom, Love, and Power of your Soulful Self on this human adventure.

A SOUL'S EYE VIEW

I needed a miracle! My marriage was on the rocks. I had two young children and even the thought of splitting up the family was torture. Nine years earlier, I'd married a man who I had vowed to make happy. I was embedded with the belief that finding a man and making him happy was the key to my fulfillment.

But my husband wasn't content. I thought I was a good wife... looking after the home, meals, the children and even sex... but still he was grouchy and miserable. The harder I tried, the more unhappy he became. Now a dismal failure myself, it was affecting me physically. Night after night, my aching feet woke me up. I could barely walk on them until noon. I could see no way out... unless he changed! However, trying to change him made things worse.

When I heard about A Course in Miracles (ACIM), I jumped at it. It was my last shot! I started studying it, but it was absolutely... FRUSTRATING! I didn't get it. The Course said to keep going even if resistance set in, so I did, even though sometimes I was uttering the affirmations through clenched teeth. Whew! I needed more help than this! In desperation, I went to see a psychic. She looked me right in the eye and said, "If you don't have what you want, it is because you are withholding it from yourself."

"How can you call yourself a psychic?" I thought. "Don't you know that this is my husband's fault?" But I didn't say that. Out loud, I responded, "Huh?"

"If you don't have the lover you want, you are not BEING the lover you want!"

Wham.... those words hit! Suddenly I clearly saw I was NOT being the lover I wanted at all. Without joy, I had been going through the motions... but they were filled with an underlying resentment; a desperation to fix my relationship. Who wants a lover like that?

Her words cracked open the heavy cloak of resentment and blame I didn't even realize I was wearing. Shucking off this cloak brought so many concepts from ACIM to life:

All that I give is given to myself. I was receiving and experiencing the unconscious resentment and blame that I was giving! This, I could change! I realized I could choose to give love instead of resentment.

A miracle is a shift in perception. I now saw that waiting for him to change and trying to make him change was how I'd given away all of my power! I was making us both miserable.

Forgiveness is the key to happiness. My resentment and blame had kept me stuck. Only I could let it go.

The realization of CHOICE powered through me. I am in charge of what I give. That changes everything! Here, all along, I'd been waiting for him to change before I could be Okay... before *we* could be okay! I went from Victim to Creator in the blink of an eye.

I can give love instead of resentment. Then, I will receive Love. I got it! I floated home, lighter than air, filled with enthusiasm and power. I CAN create the love I want by BEING it! No doubt my husband was puzzled by my new-found attitude. He probably didn't understand my words, but he felt them! We made LOVE that night. The ache in my feet disappeared and never returned.

We fell deeply, madly in love as we'd never loved before... for three days...

A friend came to stay with us. In the past, I might have felt threatened by this woman, as I knew my husband had a small crush on her. However, we were now SO in love that I didn't think twice about going off to bed early one night and leaving them to party on.

A few hours later, I awoke. No husband. I listened for voices... nothing. An uneasy, sickly feeling arose inside of me. I tiptoed through the quiet house and out into the orchard, wondering where they might be. I turned a corner and saw them!

It was a scene right out of a romantic novel... there they were, perfectly silhouetted against a giant harvest moon. She had her blouse off and he was kissing her, holding her naked breasts! (Her voluptuous, voluminous breasts, I might add!)

Rage seared through me. "How dare you do this to me?" I roared. "Three days ago, I'd have been thrilled to have concrete evidence to get you out of the house. But no! You let me fall in love with you like we never loved before, and now this is what I get." My heart was bursting; I felt myself leap right out of my body and I watched it keep moving. Storming past them I seethed, "I want her out of this house when I get back!"

Agonizing tears blinded me as I stumbled around the orchard. Through the shock and bewilderment I wondered, "How could he do this to me?" It was out of character for him, even in our dark days. As I thought of him standing there, hanging his head and watching me rage past, I got the strange feeling that he was as bewildered as I.

Taking in the expanse of the valley below, the whole scene felt surreal. Suddenly, there was someone tugging at my arm. It was *her*! "I'm so sorry Maggie! Please forgive me," she sobbed.

Vehemently, I tried to shake her off and BAM... a silent explosion right from the core of my Being shattered the painful emotional cloud around me. I expanded into the Cosmos and got a Soul's Eye View of my situation. Suddenly, I knew beyond the shadow of a doubt that I had set this all up to reinforce what I'd just learned!

I saw myself playing the role of the wounded victim, justifying my right to be angry. I could CHOOSE to kick my husband out of the house and dismiss my friend forever, break up my family and maintain my ego and pride... or I could forgive.

The earlier breakthrough to a new way of Being, Loving and Living was just a sneak preview to the power and miracle of the shift in perception that was available to me *in this moment*. I could apply that again here, or I could fall back into the clutches of the ego... "No," ego hissed, "You CAN'T let them get away with this! They deserve to be punished. They've made you look like a fool! You'll never be able to trust him again..."

As you read this, your ego may have something to say too! In fact, you may be ready to persecute them both on my behalf! Maybe it's bringing up events and emotions from your life. If so, that's fantastic! Because you too can learn to stop letting your ego torment you, running your life and relationships into the ground.

This is not a story of betrayal and revenge but of the triumph of Conscious Spirit rising above ego. That sweet victory is so much more powerful, expansive and lasting than the easily collapsible and fleeting satisfaction of ego's revenge.

From my Soul's Eye View, I could clearly see that I'd walked that ego trail for far too many a mile and experienced its misery for way too many years. I'd had a taste of Freedom, and so I *chose* the freedom and expansiveness of my Soul's Eye View. In that view, my husband and friend were players in my game... players who had come to remind me of my True Power... the power that is available to each and every one of us if we can extricate ourselves from our ego's emotionally-backed demands and stories of how our life *should* be.

That is when I realized that *forgiveness* is really about thanking the players in our game of life *for-giving us the opportunity to reclaim our True Power*... the power to remain present in every moment and to choose our state of Being that determines what we will give to that moment.

"All that I give is given to myself"... will I give hatred or Love? My Spirit soared, intoxicated with the LOVE and POWER that now filled my world. Three days earlier, I had been a bird set loose in my backyard, freed from the cage of my own making; I now discovered a whole universe beyond my backyard!

Although it has taken time to explain what happened that night, all of this happened instantaneously... one moment I was trying to shake my friend off my arm, and in the next moment I was turning to her, taking both her hands in mine, looking deeply into her eyes, and with a heart full of gratitude, I heard myself say, "No, no dear friend! There is no need for forgiveness... in fact I thank YOU!"

"Huh?" she said. I mean, what else could she say? Undoubtedly this response was the last reaction she expected from me!

Grateful and eager to share this expansive and miraculous understanding, we walked and talked for HOURS... I told her of the freedom, joy and power of these principles she'd helped me bring to life. She shared her deep self-loathing, insecurity and need to prove herself attractive and worthy. A whole new world of possibilities for living in a different way opened and deepened in both of us.

Towards dawn, I slipped into bed beside my unaware husband. The music from Jesus Christ Superstar carried me off into the ether... "Neither you, Simon, nor the fifty thousand/Nor the Romans, nor the Jews... Understand what power is/Understand what glory is/Understand at all"

For months afterward, I literally shook with the vibrancy of Joy, Love and God Power that flowed through my veins. My husband and I fell into an even deeper love. Sometimes ego would creep in with the full moon snapshot, trying to entice me to revenge. I would quickly dismiss it, choosing to live in the Joy and Power of that Holy Instant.

From this expansive state, I could see the old patterns arising that used to trap me in arguments and inner turmoil. Instead of getting sucked in, I simply witnessed them and let them go, choosing to stay in my Power and maintain my Soul's Eye View.

I LOVED this new state of being... I wanted my husband to share it with me, but he wasn't interested. How could we deepen our relationship further without Spirit? I felt crushed... and annoyed... because now, it seemed that I was doing all of the emotional work in our relationship... again.

Eventually old emotional patterns crept in as I slipped from my Soul's perch. Our relationship spiralled into confusion and pain. Try as I might, I couldn't get that state "back." One day, I curled up next to him after yet another attempt to fix our relationship through sex. "Wouldn't it be wonderful," I whispered wistfully, "to live life as Spiritual Beings on a human adventure?"

"Why do you have to ruin everything?" he spat out his annoyance. That was the end of our intimacy and our marriage. I knew that I had to move on. Having tasted Heaven, and Freedom, I needed to surround myself with others who value living as Spiritual Beings.

I am forever grateful to the role my ex-husband played in catapulting me to my Soul's Eye View. I thank him for-giving me the opportunity to understand that it is impossible to make someone else happy. I share my joy freely; yet, their happiness is their decision.

Eventually, I learned that going back to retrieve an already known state doesn't work. I need to keep welcoming the unknown. My path has been to discover many more methodologies and tools to explore and express my Freedom and experience the ecstasy of Soul moving through my life.

It is my honor to now help others experience the wisdom and conscious connection to their own Soul's Eye View. Using sound, hypnotherapy, somatic counselling, Conscious Communication Circles, art, music, movement, breath and energy work, clients experience their true power as they move from victim to Creator... sometimes in the blink of an eye! I help emerging conscious leaders dissolve the conditioning that keeps them small so that the soul can move freely and joyously through them. How will you choose to respond the next time your ego steps up? How can forgiveness free you to feel greater love and power? Which perception do you choose? It is your choice. Follow your Soul's Eye View.

IGNITE ACTION STEPS

Are you waiting for someone to change before you can be happy? If so, you are blaming them for your state of being and thus giving your power to them. *To blame others is to set yourself on fire and hope that they die of smoke inhalation!*

- **Take full responsibility for your inner state.** Firmly decide *that you want peace more than you want someone to change so that you can have peace.*

- **Go beyond the mind.** Blame is held in place by deeply- and physically-embodied emotions, and by ego's conditioning. The mind justifies the emotions and ingrains them.

- **Take it to the body.** Your body is the key to releasing blame, anger, hurt, resentment, disappointment and all that goes with it. When emotions get trapped in the body, they create discomfort. We've been conditioned to swallow our emotions and stuff them in. When you release the emotional charge this creates in the body, the associated thoughts will cease to circulate so you *can* let go. To feel it is to heal it. Here's how:

Use your posture and breath to center yourself in your body. Stand or sit with a straight, yet relaxed spine. Imagine your feet sinking into the earth.

Close your eyes as you think of someone you've been blaming. Where do you feel it in your body? Allow and investigate the feeling sensations without trying to change them. Proclaim aloud, "I give this energy permission to release." Breathe deeply into the abdomen and upper chest, then imagine filling the space up to an arm's length over your head with the breath. Trust in the energy that holds you upright. As you release the breath, let go of trying to hold yourself up with your shoulders. Allow your skin and muscles to relax around the frame of your body. Surrender to gravity and to the earth. To deepen the release, gently press three fingers vertically into the center of your chest (over your heart chakra) on the acupressure point called "the sea of tranquility."

Keep breathing, fully and deeply, as you curiously, without judgement, investigate what happens to those sensations associated with blame. How much space do they occupy? Do they have shape? Color? Depth? Texture? Movement? Release the next deep breath with an audible sigh. Hum or create whatever sound brings vibration to that area. Use your imagination to encourage the energy to flow out of your body. If energy is intense, scream or howl! Use movement, art, writing, acupressure, hypnotherapy, and other creative ways to intentionally allow the energy to release. If the mind pulls you back to blame, focus more deeply on releasing the uncomfortable energy, reminding yourself you choose the peace that comes from this release.

Feel the power in taking charge of your own triggers. No more waiting for anyone to change so that you can feel better. This is how you can heal your relationships, your health and your life! Pre-position yourself for success by proclaiming everything happens *for you*, not *to* or *against* you!

Can you be grateful to your "adversary" who helped you uncover uncomfortable buried emotions so that you could release them and move more deeply into your own power? Can you thank them for-giving you the opportunity to rise above your ego and expand into your Soulful power? Blink...you're there!

Maggie Reigh - Canada
Soul Streaming Coach and Visionary
www.maggiereigh.com

KATELIN GREGG

*" The best investment is to invest in yourself
so that you can invest in others. "*

**My intention is to share with the reader the practices I have learned
throughout my journey that have shaped the person I am today. Through
my story, I hope to inspire you to make these simple, yet effective changes
in your daily life so you can reach your full potential and feel motivated
to share it.**

WE'RE ALL IN THIS TOGETHER

"Mummy, you won't believe it! Jasmine and I are both bastards," I said to
my mother with the cheekiest grin.

She paused, unsure how an 8 year old had learned such a word.

I took great pleasure in explaining to her that it was the terminology for
children who were born into families of parents who never married. Jasmine
had shared this with me and we thought it was hilarious that we could get away
with saying such a naughty word by justifying its context.

This is an example of the humorous and positive spin I put on the circumstances I was born into. For as long as I can remember, my parents have not
been together but, in my eyes, I had the best of both worlds. Two homes, two
beds and two parents who cared deeply about me.

During the younger years of my life, I lived predominantly with my mother.
I was brought up observing the experience of her transformative journey, so it

seemed to be the natural way of living. While some kids spent their weekends at the beach or at play centers, my childhood was a lot more unconventional than that.

Growing up as an only child of a single mother, she took me everywhere. From meditation weekends away to personal-development workshops, I was her little sidekick; absorbing this fascinating alternate world at a young age. At the same time, she was directing large medical companies, so I was privileged to tag along to medical business conferences all over the globe. This gave me a perspective on the world that was so different from that of my peers; however, for me, it just seemed to be the norm.

When I was three, I was taught a baby mantra with transcendental meditation. At age 12, this was transformed into an adult mantra, one which I still use to this very day. In addition, if I was struggling in school with stress or friendship dramas, Mum supported me by offering kinesiology sessions and alternate healing processes.

I was in awe of my mother. She ingrained in me the importance of always taking responsibility for my life, and using my imagination to create my dreams and follow them. This was complemented by my father's self-starting nature, which proved that, with hard work and persistence, anything I put my mind to was possible. I considered myself fortunate to spend time with him and his wife Elaine, at a young age, I learned ambition and the desire for hard work and success.

My mother also believed you could achieve anything you put your mind to. Being a very supportive parent, she religiously attended my Saturday morning tennis competitions. However, one weekend she became quite disappointed in my lack of determination, describing the situation as, "Dragging your tennis racquet across the court and having lost complete and utter interest." I was down 0-5 to the opponent and my chances of winning were slim. This simply was not good enough and, during the changeover, she whispered in my ear, "I am going to the car now. For every game you win, I will give you $10. Remember your affirmations, you CAN do this!"

I bounced back onto the court, with a goal in mind and repeatedly thought, "I am dedicated and focused on playing to the best of my ability."

Ten minutes passed... then 15... and by about 25 minutes, she started to worry as to where I was. To her surprise, when she returned to the court, not only had I won my match, but she now owed me $60. This simple demonstration confirmed in me the power we have; the ability to achieve anything that you put your mind to.

In my mid-teens, however, I transitioned from living at home to boarding at my high school. Being around other girls 24/7, I found myself easily distracted. Without daily exposure to the practices I had grown up immersed in, I felt my interest gradually decline. Daily meditation rituals turned into texting boys; mindful weekends away were now sleepovers with my friends. I was sidetracked by the excitement of adolescence and experimenting in a whole new world; one that fascinated me. Veering away from the activities I had learned and shared with my mother created distance in our relationship for quite some time.

What seemed to be the natural next step in life was attending university. I enrolled in a Bachelor of Economics and Marketing at the University of Sydney straight out of high school.

But this wasn't my passion.

I just believed it was the sensible thing to do; that it would open many doors.

Although I longed for adventure and independence, I never went traveling after high school like many of my friends. I found myself going from one strict, rigid boarding institution to the next, without a break, living on campus at an all girls college within the university. I had not considered how much freedom would come with the turning of age. Feeling suffocated by the constant rules, curfews and regulations sparked resentment in me. I masked my emotions through alcohol and partying.

Fully engaging in *campus life,* I found my grades slipping and my motivation rapidly heading into a downward spiral. By the second year, I had failed Intermediate Microeconomics — not once but twice. As this subject was a core unit, it was essential that I passed it in order to graduate.

The real issue was the detriment this had on me. If one word could describe how I felt, it was *worthless*. I had tried and failed not once but twice and now questioned my ability to complete my degree altogether.

I was transported back to a time in Year 9 when I suffered severe glandular fever and took 6 weeks off school. On return to class, I failed maths, test after test, to the point where I was advised to drop a class level. This was a period of my life where I felt ashamed, doubting not only myself but my future. The anxiety this experience instilled in me around resitting exams made finding an easy escape route seem like the only possible option.

I didn't have the guts to tell my parents what was going on. I couldn't dare risk the disappointment of them knowing their daughter was yet again failing her studies. I knew what would happen if I approached my mother: She would want to talk about *feelings*. I could already picture the look on my father's face.

After years of investing in my education, I had failed his expectations. All I wanted to do was run.

With a total lack of confidence and faith in my ability, I resorted to flight mode: I impulsively packed my bags, deferred my degree and moved to London with my best friend with the intention of never returning to complete my studies. Seeking a glamorous life overseas seemed to be the solution to all my problems. This decision was spontaneous. It was completely unorganized and lacked structure to the point where my friend had even run out of time to apply for a visa. We had no clear vision or plan; we were just *winging it*. I knew I was running away and escaping. Not motivated to stay and complete my studies, I felt that going to the other side of the globe would allow me to avoid dealing with everything.

Living in the center of London, we did what any 20-year-old girl would do when overseas for the first time. We drank, partied and occasionally saw the sights. After huge nights out, my friend and I would curl up on the couch all day watching Netflix and planning what meal we would order next. It wasn't long until we had formed a friendship with our delivery driver, Ben, as we regularly indulged in these take-out meals. During these times, I felt a deep sense of loneliness and sadness. Despite being on the other side of the world, my escape plan seemed to be failing me. I may have left my responsibilities back home, but I took with me the fundamental issues that had caused me to leave in the first place. I could escape my failures — but I could not escape myself.

It was not all gloom and despair the whole time we were away. We did take advantage of our geographical location, traveling every weekend to breathtaking destinations, which fulfilled the burning desire for adventure I had always had within me. It was at these points I felt at peace; as I indulged in nature's beauty and saw sides of the world I had only ever dreamed of. After a while, that lifestyle was unsustainable, both health-wise and financially... thus my indefinite trip overseas came to an end. After four short months, it was time to head home.

On return to Australia, I struggled. I began to question what my purpose in life would be. I felt a lack of direction; an emptiness that was desperate to be filled. I also knew that I did not want to return to living as before. It was time to change and revert to the roots that had been embedded within me as a young child.

Moving back in with my mother created a significant shift in my attitude. I was back in the space that had once uplifted me. I evaluated the person whom

I was compared to the person I wanted to be. It was clear I needed to transform — to become the best version of myself.

This involved turning to daily practices that could elevate me to reach my full potential. I created a routine incorporating meditation, self-reflection, and a morning ritual dedicated to writing out my gratitude, affirmations and goals for the day. As I was familiar with these practices, I knew the benefits of putting a small amount of time aside each day to work inward. Almost instantly, this new outlook gave me a burning desire to give my degree another shot. I was going to sit Intermediate Microeconomics again, but this time I set an intention to get a High Distinction.

Writing out my goals for the semester, I developed a structured plan in which I would achieve a result of 85 per cent or above. The negative thoughts that questioned my ability were reframed with positive affirmations such as, "I study effectively, efficiently and purposefully to achieve my goals." This positive self-talk transformed the way in which I thought about myself and totally boosted my confidence. I made sure that I practiced meditation daily, particularly right before an exam that I was nervous about. Realizing that the only limitations we have are the ones we put on ourselves, I committed whole-heartedly to my studies. To my surprise, I received **100 per cent** in the exam — and thought, "How could I receive a top mark in a subject that I had failed twice?" *I really could achieve my goals* if I set the right intentions and put my mind and heart to it!

This Ignite moment confirmed the power I had within me to take back control of my life and write my own dream; something I had been taught as a child but overlooked recently. As I had not been leading myself in the right direction, steering by the correct values and principles, I had prevented myself from being the best version of me possible. I undertook this new practice for each of my subjects as I completed the rest of my degree, graduating with distinctions! It was quite the opposite from the merely passing and even failing grades that had once defined me.

During that time, I was also fortunate enough to attend a conference that brought together empowering people who have visions of changing the world. I spent four days surrounded by like-minded and motivating individuals that not only want to uplift themselves but everyone around them.

When I arrived, I felt shy and reserved. Never had I been in an environment with so many people that resonated with ideas similar to my mother's! By the end of the conference, I had laughed, cried and made so many lifelong friends. The energy and vibrancy I experienced over those few days was captivating. It activated something within me to return to Australia with the mission of sharing everything I had learned with everybody that I could. My consciousness was awakened. Instead of focusing on individualistic thinking, I would put my energy toward growing collectively and leading others by example.

This new-found ambition inspires me every day to share with those around me how they, too, can make small but effective changes in their life. I work towards motivating individuals who may not have as much knowledge around personal development by suggesting books I have read or encouraging them to try my favourite guided meditations. By being able to share this, I not only uplift myself, but I uplift others. I love to see the positive impact I can have on someone by encouraging them to invest more in themselves.

Now, I am driven to be a lifelong leader; to continuously upskill myself and others by passing on the message of leading yourself in a holistic way. I speak to millennials about how important it is to consider your actions and why you are doing them. By setting your goals and embracing your values, you can define where you are going and what it will take to get there. Being clear on where you are headed encourages you to prioritize your time and to lead a purposeful life every day.

We are all in this together, so why not do everything we can to maximize each other's knowledge and elevate collectively? Working together, the power we have to achieve in this journey is infinite.

For me, this is only the beginning of a lifetime of serving each other. For you, there is no better time than now to invest in yourself and the life that you love.

IGNITE ACTION STEPS

Methodology for self-leadership

I believe that it does not require drastic changes to navigate your life and ensure you are on the right path. In order to live my life by design, I incorporate a few techniques into my day, allowing me to be fully aware and present in where I am going:

- **Affirmations**
Affirmations are short phrases you repeat to yourself to affirm something you wish to happen. A good affirmation is personal, positive and present. The trick is, when you are saying your affirmation, you visualize and feel the emotion. You can instantly brighten your attitude and outlook of the day

by repeating positive affirmations that restore confidence in yourself. Say your affirmations three times in the day: Once in the morning, once right before bedtime and once throughout the day.

For example, an affirmation of mine is, "I have what it takes to succeed and help others succeed."

- **Meditation**

I spend 15 to 20 minutes alone each day meditating, completely undisrupted. Preferably, I sit in the park among nature. For beginners, I recommend guided meditations, which can be easily sourced from the App Store, such as *Headspace*, *Calm* or *Insight Timer*. You can start off with shorter meditations and gradually build up toward 20 minutes.

- **Self-Reflection**

My favorite part of the day is when I sit comfortably and either type or hand write a reflection of how my day was. Usually, I will write out everything that occurred during this day and reflect on how it made me feel. If I faced any challenges or obstacles, I discuss what to do differently next time. By stepping back and analyzing each action, you are able to understand the person you are and identify what it is going to take to become the person you want to be.

Katelin Gregg - Australia
Strategic Marketing Manager
www.mondeal.com.au/
*www.instagram.com/cosmechix_*

JOANNE HUGHES

"Life is a collection of experiences that you choose to experience. There should be no judgement, no right or wrong. They simply are experiences."

My hope is that you find a light within that will guide you through your journey and inspire you to listen to your soul; that you find and do the things that bring you happiness. In every one of you lies a Conscious Leader. By living your life as the best possible version of you, you will inspire others to live their lives that way as well.

A JOURNEY BACK TO THE LIGHT

My parents taught me from the beginning the importance of being good to your neighbours, and the value of community and acts of service. My Mom always marveled at my writing. She was the biggest supporter of my poems and stories. To honor her, I am writing this story two days after she has passed. She was my biggest cheerleader and I dedicate this story to her. *May you rest in peace, Mom, and journey well.*

It took me a long time to begin this story. Modesty was another lesson my parents taught me. For the days and weeks before I sat down to write this, I thought about my life, growing up, and how I got to the place that I am in at this very moment.

Surrender, letting go and realizing that by simply living my life, I feel I am a Conscious Leader. There is no big multi-million dollar company that I run, nor am I making seven figures running workshops, but I do remember the journey that I have been on and the many dark spaces I travelled through to get here. It is some of these stories, these *aha* moments and revelations, that I would like to share with you.

The Abyss

One of my earliest memories is of wanting to be more than what I was. As a child, I felt a sense of *not belonging,* not being a part of, or that I had no roots set anywhere. That I was floating in a great vast universe, not really belonging to anyone or anything. I felt like I did not fit in. I felt awkward, ugly and small. Yet at a very young age, I had knowledge of people living on the streets. I remember having, one Christmas Eve, an experience where I felt I was outside of myself and looking in. Looking in at all the presents under the tree, at all the food on the table and at my Aunt playing Christmas carols on the piano with my family around. It hit me, in that very moment, that there were people outside with no shelter, no food and, most importantly, no family; and therefore, no love. In that moment, I was determined to march downtown and bring them all home to my house so that they, too, could experience the love that I felt as I stood there looking at the abundance I shared with my family. But as I got on my coat and opened the door to go get them, I realized that I had no idea how to get there. It was dark and cold, the world got so big and I was so small.

This is the part I call *the abyss.* In the path of consciousness, I believe we start out feeling small. From there, it is a journey to get to that place of awareness. I never did go out and bring whomever I found on the streets home that night, but my Mother always set out an extra plate around Christmas time, which in turn allowed me to become aware of others. I would say a prayer or set an intention that whomever needed family or food would find their way to us. I, of course, never thought of it that way as a child, but I know now that it was where things began for me. As we set out in this life, we are taught by our parents, society and external influences. The beginnings are both simple yet excruciatingly hard as we begin to grow and formulate opinions and perceptions of our own.

The Journey of a Thousand Miles

I call it *the journey of a thousand miles* because we get to that age of finishing high school and our life seems to begin. Suddenly, we are thrust out into the world as an adult and we have to make conscious choices. Some choose a path based on what their parents want or think they should do. Others follow the path of money and what feels best. Some decide to go out and experience life and all it has to offer at that tender young age before choosing the career path they ultimately will be on until they retire. My Mother, who was a nurse, thought that nursing should be my path; but, as I became an adult, I knew I wanted to help women and children. Instead of becoming a nurse, I became a Child Support Counsellor and dedicated part of my life to being of service.

I loved my job. I worked with youth who were exposed to domestic violence, and with women who fought many battles and lived through some of the most horrific experiences. People told me they could never do the job that I had. For me, I got to meet some of the most courageous women — heroines. Every day, I listened to their stories and helped them find some peace of mind and make sense of it all. I also helped young children and youth work through their loss, grief and trauma. Every person I spoke to touched my heart and soul. But then came my own trauma and challenges...

The Tower

In a tarot deck, the *Tower* card is illustrated by lightning striking a tower and a man falling to the ground. The card's meaning is "a shocking revelation or event that forever changes the way you see yourself and the people around you."

My husband, whom I married during my career, was a Professional Engineer who began to drink after he was wrongfully let go. Then, he became paranoid, manipulative and abusive. My world began to crumble. The very ground I walked on dissolved beneath my feet. At work, I listened to other women's stories of abuse and I understood more than they knew. It was hard to focus on their lives when I lived in fear myself. My stomach felt queasy and sick because it was also happening to me.

I wanted to scream out, "Don't make me leave, let me stay!" I had a little boy and a baby girl that I needed to go home to, so I did. I found strength in the women I worked with. I knew that if I was going to walk my talk, I had to leave my situation. In spite of being worried about judgment, uncertainty and fear of retribution, I knew that, for the sake of my children, I had to leave.

The things I grew up believing... that fairytale I had always been told... was shattered. I had to put the pieces back together. How does one do that, you ask? You begin to examine everything you were told; things you thought and dreams you had. You begin to rebuild yourself again, piece by piece. The situations that no longer work, you simply have to let them go and begin to decide who you are as a single, separate being.

The trauma wouldn't end there, though. Two months after leaving my husband, my child, only six years old, became ill. We spent many days and nights in the hospital. One day, a doctor walked in and took one look at my child, then looked at me and said, "He has cancer." That night, we were admitted. He was diagnosed with anaplastic large cell lymphoma. We began a year's journey of chemo, outpatient treatment and hospital stays. My world began to crumble. The tower had fallen.

This part of my life was challenging and extremely hard, but we made it through and, after the year was over, the cancer was gone. That lead to another part of our journey.

Healing and Self Discovery

I had always wanted to live outside the city, but I was a daughter living at home in the middle of town, then a wife. Then, I was a mother raising her children on her own. I bought a house outside the city in a rural town in Alberta, Canada. There, my children and I began to heal and regroup, to pick up the pieces of the ending of my marriage and our family as we knew it.

The disappointment that my parents felt about my marriage ending added to the difficulty of trying to embrace the image of myself in the mirror — an image I no longer recognized. I felt like everything I had been told while growing up was a lie; more importantly, I bought into it.

Life began to change for me, but the good thing was that I was the one who began to put my life and self back together — the way I wanted. I began to look at every part of me, of life, and what it was that I wanted for myself and for my children. During the time after my son's chemo, I volunteered with the Royal Canadian Mounted Police (RCMP) as a Victim Services Advocate. I did many ride alongs with the officers when they did next of kin notifications, to support them.

I worked as a Crisis Counsellor at a shelter for over 20 years. During that time, the job began wearing me down. I felt like I was led to see or become much more than what I had become. I no longer felt I belonged where I was. I wanted to give my children an experience of childhood similar to the one that I had growing up. Being in a community; feeling the freedom of running around with a group of kids, playing in the hills, at the park, in the streets; playing hide and go seek or kick the can; and swimming in the river all day long. It boiled down to community and feeling safe. The road to healing didn't happen for me as quickly as I thought it would. Being out of the city helped, as there were moments we played and times when I had peace and quiet just for me.

I wanted to give more of myself. To be bigger and better than who I was. I knew I had to make more money and thoughts of that consumed me most of the time. I did some home-based businesses and I continued to volunteer with the RCMP. At this point in my life, I rather enjoyed the organized chaos and crisis that my life seemed to be. I enjoyed being of service and the adrenaline rush I felt when I was in a police cruiser, rushing off to a call. My first experience was a triple homicide — not what I expected my first time out, as if I had any say in the matter. I do remember sitting in the back of the police car with a lady who had just lost her daughter and grandson at the hands of her son-in-law. She felt such grief and pain. I felt like my being there was intrusive. I couldn't imagine how she must be feeling, but I did know that I had seen the worst of the worst of humanity. My spirit began to wither even more.

Metamorphosis and the Awakening to Consciousness

During the next phase of my life, I decided that I wanted to give my children — and myself as well — the opportunity to experience innocence. I thought long and hard about the decisions I would make. I felt severe anxiety at the thought of quitting my career, leaving our home, my family, and everything we had known to move to a little town in the middle of the mountains, Yet, somehow, I knew that was the path that I must take, and so we did. I wasn't very popular with my family after making that decision, but it ended up being the most important decision I ever made.

We arrived in that small, surreal town. The air felt so clean and oxygenated, the nights were utterly quiet, and it was coal-dark outside at night. You could see a billion stars and galaxies. I realized how much we are bombarded daily by white noise, sirens, distractions of every kind. In that little mountain town, time seemed to stand still. The things that seemed to matter so much in the city had no value there. There was no need for designer labels; or any labels, for that matter. There was no need to put on fake nails and eyelashes. Kids didn't sit inside all day and play on computers or watch tv. It really was like my childhood. The best day was when a group of local kids knocked on our door to welcome us to town. There it was, so simple. My kids had made a bunch of friends. After that, my house was always full of children, tons of love, laughter and late night sleepovers. I was able to walk to school with my kids, right across the street from where I worked. I stopped chasing the almighty dollar and was gifted *time*. I was able to spend the most important years with my children. They were able to experience feeling safe and free without any worries.

There in that little town, I felt ignited. I let go of my ego and every perception of how I felt others had seen me. How I had seen myself previously... just melted away. What mattered was *being* instead of *doing*. I had the time to look back and realize how much all the ups and downs, the trauma of existing in a world of crisis, truly affected me and my spirit. I did eventually leave our beautiful home as one more crisis happened, but I stopped looking at things as a crisis or a failure. I started to see what it truly was: another opportunity, another stepping stone on this wonderful journey called life. After losing all of my belongings, being stripped of my labels, no longer having a career or all the beautiful things that filled my home, I had nothing; and yet, I gained everything! Yes, it was very traumatic to lose everything, but when I had a bit of time, I realized that no matter where I am, I am home.

Family came in the form of the people I met along my journey. Love came from my children and the children of the town; from my friends and the love that I felt for myself. What I came to understand at that moment truly changed the course of my life... I came to the understanding that life — all of life, the good, the bad, the ugly, and the bliss — made life rich. That I didn't have to prove anything to the world, to my parents, to my friends or even to myself. I realized that life is a collection of the choices that we make and the things we want to experience. If you can stand back and be outside of your situation, you can look at it as it is. With no judgement, it simply is. If I didn't want to do a traditional job, I didn't have to. If I wanted to experience life my way and it made me happy, then that's what I began to do. I know that I am okay, I am capable and I am loved. Knowing this fills me up everyday and allows me to be free. Free from any kind of attachments or *shoulds*. Now, I experience everything through my heart, being conscious of the things that bring me joy. I have learned I always have a peace inside of me that I can access in times of turbulence. I know that I have also given my children the knowledge and experience of being free.

It is my hope that, by reading this story, you discover you are powerful and see that you have abilities and opportunities all around you. If you are aware and present in your own life, you can begin to do the things in this world that will bring you Joy, as Joy is your birthright and Love is who you are. Life is rich; take it and live it the way you feel in your heart. You are powerful beyond belief in both consciousness and leadership. Life is all about your choices, so choose what is in your heart to set you free. *Namaste...* may light find you in times of darkness.

Ignite Action Steps

- **Find ways daily to connect with your truth**, be it through meditation, journaling or spending time out in nature.

- **Be Present — with yourself, your loved ones, friends, children.** Time is the greatest gift there ever will be. Be present for those around you, and for yourself. If you are present, you will hear what they are saying, what they need. Your inner voice is your knowledge, wisdom and knowing, so listen. Listen deeply.

- **Your body is literally your home**, treat it well and put good things in. Drink a warm glass of lemon water every morning to awaken your cells and hydrate. Listen to the wisdom your body has about the foods, liquids or chemicals you are putting into your body. You will feel so much better for doing so.

- **Play — don't take life so seriously**, time is so precious. We have *right now*. Being able to go back to a time of innocence is so needed. Play games with your kids, swing on a swing, take your shoes off in the middle of the day and feel the earth under your feet. It's grounding and good for the soul.

- **Stop looking for happiness on the outside or from things.** Happiness comes from the inside. You, and only you, can make you happy. Start to make choices in life that increase your happiness. Leave behind the things or people that do not value or respect you. Be more careful with who you stand beside and allow into your energy.

Joanne Hughes - Canada
Spiritual Coach-Mineral deficiency/facial analysis Practitioner
joannehughes.simpl.com

MATEJ ŠIMUNIĆ

"Plants, for the future"

When we say Nature, we think of animals, plants, rivers, mountains, oceans and clouds. What I want to tell you is that You are Nature as well. People say that Earth is going to take care of her problems. She will. She is. Nature is calling You to take care of your future by planting trees.

YOU ARE NATURE

Letter to the Earth

Dear Earth,

Today was an excellent day in school. We got to see what coral reefs used to look like in the virtual reality classroom. The teacher said that she still remembers the day the last one disappeared. She tells me the whole world was sad then. I am sorry for what we did.

I remember when granddad told the story about how he tried his best to save the reefs. But that people ignored him until it was too late. I am proud of him and all the people that worked alongside him.

How did you feel that day, Earth? It must have hurt you really bad.

I am so bored, and I want to play outside. I hope we can leave the house soon. I want to ride my bicycle.

I don't want to eat this substitute food anymore. I miss my non-robotic nanny. She would still cook at the stove. This heatwave is the longest ever. It is already the seventh day that we can't leave the house. I wish I lived in a world like it used to be.

Sadly,
Earth Child of 2100 (if we do nothing...)

A Lone Candle in a Dark World

I was 31 and living in Pula, Croatia; my birth town. Even though I hadn't lived there for more than 10 years and I had never thought I would come back, the sudden change of mind turned out to be my intuition speaking. Within a month of my return home, I got to run a coworking space called *Kotač* which, a month later, was transformed into a power event hub. For three weeks, highly successful, beautiful and impactful people talked openly, created masterminds and conducted workshops. The collective influence they brought gave birth to a life purpose that wanted to manifest itself in the world.

I had heard of little Greta Thunberg, that brave girl who took a 32-hour train journey to speak about climate change in Davos, Switzerland. So when I saw her newest speech on my Facebook feed, I sat down and watched. As I listened, her words were engraved deep in my soul. "If we haven't made the changes required by approximately the year 2030, we will probably set off an irreversible chain-reaction beyond human control. Then we will pass a point of no return, which will be catastrophic."

Sitting at my work desk watching the video, I was shaken to my bones.

At first, I could not believe that the world remained silent while this information was public for 9 months[1]. My body was frozen. My eyes were fixed on the screen. My mind was searching for an escape, begging for denial, so that it could remain in its comfort zone of not knowing. But my soul was awakened. The screaming awareness of every electrical impulse happened in my body and brain. Because I was aware, I had complete freedom of the next choice. That choice was opening my eyes to the truth.

We are entering the sixth mass extinction and no one is talking about it. Up to 200 species are going extinct every single day — that number is unheard of in our known history. We have less than 10 years to act before we cross the dreaded limit of 1.5 degrees Celsius of global warming. It's not in the News, nor social network channels. I don't hear politicians seeking change. Nor are my friends or work colleagues aware of it. Are You?

Why don't we talk about it when we meet for coffee or tea? Why isn't this problem the topic of our day-to-day conversations? How come we haven't decided as a species to focus our collective attention to this alarming crisis?

There is a premise in my life that I live by: "Everything that happens to me is my own responsibility." That includes every single event and observation that enters into my consciousness. Accepting that I play a part in it gives me the power to act. There is no outside force where I am just a puppet on a string. I will take responsibility and I will make a change. Embrace this power within us and we can all make a change.

The Seed

Plants have played a big role in my life when I was a kid. My grandmother was making natural balms that I would put on my skin when I was hurt. My aunt was picking the fragrant teas from the Bosnian mountains, a flavor I can still remember vividly. All my adulthood, I explored healing and consciousness with different traditions around the world. Finally, when I was 27, I found myself back in touch with plants. Although I wanted to devote the next chapter of my life to studies of nature's medicinal properties, life had other plans for me.

In pursuit of this knowledge, I ended up living in the Amazon jungle at the border of central Peru and Brazil. Love for plants and old cultures brought me there. In my mind, I was expecting the scenes from documentaries — Rainforest, full of animals, and life. What I found instead was destruction. Indigenous tribes were living on the land that the government *allocated* for them. They were chased away from their forests. Trees were cut down as far as you could drive in an entire day. They *lived* on borrowed land chosen for them, but only until the government said otherwise. It was not theirs.

When a tourist first comes to the jungle, they usually come with certain expectations and demands. In exchange for money, the villagers will provide the service (usually psychedelic experiences triggered by different plants). But when they accept you as one of their own, that facade falls off. People there, they are one foot in the other world. They experience the plant world as spirituality, all of the time. For them, it is an integral part of their way of being. If I would make a metaphor; they have multiple radio stations playing and they learned to tune in to all of the melodies at the same time. We, westerners, are mostly aware of only one.

Just spending time living alongside them, I started to learn how to tune in to different worlds. I learned like a child, with observation and imitation. Just words and superficial ways of communication play a very small role in their social exchanges. The telepathic movements in "other worlds" was where their consciousness is constantly connecting with other villagers and in between themselves. I was eventually invited to be a part of the family. That changed my perception of reality.

I learned a lot about the plants as well. When the time was ripe, I was sent to spend some time alone with the plant spirits, as the tradition asks. Weeks of isolation from people, noise, flavors, and food. I only eat to survive. Tasteless food, without salt, sugar or oil. The only friend I had became the plant I consumed. She directed my dreams and my thoughts. She even manifested as a person and, in discussions with her, I learned a lot about myself. After weeks of outer silence and inner dialogue, I got to know the essence of that plant; how it affects every part of one's being, what organs are being healed and which emotions it is processing. This process is their ancient technology of finding the medicinal properties of plants, called *dieta*.

The *dieta* connected me to the living world. I understood that I was a small part of nature. Plants became a part of my being.

As an exchange, I contributed by applying my tech knowledge in the rural community. The family needed help setting up the first WiFi in the village so that they could make their living off of it. I helped with the creation of a website where volunteers could come and contribute. Now, whenever I go back, I am happy to see what they created together with all the new people that visit, and how their wishes have been fulfilled.

Papa Julio, the grandfather of the family I stayed with, used to say: "Before, if we wanted to build a house, we would cut down a tree. If we wanted to build a canoe, we would cut down a tree. When we went fishing, you could knock with the oar on the boat and fish would jump inside on their own. Once a year, we would call friends and family, and we would plant yucca and plantains that could last us for a long time. We, *Shipibos*, never worked more than a couple of hours a day. The jungle provided us with all we needed. Today, you need money for anything and everything. Kids go to school, you need money. You want to build a house, you need money because there are no more trees to cut. You want to eat, you need money, as the land is poor and the big boats took all the fish. To earn that money, we need to go to the city and work 10, 12 hours a day."

Even though everything was taken away from them, they still kept their essence. The family was together. Grandfather and grandmother, all the way to their great grandchildren. Every day there would be another sister or daughter to share the food. Kids were playing in the dirt and climbing on the mango trees in the backyard. In the night, everyone would sit together and talk. There was a simplicity of life. Even joy. I wanted to stay and live there, and I started to build a house in the fields, but there was something else inside that urged me to continue with my journey. With all the suffering I witnessed, I didn't recognize that I could play a part in making the change. Like the others, I thought that somebody else would take care of it. Nature would take care of this. But inside, the seed was planted. It took its root so strong, it's as if it was there all along.

I found out later that I saw Greta Thunberg's video at exactly the same time that huge sections of the Amazon forest started to burn. It was no coincidence. The facts she pointed out consumed me. I was struck down by her honesty and simplicity. How come I am doing nothing about it? A highschool girl is putting her life second for the cause and I was sitting here, in my office, doing nothing. That day, I was reborn. Reconnected. With impeccable focus, I started my research. Tree planting websites. New green movements. Companies that are using their profits to plant trees around the world. How can we make an impact that matters? Me buying a few hundred trees was not going to make the change that the world needs!

So, I made a simple calculation. I took the amount of CO_2 emissions that we produced per year and divided it by how much carbon one young tree can absorb in a year. Young trees, because we have less than 10 years to act.

The number? — more than a trillion trees are needed globally to reverse the effects of human-emitted CO_2. An average person needs to plant around 4200 trees to become carbon neutral before 2030.

With my mind still contemplating the numbers I calculated, the Amazon fires became viral. Everyone was sharing the news, after three long weeks of silence. Finally, I understood. Mother Rainforest, she was calling me from within all this time. The seed that took roots sprouted to life. The trees, plants, and rivers of the Amazon were living inside me. And they called for help. She cried for help.

Knowing that I received a purpose, I recorded a live video on my Facebook, urging people to start planting trees by any means possible and sharing the information I had. As the video was going viral inside my friend circles, I got contacted by Eriko, a PR manager from Peru, and Gustavo, a product manager and my mentor from Venezuela. Few online meetings, and a couple of in-person brainstorm sessions and the project took its form. **Youthetree.org** supports planting trillions of trees, starting with a first million. We created a nonprofit transparent platform for tracking the donations for tree planting. You are able to see your tree growing from little sapling until it forms the canopy that can be seen with the satellite images.

Letter from the Earth

Dear Human,
Thank you for taking responsibility for yourself. For every action that you do. For all the choices that you make. Know that they impact me. Your choices can hurt or help. Educate yourself on what You can do. Invest your time in learning the truth.

I need your help. There is still time, if You act now.
Earth

Being a conscious leader means that first, you are conscious of yourself. When you are aware of your virtues and your shadows, you can hold the integrity to lead others.

IGNITE ACTION STEPS

- **Start using www.ecosia.org as your search engine.** This is the easiest way to start. We can give support to the companies that use their profits to plant trees. They have planted 65 million trees and that number is growing.

- **Support the products that don't use soy or palm tree oil,** as those are one of the leading products in agriculture responsible for big deforestation in Southeast Asia. [8]

- **Support local products that don't need tankers to reach you.** Shipping is responsible for more than 3 percent of global greenhouse emissions. On top of that, they burn the crudest "bunker oil" that is left after extraction. It is high in sulfur content and is responsible for acid rain, and for many respiratory problems in cities with ports.

- **Fly less with planes** They contribute more than 5 percent of human-caused global warming. [2]

- **Eat fewer dairy and meat products.** Meat and dairy, particularly from cows, have an outsize impact, with livestock accounting for around 14.5 percent of the world's greenhouse gases each year. That's roughly the same amount as the emissions from all the cars, trucks, airplanes and ships combined in the world today. [3]

* **Get involved with tree planting movement.** There are currently 3.5 trillion trees on the planet. Just in the deforested area, we have room for about a trillion more. [4] [5] There are already scientific works on reforesting deserts and creating new ecosystems with new technology. [6]

* **Invest in a renewable source of energy.** Long term, we only have one solution, and that is to stop burning fossil fuels. The more each individual supports the renewable economy, the more the prices go down and it becomes available to everyone. [7]

* **Educate yourself on climate change.** Every choice we make needs to be guided with the north star of saving our planet. We should all align with the same purpose and act today. Instead of reading about celebrities and yellow stamp, let's read what the science is saying about the future of our planet and our children. Listen to climate change podcasts. Start following climate change movements. Become a part of it.

* **Spread the knowledge to your friends and your children.** The awakening that is happening about our connection with Nature and our responsibility for our actions is beautiful and wonderful. Many people want to make a change but don't know what to do. A lot of people are still living in the dark, not knowing what is happening. We can make a change by lighting the candles of others. There is still time to act, and every flame is important. You are The Tree.

Matej Šimunić - Croatia
CoFounder of Mokuteki.io
youthetree.org

CATHERINE MALLI-DAWSON

"With awareness comes mindfulness; with mindfulness comes connection, gratitude and compassion."

My intent in sharing this story is to help leaders find the quietude in the chaos, move beyond command and control tactics, so they can think more clearly, act more purposefully, and lead others through respect and compassion.

MICRO-DOSING MINDFULNESS

Deadlines were looming. Critical milestones were being missed. Staff were leaving due to overwork and stress. I was in the middle of a typical healthcare electronic medical record conversion project. The Program Director had let us all know, not too kindly, how critical the situation was for meeting the timeline.

"How do you stay so calm when everyone else is running around and panicking like the place is burning down?"

The question was posed innocently enough; however, I really had to think about what it was my staff member was really asking me. I had never given much thought to why I don't react the same way as other leaders when something challenging comes up. This is not to say I'm a saint; I most definitely lose my temper from time to time or express my frustration in various situations. However, on the whole, I really don't let things get me too excited. I would also stress that I can work with the same sense of urgency as anyone else. I just do it in a calm, rational way.

After giving the question posed by my staff member some thought, I concluded it must be because I meditate every morning and practice deep breathing exercises throughout the day. But instead of saying that, I gave the token answer, "First of all, I've been through many situations like this throughout my career, so I know that getting anxious about a particular issue may seem urgent and critical at the time. However, I recognize there are usually underlying circumstances that we may not be aware of and therefore some investigation is needed to fully understand the situation."

While that answer placated them somewhat, I could tell they weren't convinced that was everything. So, I continued and admitted, "I also meditate every morning and practice deep breathing exercises that help calm my nervous system and allows me to respond more rationally."

Her eyes lit up and I could tell I had hit on something. She asked, "Could you teach us your secret?"

I looked around the table at my ragtag band of technical analysts and wondered how on earth I was going to get out of this one. "How many of you are interested in learning some basic meditation techniques?" To my surprise, all their hands went up and they nodded their heads as they glanced at each other. "This will need to be either before or after work, as we can't disrupt the day's work schedule. Is everyone OK with that?"

I could see there was a little more hesitation with that question. I recognized the majority of the team were staff level and accustomed to working 8-5, Monday through Friday. They put in their time and went home to their families. Some of them had long commutes and traffic could be brutal. We agreed to try out a schedule of two mornings a week, on Tuesdays and Thursdays. We agreed to start the following week, but I wondered how many would actually commit to coming in an hour early just to learn to meditate.

Back in my office, I opened my calendar and checked room availability. To have the least amount of disruption, I booked the conference room at the far end of the building. Then, I sat back in my chair, took a deep breath and wondered what the heck I had just signed myself up for. The fear and self-doubt started flooding into my brain. I may have been meditating for over 20 years and attended plenty of guided meditation sessions, but I had never led a meditation session on my own. What did I know about leading others through a meditation, let alone teaching them to meditate?

After berating myself for giving them some false sense of hope, I decided I was committed and I couldn't let them down. I had some homework to do before we got started next week, but that would need to wait until later. I needed to get started on the agenda of the day. A few hours later my cell phone rang with a number that I vaguely recognized. I answered and was greeted with a familiar voice. "Hi Catherine, this is Merwan from the Chopra Center. How are you doing?"

Pleasantries exchanged, he then got down to business, "I'm reaching out to you as you had expressed interest in the Teacher Training Program for Primordial Sound Meditation. If you're still interested, we have a new class starting in a few months and I wanted to see if this was a good time for you to start."

I raised my eyes to the ceiling and mouthed a silent, "Thank you."

"Well, Merwan, it's funny that you phoned me today as I just committed to introducing my team to meditation." I shared with him my doubts and concerns. He reassured me that even though I'm not a certified instructor, I would do fine with leading them through some basic meditations and he offered to send me some simple guidelines. I signed up for the course that was starting in three months. Following my conversation with Merwan, I was much calmer. I was now looking forward to researching different meditation techniques, styles, and programs and preparing for my first session leading the team through their introductory experience.

Tuesday morning, I arrived early to prepare the space. The conference room was often used for some very heavy meetings and heated discussions, so I wanted to raise the energy before we got started on our meditation. There are several ways to do this: burn some cleansing incense, perform some meditations and mantras prior to others arriving, or use sound to raise the vibration. I knew I couldn't use incense, so I chose some aromatherapy spray and brought my Tingsha bells to cleanse the energy in the space. I then sat quietly with my eyes closed, played some soothing music, recited some mantras silently and waited to see who would arrive. I heard them as they slowly filed into the room, quietly selecting their seats around the table. I let them get settled and noted about a third of the team had arrived. A few I expected; a few others I was excited to see join us.

"Welcome, everyone. I'd like to walk through some basics before we get started. How many of you have meditated before?" I asked and looked around to see three out of the eight raise their hands.

"Okay. For those of you who have meditated, please bear with me as I give some background to the others. Meditation is a centuries old practice that spans all of humankind. It is not a religious practice, although many would compare it to prayer."

I went on to explain that there are many forms of meditation, from silence on one end of the spectrum, mantras, guided meditations, and active meditation like walking in nature and just observing your surroundings. These are all forms of meditation and lead to mindfulness and opening your awareness. I expressed my gratitude for them inviting me into this opportunity and I then explained what tools I used for my practice.

"I use various mantras during my meditation as I've found that it helps to quiet my monkey mind." This got a little chuckle from them and a few head nods. "In our current society we are bombarded with so many incoming thoughts, messages, interruptions, demands, etc., that we all struggle to 'quiet our minds.'"

I could feel my confidence growing as I shared, "Many people think of meditation as the silencing of the mind. While quieting is the intent, silencing is impossible because that would mean we were dead." This got another little chuckle from them and I could see them relax. I continued, "The use of a mantra allows the mind to focus on something during meditation. We will have thoughts float into our mind. We can acknowledge them and then return to the mantra. It is simply a vehicle to quiet and focus the mind."

They all agreed this sounded like a good place to start. I walked them through the basics of what to expect and let them know we would be starting with a blend of guided and mantra meditation. I looked around the room and could see a mix of apprehension and excitement on their faces. I asked them to please close their eyes and we would begin the session. I queued the music and directed them, "With your eyes closed, take three deep, slow, cleansing breaths. Breathe in through your nose and out through your mouth."

With the gentle music and the deep breaths lulling them into a calm, relaxed state, I walked them through some affirmations of gratitude and awareness. I led them on a gentle inward journey of relaxation and retrospection, asking them to focus on releasing stress from various parts of their bodies from their heads to their toes. Then, we spent a few minutes silently repeating the mantra I had shared with them before I softly brought them back into a waking state and asked them to slowly open their eyes.

After the session, I could see their shoulders were more relaxed and they sat more comfortably in their chairs. I sensed a peacefulness that settled in the room. I let them sit in the quietude for a few minutes and regain their awareness. "Does anyone want to share what their experience was like?" I asked quietly.

Sarah, who I could see had light streaks of tears drying on her cheeks, spoke up first. "I just want to say that it was one of the most profound experiences

I've ever felt. Thank you for leading us through it. I'm feeling a little emotional and I'm not sure why."

I explained to her that when we quiet the mind and go within, we touch a part of ourselves that is where we connect with God, the Universe, and our true selves. It doesn't matter what you call it, it's all the same. Sometimes when we connect for the first time, we can have an overwhelming feeling of 'coming home' and this can trigger an emotional release.

"Did anyone else feel this connection?" I asked the rest of the group. They all raised their hands in unison.

"Thank you, Sarah, for being brave and sharing what you felt." I asked if anyone else would like to share. Mike raised his hand and asked to go next. "I felt a deep sense of calm and I saw some amazing colors. What does that mean?"

I was happy to explain, "Well, I think when you see colors during meditation, it's your mind's way of playing with the energy that you're feeling. This is quite common during meditation and especially for those who are new to the practice." I didn't want to go into too much detail about what each color might mean, as they mean something different to everyone. I went on, "As we get further into experiencing deeper calm and silence, the colors may disappear. Right now, your mind is still very active and will take time to fully relax and let go."

A few others shared what they felt during the session. They used words like calm, relaxed, connected and even excited to describe their experience. Overall, they all agreed it was a great experience and they wanted to continue.

Throughout the next several months, we met regularly. Sometimes it was twice a week and sometimes only once a week, depending on the demands of the current project. Occasionally there was only one person who could join. Other times, we had a good- sized group. Overall, they seemed to enjoy the sessions and I could see small shifts happening across the team. Where once there was sniping, whining and complaining, now there were smiles, compassion and offers of assistance.

One of the most amazing things I observed was that the shift didn't just happen with those who were participating in the meditation sessions. It was happening across the entire team. Being in the maelstrom of a major electronic health system conversion for a hospital system can raise anyone's blood pressure a point or two. These projects have proven to be life threatening and people have died due to the stress they are under. The demanding timelines, ever changing scope and lack of sufficient resources to do the work can crush even the most resilient person.

I was one of five leaders across the program and we were all feeling the pressure as the deadline grew ever nearer. When I first joined the program, I quickly realized that my team was undoubtedly the greenest and had the least amount of experience for the work ahead of them. Most had barely passed their certification exams and were struggling to comprehend the day-to-day activities they needed to achieve their milestones. I did what I could to help them with the technical aspects, but I recognized it was the stress that was going to sink them if we didn't do something to address it.

Incorporating meditation practices into our weekly schedule had a significant impact on the overall morale of the team. They became much more supportive and collaborative with each other. For those who couldn't attend the morning meditation sessions, I shared with them various tools and applications they could download to their phones to use at home on their own. I walked them through the basics of meditation and encouraged them to find the time to take care of themselves so that the stresses and strains of the project didn't impact them negatively.

Over the course of the program, I noticed that some of the more senior team members started to share their knowledge more freely and include others in work discussions they felt they would benefit from attending. Several would regularly go out to lunch together and they made a point of recognizing each other's celebrations along the way. Whether it was a birthday, an engagement or a son's graduation, they were all acknowledged and celebrated by the team.

This collaboration and engagement created a more supportive environment and enabled the team to deliver the project while practicing self-care. As a conscious leader, I was able to accept their challenge and guide them into a more relaxed, mindful state of being so they could complete the work needed without compromising their health and wellbeing in the process. I would encourage all leaders to take steps to incorporate more mindfulness into their daily activities, both for themselves and for those they lead. Small steps can open up feelings of connectedness. This feeling of connection enables people to interact with love, compassion and gratitude, which ultimately leads to better outcomes for everyone.

While my story was an example of introducing a meditation practice into a team I was leading, the real benefit came from building a more mindful approach to engaging with each other. Meditation was simply a tool to enable them to become more aware and compassionate with each other and with themselves. There are many ways to incorporate mindfulness into your daily life that can be applied to all aspects. Whether it's practicing deep breathing while at work or active listening with a family member, mindfulness can be incorporated in many small ways. Micro-dosing mindfulness leads to daily self-care that becomes second nature and vital to your overall well-being.

Ignite Action Steps

Meditation: Gauge the level of understanding with your team about what meditation is or isn't. What do they feel most comfortable with — guided, mantra, movement, or silence? Then, either establish a regular time to allow them to practice or hire someone to lead them through the session.

Reflections: Start each team meeting with a reflection that is selected by a different team member each time. This could be a poem, favorite quote, prayer, etc. Choose anything that is inspiring, uplifting or motivating. Allow 5 to 10 minutes to discuss how the reflection relates to the team and how they can incorporate the learning into their day.

Gratitude: Start each day by writing or stating two to five things for which you're grateful. Encourage your team to incorporate gratitude practices into their daily routine. This could also be incorporated into meetings by having one or two people express their gratitude for something or someone at the beginning of the meeting. It doesn't have to be about work or other members of the team. It could be that they are grateful for a family member, the barista at the coffee shop or even that they have a car to drive.

Catherine Malli-Dawson - USA
CEO & Founder LifeWhys LLC
www.lifewhysllc.com

CLAIRE WILD

"Leaders neither push nor pull; they allow. Their experience inspires and gives permission for others to walk in their steps."

This is a reminder and an invitation for you to allow yourself to consciously be who you are and to express it fully through leading an intentional life, true to yourself. May you step into the leader you already are and become a life sparkler.

WHAT LEADER DO YOU CHOOSE TO BE?

Cooking crêpes is quite an impossible mission while sailing, but it wasn't that day. In the cockpit, under a bright sun, with nothing else in view than a lake-like ocean, we enjoyed the impromptu tea-time, sailor's version: crêpes and rum.

This remarkably un-windy day found us between Cape Verde and Canary Islands, far away into the Atlantic Ocean, aboard our engineless boat. When the last bit of wind died, we opted for lowering the sails and enjoying the calm. Sailing, you go so slowly sometimes, you would arrive faster walking. On that occasion, we actually went backward, thanks to the current! Yet, mile after mile, we eventually arrived at Gran Canaria.

Even in the form of a nautical mile, never underestimate the power of a single step: the first one. Nothing predestined me to taking that step... aside from my obstinate mind. For as long as I can remember, I have dreamed of traveling. That vision developed into living on a floating home. I never lived by the sea, though, and had just one experience of a few days sailing when I was a kid.

At 17, I had to choose which diploma would be my gateway to further studies. A teacher kept me after class: "Have you decided yet? I know you prefer literature and philosophy, but science will open every door." He tried to convince me. This conversation just increased my misfit feeling. Asthma kicked in again. The more I grew up, the more I felt like everyone wanted to make me fit in a box too small for me. I was suffocating.

Listening to their *reasonable way* had me utterly uninspired. They awakened my fears that that path might indeed be the only option, and, should I try anything else, I would obliterate my future. Yet, the same desperate hope kept coming up, "There must be more to life than this."

I sensed that shutting down my nature to force myself into that tight box would suck the life out of me. But in that pre-Google age, I knew no alternatives except the ones from my imagination.

I had not been considered politically correct since I was eight, thanks to my father. He had shown me that a happy face doesn't equal a happy person and that adults, too, can make bad decisions... when he suicided without even letting us know why. That was my best-kept secret, adding to the misfit syndrome. I learned from that period that appearances can lie and that you only discover your power when you really need it.

All of this summed up into determination. Was it conscious? No. It was not even completely intentional. But damn, was it strong! My vision became unshakeable: I didn't wonder "if," but "how." I would eventually sail on my boat, but I had to climb so many steps before that day.

Finding a partner was a crucial step, though they say two captains is one too many.

I can still see him looking at me with curiosity across the table. We were at his place, a few months into our friendship, yet only one week into our love relationship. I could sense the potential for something serious between us, though. So, with my usual brutal honesty, I asked him, "If you want to be with me, there is something you need to know. Sooner rather than later, I will buy a sailing boat and travel the world on it. If you want to try this with me, I love you even more. If not, I'm afraid our relationship won't last long." I'm smiling each time I remember this cheekiness.

And he — maybe because hormones were messing with his rational thinking, maybe because instead of questioning my dream, I boldly declared it — he courageously decided to follow me. I had met my first tribemate. Everything becomes easier with community. It starts with just one person telling you, "That sounds crazy, but I am in." Growing away from "the misfit," I was taking over my life, one step at a time.

There I was, crewing with my partner across the Atlantic. Three weeks into the transatlantic passage, coming closer to the Azores, I was fighting sleep, eyes on the compass, hands on the steering stick. The skipper's head popped out from below deck with a suspicious look and then disappeared back inside.

I was exhausted, physically and emotionally. The hydraulic wheel had broken, forcing us to steer day and night with the back-up stick. The back-up stick was so hard to move that I had to use both my arms; yet, as soon as we stopped holding it, it didn't stay on course. I was taking turns, just like every-one else, but as much as I tried, I never got a chance to get involved in the decisions. It seemed I was only good at being told what to do, only to be met with the skipper's unspoken suspicion.

After hearing strange watery noises for hours, I suddenly saw a whale crossing our route. I was fascinated... and staring so much that I almost ran the boat into her baby, who was swimming behind her.

In a glimpse, I knew: It was all worth it! All the efforts. Going to live by the sea, learning how to sail, all while saving every penny. Going around in search of what still seemed impossible: an affordable aluminum sloop. Those long days and nights on this less than optimum boat with a misogynistic captain... It was all worth it! Never had I come closer to my dream. And then, I had something more: confidence. After this transatlantic passage, I knew it: I was ready. I still had a lot to learn, yet I had earned my captain's hat.

A few months later, I was learning at the speed of light. I had finally found my own boat in Senegal, Africa, and we were sailing along the coast. Not much wind, combined with waves, made the perfect cocktail for an extra rocky cruise. That was when I noticed the electrical system still needed improvement. It was playing the on-off game, rhythmically with each wave, just like a blinking Christmas wreath. Not that we had a lot of electronics on board, but everyone enjoys a bit of light, GPS and a radio at sea.

That was one of my first "learning opportunities" as a captain and it was a gentle one. Until I began, I couldn't really know what I needed to know. I could prepare — and I did. At some point, though, I had to accept that I wouldn't know everything; more importantly, I had to be cool with that. Being afraid of trying new things was not an option. I needed to experiment and rise to the occasion; even better if I enjoyed the ride.

There would be many occasions to rise to. I could write a book just with them! Some bitterly funny, like this one, some tougher. Steering day and night under stormy weather for so long that all I wanted was arrival and sleep... At the same time, getting dangerously absorbed into the beauty of the ever-changing color of the waves. Or entering the Casamance River with too little wind, still no engine, random sandbars and strong currents. Or nurturing love while living in a tiny, closed space with another human being while sometimes discovering parts of myself I had never met before.

All of these experiences were increasing my awareness and shaping my inner leader. I wasn't only gaining practical skills. Without even realizing it, *the Ocean, the Wind, the Stars, the Boat...* they were teaching me: meditation, emotional and relational awareness, equanimity, patience, self-confidence, trust, consistency, discipline... They were my first and wiser spiritual teachers, rewarding me for taking a leap of faith.

With tough love, these *elements* were forcing me to take total responsibility for my life and actions; and reminding me that, in the end, they were bigger than me. All I could do was embrace the attitude of learning through experience and trust that, as I would need it, I would find answers and develop skills.

Being at sea somewhat highlights the challenges because it often brings you back to basics: life and death. Whenever you choose to go off the beaten path, you will be tested and grow accordingly.

After four years at sea, I was pausing before the next departure and I happily reunited with my family and friends in France. During my travels, I had met my sailing tribe. They got me. With them, there was no need to explain about pirates, storms, or dolphins. Here in France, I was the misfit again, in a new way. I had changed so much. They hadn't.

I was getting a lot of: "You're so lucky! I could never do that because of... my kids / job / cat." At first, naively, I would try helping them. I knew enough practical solutions and examples, from both my personal experience and that of my fellow explorers, to overcome any objection. That led me to quite a few passive-aggressive interactions.

Until I understood that sometimes the intention behind the words was, *"Don't help me get over my limitations; rather, feed my belief that I can't change."* Soon enough, then, I answered directly to the intention: I talked to their fear, from love, which led to some wonderful, heartfelt conversations.

There were also the "How can I...?" questions. I even received a few emails from strangers through my blog, stating "Thanks for the inspiration!" There I was, on the other side... changing their definition of *possible*. A few years before, I was the one reading those books and blogs for inspiration and validation that I wasn't so crazy after all.

These many questions showed me that, all this time, I was seen. I was not only creating and living life in my own way. I was always leading by example — only now, I was conscious of it. I began to acknowledge how much I could impact. Very often, the conversation started from a curiosity about my specific story. Many times, we arrived at deeper and more universal topics: facing our fears and insecurities, building healthy relationships, redefining aging, and more...

"Do you ever stop during a navigation? What do you do at night?" they would often ask.

"You go on! You can't stop. One is always on the deck while the other sleeps. If needed, you go and give a hand, even if it is your turn to rest."

"Wow. But then how do you deal with the tiredness?" Or also: "How do you make money on the go? How do you find the courage to go on long navigation without assurance of good weather all along? How do you deal with living as a couple in such a tiny space? Do you miss family and friends? Did you lose friends from being away for so long?" And so on..

Want it or not, I was challenging lots of beliefs through my unconventional lifestyle. More and more people opened up about their hopes and fears, looking for answers. I was surprised by how many of them are not happy with their life, shutting up their doubts, and shutting down their dreams. The funny thing was I had become passionate about living the questions. I didn't have their answer, but I could help them to find it by themselves.

Was I a leader? I certainly didn't consider myself one. Had you told me back then that I would participate in this book, I would have laughed in disbelief. I mean, The Dalai Lama, Aung San Suu Kyi, Rosa Parks... *these* were leaders.

As I sat down to write this chapter, what I am doing now came to my mind first: empowering unconventional humans to be unapologetically themselves and embody this freedom into their personal and professional lives. Transforming lives through resilience building, embodiment and body-mind tools to overcome overwhelm, stress, isolation... This is consciously leading, right? But how did it all start?

I kept going backward in time until it hit me... My Ignite Moment, rather than a point in time, was a process: that of taking the lead of myself. That was my first step... the one that made everything else possible, including what I didn't even know I could do.

Everything I did afterwards was about scaling my leadership and stepping deeper into consciousness. I started the "Integrally Alive" movement and community. I overcame all the "who am I to do this?" stories, helped by the humbleness of knowing that my purpose was bigger than me. I accepted that I needed to be an increasingly public figure to expand my reach and increase my impact.

Whatever the range of your influence, from "just" your family and friends to a more global community, or your team... you are seen. It all starts with yourself. The first and most important step to conscious leadership is leading your life intentionally. Choosing day after day to embody your truest and best Self, and taking responsibility for the impact you have.

If you knew your choice would inspire thousands of people, how would you live your day today?

IGNITE ACTION STEPS

Three pillars support your actions. Though they develop in this specific order, you will keep revisiting and strengthening them.

Awareness

Even when you don't know what your motivation is, your actions and words are showing it. Why not make it conscious? What do you want? Why is it important? What would it change for you? And for your surroundings? Sometimes what you don't want comes easier than what you want. **Keep digging.**

The clearer your intention, the more unshakeable you become. Let it evolve. But don't let anyone, even yourself, question it. People will listen because you firmly know and claim your truth. Some might call you crazy and reject it; others will love you... for exactly the same reason. Allow your tribe to find you.

Freedom

Embrace the freedom to transform: Both as a prerequisite for and as a result from action. Action will question everything you think is true.

- What do you take so seriously that it blocks you?
- How can your actions feed your awareness?

Rather than "if," ask yourself "how."

Begin as soon as you get ready enough. You will never feel completely ready, and that is OK. You can't have all the answers. From where you are standing, you can't even imagine what opportunities become available once you move.

Start with the next step, staying open to learning on the go — exactly what you need, when you need it. Can you explore playfully, rather than ticking off your to-do list?

Connection

Acknowledge and take responsibility for your impact. Live every moment like you had followers who would hold you accountable for what you say and do. What would you stop doing or saying if you knew someone was watching? Connection forces you to lead intentionally.

One of the best ways to integrate your learning and grow further is by giving back. What knowledge would have helped you ten years ago? Don't impose your experience on anyone, but notice the requests for help.

Always choose love over being right: not everyone will follow you. And that's OK. Focus on the ones who need you and let the others make their own choices. That doesn't mean you had no impact on them. Maybe you helped them get clear on what they want... by showing what they don't.

Use these pillars to discover the leader you already are and become a life sparkler!

Claire Wild - France
Bodymind Therapeutic Coach
www.integrallyalive.com

Natalie Matushenko

"Be gorgeous, successful, sexy and vibrant at any age."

I wish to inspire you to notice where you are being called to step up as a leader; to overcome your internal obstacles to serve that calling so that you can make the impact you are meant to make in the world.

Say Yes, Then Figure It Out

My new purpose hit me like a ton of bricks and my first thought was "Oh no! Not this!" Followed by "Seriously, Universe? Why me?"

I was surrounded by about 300 people, sitting in a huge conference room at a personal and business mastery weekend in Jamaica. There was a really dynamic speaker on stage, but I wasn't really listening. I was struck by how out of place and disconnected I felt.

I had no reason to feel this way. Everybody was very friendly and there were many social activities to enjoy, and I did enjoy them! In fact, the whole weekend was a big, fun party as we mingled in between break-out sessions during the day, ate our meals together and danced the night away at beachside restaurants. It seemed like everyone else was having a fantastic time; but for me, something was missing.

I found myself feeling critical. "The sessions didn't go deep enough. This is Personal Growth *Lite*. What's up with all of these scantily clad young women all over the place? Look how hard they are trying to get the men's attention. Could they wear any less clothing? They look so desperate and ridiculous."

All these judgements were swirling through my brain. (I am not proud of it, but it's true.)

I was 46 years old at the time and, truth to tell, I felt attractive. I was fit and full of energy. Yet as I looked around, I was struck by how young everyone else was. They were all in their late 20's and 30's, and I started to notice that there was a sort of "mating dance" going on around me and I wasn't a part of it. The men were busy checking out the young women and I had become somewhat invisible.

Mind you, I wasn't interested in finding a partner or having a fling. I was at this conference with my husband of nearly 20 years and my main desire was to forge a closer connection with him. At an even deeper level, my top priority after focusing so much on the needs of others for so many years was re-establishing a close relationship with myself.

I used to joke with my girlfriends that if my husband and I were to ever split up, the last thing I would want is another man around. All I seemed to crave was alone-time, followed by time with close female friends. I missed the deep connections that I had with other women before our children and family demands took over.

So why was I so annoyed watching the mating dance around me? Why was I so critical? And, I hate to say, somewhat jealous of the scantily-clothed young women all around me? I wanted to scream when I saw all those medically-sculpted bodies.

The answer to this goes way back.

My mother was a Soviet engineer. She is a very pragmatic person. She is not given to emotions and tends to respond to life in a very practical way. I have only seen her cry a handful of times in my entire life: when she was planning to leave my father, when my grandfather died, when we emigrated from the Soviet Union during the harsh Brezhnev years and didn't know if we would ever see my grandmother again, and when my grandmother passed away.

Yet I remember my very stoic and practical mother being depressed on her 40th birthday, unwilling to get out of bed and get ready for her own party. I was 18 years old at the time and I got the distinct impression that life was kind of over at 40.

Looking back even further, I have a memory of my mother being very sad on her 32nd birthday because she thought that she was getting old, and she scrutinized herself in the mirror, looking for wrinkles. There's also a memory of my mother at 30, telling me with great sadness in her voice that I was getting so big. I distinctly remember thinking that I didn't want to get any older and I pretended to be younger than I was for the next couple of years.

So yes, I had issues with getting older as far as I can remember. But I grew up and became a mom and, all of a sudden, I was obsessed with getting a decent night's sleep. I did tons of personal growth work. Birthdays rolled by and I thought that age was just a number. Certainly, not something for me to worry about. Until I sat in that conference hall surrounded by all those young, beautiful and flirty women.

I suddenly started to wonder what I looked like to those around me. Did I look like the middle-aged woman that I was? Was I no longer attractive? For the first time in years, I started to worry about becoming invisible to younger people. The vain part of me was trying very hard to hold on to my self-image as a beautiful and desirable woman.

I also realized that while these young women seemed so concerned with finding a mate at the conference, I was more interested in making personal and professional connections with — do I dare say? — other middle-aged women. I was interested in figuring out how to handle my fluctuating hormones and their pesky, uncomfortable side effects. I longed to be in wisdom circles with women my own age and share deeply, from our hearts, about our biggest joys and deepest sorrows.

I realized right then and there, sitting in that conference room, that something deep inside of me had changed. I was entering into a new phase in my life and it was nothing like I had ever experienced before. A phase where the internal world mattered much more than the external one and where time, alone, was prized over mindless banter with others. It was a time in my life where I was on a quest for deep wisdom while so many things around me seemed silly and frivolous.

I felt a deep inner longing to create a community of women over 40. The Universe seemed to support this idea as I attracted, as if by magic, other women over 40 who seemed disgruntled by the offerings at the conference. They shared with me that they, too, wanted something deeper and more transformational. They also wanted to let their hair down and connect in ways that only women can.

I knew that this longing to create a women's community was my future. Yet, I resisted it. I have grown my business by writing a weekly blog in which I shared very openly and honestly all of my trials, tribulations and learnings along my life's journey. I had never, however, shared my feelings about getting older — my hair thinning, the extra pounds I had put on around my waist (that just would not come off no matter how healthy I ate or how much I exercised), my moodiness, my waning libido, and (I cringe to write this even now) the arthritis I developed in my hips the year I turned 40.

I realized that I had internalized, a long time ago, watching my mother struggle with her aging. I had internalized that getting older is bad and somehow shameful. I did not want to admit that I was getting older. It felt like giving up my last pretentions that I was beautiful, desirable and worthy as a woman. And I realized how ridiculous it was. Anybody looking at me could tell that I was no longer a young woman; yet somehow, I just could not talk about aging openly. So I shuddered when I received that intuitive hit that I was supposed to start a community of women over 40. I pushed it away.

My hormones, however, would not let me off the hook. I became moodier and crankier. I began questioning everything in my life even more than before. My life's work, my relationships, my surroundings — everything went under the microscope and usually came up short. I had this sense that I hadn't done enough, been enough or lived enough. "Life is to be lived now" became my new motto as I planned long trips around the world for my family of five, went hiking in the Colombian jungle with a group of women and jumped out of a perfectly good airplane at 14,000 feet for the first time (with a parachute, of course).

I felt as though my rose-colored glasses had come off and I was finally seeing clearly the ways in which my life wasn't really mine. All the ways I had put my own desires and dreams on hold in order to meet my family's needs. All the opportunities I failed to pursue because I was afraid to leave the warm comfort of the nest I had built for myself. All the times I said "Yes" when I really meant "No."

That was not all. My body was speaking to me in ways it hadn't before. I started to experience serious night sweats, waking up five, six, seven times at night feeling like I had a coal-fired heater inside of me. Needless to say, I was not sleeping very well and was feeling exhausted and anxious as a result. My body often ached in strange places and, much to my husband's dismay, my libido seemed to have gone to live with my former self. All I wanted to do at night was get into bed in my comfy pajamas, watch some Netflix and pass out from fatigue.

I have to confess that despite all these discomforts and over-tiredness, I loved the kick-ass, take-no-prisoners new me. I was always so sensitive and concerned with the feelings of others. I loved that I stopped caring so much about what other people thought and started speaking my own truth more often than not. I happily stopped caring so much about being attractive to others and was more interested in my internal world and qualities. I no longer suffered fools gladly. In fact, all of a sudden, I developed a strong inner need to set firm boundaries with loved ones and tell off just about anybody who did me wrong, even if it was in the smallest of ways. After years of *playing nice*, my inner bitch was finally free! And I really liked her.

What I really didn't like were all those physical and emotional symptoms of perimenopause that I mentioned. I often felt like my body and psyche were out of control and I started to search for answers.

I am very holistically oriented and tend to be anti-medicine, so I searched for all of the natural remedies out there. Herbs, supplements, eating regimens — I tried them all. I was amazed to realize how confusing it was. It seemed that all of my friends and clients were in the same situation. There was actually very little information out there about how to balance our hormones or make sense of this stage of life that often left us feeling like the rug was being pulled out from under us. We were all feeling like our lives had turned upside down and there was little we could do about it. Friends would mention an estrogen patch or a progesterone cream, but no one seemed to have a comprehensive understanding of what was happening to our bodies and psyches.

I started to realize how important this stage is in a woman's life. We are no longer young and child-bearing, but we are not yet old either. It seemed to me that this stage was little explored by our society. In fact, the messages all around me were that women go from child bearing to menopause to old age as though there aren't decades of productive and bountiful living in between.

The idea that I should interview experts on all the areas important to women at this stage — hormonal balancing, relationships, health, sex, money, success, parenting, personal transformation, spirituality and beauty — grabbed a hold of me and would not let me go. I kept telling myself that I did not have the energy or the time. My schedule was already filled to the brim with my business, husband and three daughters. Plus, where was I going to find these experts when I had not been able to find the answers that I needed so far?

The idea kept swirling in my head, however. I knew that it was my calling, yet I was reluctant to answer and walk through this portal of the wisdom stage of a woman's life. This went on for a couple of months until, one day, I awoke and read a pair of quotes by Richard Branson that said, "Opportunity favors the bold," and "If somebody offers you an amazing opportunity but you are not sure you can do it, say yes — then learn how to do it later!"

I read the quote and said, "F—k it!" I opened up Facebook and wrote to all the groups that I followed. I mentioned I was looking for experts in all these different fields for an online summit. I knew that once I put it out there publicly, there was no going back.

I then googled, "how to do an online summit" and spent the next couple of hours reading and taking notes.

What followed was really quite amazing. So many women reached out that I had a hard time speaking to everybody. Experts recommended experts and, before I knew it, I was knocking on the doors of my *sheroes* — transformational leaders and best-selling authors whose books have literally changed my life. Women who had millions of followers, who were so in demand that their calendars were booked four or five months in advance and who never said "Yes" to online summits... said "Yes" to this one.

When I interviewed them, these experts told me that the reason they said "Yes" was because no one is talking about this important time in a woman's life and because they, too, felt lost in the years between 40 and 55. We laughed together and connected. We shared stories and they offered their wisdom. I learned so much and I became so excited to spread this information to as many women as possible. I realized that while I was putting these experts up on a pedestal, these women were just like me. I started to trust even more in my own wisdom.

It took about five months of sweat (and sometimes tears) to pull that summit together. I was the interviewer, writer, videographer, project manager and publicist. There were incredible highs, like the connected conversations I was having with the experts. And there were some pretty bad lows, like when the company I hired to help me with this summit missed an important deadline and then quit the job two weeks before we launched. This, however, only made room for miracles. A friend lent me her tech support person and taught me how to assemble a team to get it all done in time. Within two days, I was managing a team that spanned the globe and feeling like I could do anything.

The knowledge I gained from interviewing the experts helped me balance my hormones and feel good in my body and psyche, yet my bad-assery power remained. I could feel my wisdom, courage, strength and perseverance. I could feel my inner drive to make an impact on the world. I am now so clear on my purpose: It's simply to help women claim their wisdom and to change the conversation of what it means to be a gorgeous, sexy, successful and vibrant woman in her 40s, 50s and beyond.

Being a conscious leader means paying attention to where you are called to make a difference in the world... and doing it! You might have to overcome some internal obstacles and find the strength, courage and determination within yourself. It will propel you forward towards your true purpose and allow you to create a life that is more meaningful than anything you could have imagined.

Ignite Action Steps:

1. **Get clear on where you are being called** to step up as a leader and where you are holding yourself back. Pull out some paper and a pen and answer the following questions:

    a. What issue am I passionate about?
    b. What issue really angers or bothers me?
    c. What's the injustice I feel called to address?
    d. What pain have I overcome?
    e. What have I learned that I can teach?
    f. What is my intuition telling me?
    g. What reasons do I give myself for not serving my calling?
    h. Where could I be doing more?
    i. How can I overcome my excuses?
    j. If I were to say "Yes" and figure it out later, what would be the first step I would take?

2. **Now go out and take that step!**

Don't hold back. Life is short. Make the difference you're meant to make.

Natalie Matushenko - USA
Transformational Teacher
www.extraordinarylifeafter40.com

SARA FELDMAN

"It's in the messiness that unexpected beauty can emerge."

My intention is for the readers to consider self-acceptance and vulnerability in their leadership. On my journey, I have learned how important it is to accept all the parts of ourselves and show up in our own truth. Through doing this, we can have deeper, more fulfilling connections with ourselves and others.

THE EXQUISITE MESS THAT IS BEING HUMAN

I have learned more than I could ever have expected from juvenile sex offenders, survivors of torture and refugees. What they have taught me can be used in all of our lives to create deeper, more fulfilling connections. It all relates to a concept that I call *The Exquisite Mess,* which is about the inherent complexity of life. A lot of life and being human does not fit into neat little boxes or simple categories. Life is messy. It's only in accepting that messiness that we're able to live wholeheartedly and connect with ourselves and others in the deepest possible ways. Learning this helped me to become a more conscious leader.

I was born and raised in Los Angeles and I grew up around the entertainment industry. As much as I thought about it, I thought that was where I was going to end up. I did for a little while, but despite being raised in Hollywood, I wasn't made for it. I felt called to work with people. Not knowing how to do that, I started volunteering and interning at various organizations. A woman I met at one of these organizations said, "If you want to work with people, you need to get a master's degree in something like social work." Without any idea of what social work was, I pursued it. I went to graduate school and earned my master's degree. Social work has taken me to places I never would have imagined that I could go. I've had experiences I never could have dreamed of, and I've met people that I had no idea even existed.

My first job right after graduating was working in a residential treatment facility with juvenile male sex offenders. I'll admit that when I started, the concept of working with 'sex offenders' made me very nervous. I didn't know what sex offender treatment was, but given my determination, I was up for the challenge. I dove in and quickly found out.

I spent my days talking to kids who had molested other kids about their thoughts, feelings, and behaviors. We talked about what they had experienced and what they had done with the goal of making sure that they never, ever did it again. I created a safe environment for them to share and move forward, and we had lots of difficult conversations about all kinds of things.

I remember how those kids used to come into our program. They would be posturing, trying to look tough. Of course, I could see right through them. I recognized that they had built up defensive walls around themselves and that behind those walls, they were terrified, ashamed, and alone. They were totally disconnected.

I would spend time talking with the kids and, eventually, the walls would start to come down. The kids would start to disclose the things that had been done to them — almost every one of them had been abused or neglected in some way — and as trust grew between us, they would start to open up about the things that they had done.

One of the aspects of our treatment was to have the kids tell their families about the abuse they had endured and the abuse that they had perpetrated. Sitting in those meetings, the tension was palpable. I would feel nervous for the kids as I watched them walk into my office all hunched over, staring at the ground, sweating. They would sit down. It was time for them to open up, but some weren't ready and they would shut down, stay silent. Others mustered all of their courage and started talking, their voices shaking.

Those who came clean would begin the transformation process. It was visible in their physical appearance. They would lose weight. Their posture and facial expressions would change. We would see them start to smile and laugh freely at appropriate times. Their relationships improved. They would build genuine friendships and connections with staff. Some of them were even able to have real loving, close relationships with their families, something that they had thought was impossible. Kids who thought they would never graduate from high school were going to college.

All of this positive change came from accepting the parts of themselves that were shameful to them — the messy parts. They showed other trusted people those parts, too. Through doing so, they actually changed the trajectory of their lives.

They taught me something. They taught me that they weren't *juvenile sex offenders*. They were *people*. Kids, actually. They had some good qualities and some areas that needed improvement. They had made some good choices and they had made some very, very bad choices. They had made the kind of bad choices that hurt a lot of people; however, those bad choices didn't have to define them. These kids weren't just that one thing. *None of us are.* Through understanding and living that truth, these kids were given a second chance at life, and I learned that the healing process requires self-acceptance and integration through acknowledging who we really are.

I left that job to pursue my dream job, moving to the Democratic Republic of the Congo to run a psychosocial program for a nongovernmental organization working with survivors of torture and war. I used to fly more than 20 hours from Los Angeles International Airport to Lubumbashi in the eastern Democratic Republic of the Congo. I would then be driven over roads ranging from decent to absolutely terrible for three whole days. Out of the window of the Land Rover, I would watch as we bumped down mud and dirt roads, occasionally passing demolished buildings and overturned tanks along the way, remnants of the war.

After three days, we would pull up to this little town set on a lush plateau overlooking Lake Tanganyika and looking like it was frozen in time. It was beautiful.

It was hard to believe that just years before, it had been a war zone. The people who had lived there have been faced with impossible choices: To stay in their homes and risk that they would be attacked, beaten, sexually assaulted, enslaved, and possibly murdered; or to run, and risk the same fates, being ambushed while on the roads or in the bush. Some stayed. Some fled. Many survived. And when peace was restored, many returned.

Every morning, I would wake up before dawn and walk down the paths near our residence as the sun rose over the landscape. I would pass people – women hiking up the hill from the lakeside carrying large plastic bowls of freshly caught fish or coal on their heads to sell at the market; men pushing bicycles; and children, some following their parents, others dressed in uniforms and on their way to school.

I would admire the beauty of the landscape and the sunrise. In the quieter moments of the morning, I would reflect on the people I encountered, then I would go to work and spend the rest of the day hearing about the darkest things that human beings can do to one another. I struggled to understand how there could be so much beauty and so much pain in the same place at the same time.

My job was to work with local counselors to bring people together to talk about what they had experienced with the goal of healing themselves, their families, and their community. We would drive into remote villages in farming areas. The chiefs would gather villagers together so that we could share with them about trauma and all of its effects. We would explain how those effects can manifest as symptoms of conditions such as depression, anxiety, and post-traumatic stress disorder. Then, we would invite people to come and talk to us individually to let us know if they thought they might be experiencing these symptoms of trauma. We would organize our clients into different groups based on gender, age, and experience, and they would attend sessions in huts once a week over a period of 10 weeks. Our clients would enter those huts and try to cope with pain, fear, and sadness. Their defensive walls were up; it was visible in their bodies as they sat down.

In session two, my favorite session, the feeling in those huts would change for just a little while. Session two was themed 'Happy Memories from Before the War.' Our clients would reminisce about the games they played as children with their friends. They would share about time spent with family. They would talk about celebrations and holidays. Their stony faces would melt into smiles. Giggling would start, then laughter. As their joy and giddiness became contagious, I could feel the energy in the entire hut shift. The protective walls our clients had built would start to come down. They began to connect to each other and reconnect with forgotten parts of themselves.

In subsequent weeks, we would talk about more difficult things: the way they had changed from before to after the war; the most traumatic moments; the people they lost; the ways they survived, the resources available to them, and their plans for the future.

One of the most touching memories I have is from the tenth and last session of the group. One of the women's groups decided to decorate our hut with flowers and branches, like they do for weddings. It was a real celebration. In that last session, we would share a meal and talk about what had been learned. We would all leave changed. The counselors and I would leave wiser. Our clients would leave reconnected with themselves and the people around them. They would take that back to their homes, their families, and the community. They would start to rebuild again.

I truly believe that it wasn't about what we facilitators said in those groups. It was really about the clients showing up to see and be seen, to hear and be heard, and to understand and be understood. I learned that, through accepting what happened and allowing other people to hear their truth, they were able to begin the healing process.

After closing the program in the Democratic Republic of the Congo, they sent me back to East Africa to open a new program in the refugee camps in northern Ethiopia. Eritrea is a small bordering country, which actually used to be part of Ethiopia. It gained its independence during the Ethio-Eritrean war. Not many people know that Eritrea's government has been considered to be more oppressive than that of North Korea. One of their brutal practices was the forced military conscription for males around the age of eighteen. When I say *military*, it's different from what we imagine the military to be. I heard of boys who were sent to military school and if they tried to leave, they were hunted down, tortured, and sometimes killed. I heard stories of boys forced into labor. If they fled or refused to report, they could be imprisoned and tortured.

As you can imagine, a lot of people were trying to get out of Eritrea, but even that was a high crime tantamount to treason. The Eritrean side of the Ethiopia-Eritrean border was guarded by soldiers with a shoot-to-kill order for anyone who tried to cross. Even so, many people poured over that border. Some went directly to the camps in Ethiopia. Others tried to make the risky journeys to Libya, Saudi Arabia, or all the way to Europe. Some would board the refugee-filled ships that have been known to sink into the Mediterranean. Others would be kidnapped and become victim to the human trafficking/ransoming/torture business that operates in the Sinai desert. Those who were lucky enough to survive and be released would be thrown like garbage at the Egyptian-Israeli border. There, the Egyptian officials would scoop them up and give them a choice: Return to Eritrea, where they would be imprisoned as criminals and possibly tortured or killed; or pay money to go to Ethiopia and live in the refugee camps. As you can imagine, many of them would end up in Ethiopia.

One of my first groups in the refugee camps was comprised of male torture survivors with a broad range of age and of experiences endured. When they arrived, a lot of them were expressing feelings of isolation but also felt incredibly irritable and aggressive. They were lashing out at the people around them. They had built up defensive walls around themselves, but those walls only made them more isolated, leading to them suffering from increased loneliness, agitation, fear, and depression.

From the first day, I watched in awe as these men intuitively created a safe space, speaking at length on the theme of brotherhood. The walls started coming down quickly and they began sharing what had happened to them. In the process of talking about their experiences, the men got to know each other. As each man took a turn sharing, he received the acceptance of the others. I witnessed the support of the group and the camaraderie that grew.

On the last day of the group, as we planted a tree to commemorate our time together, the men were celebrating, joking, and talking about all that they had gained. I was deeply touched to see that the healing process had begun. They weren't isolated anymore. In those 10 weeks, I had the privilege of witnessing the powerful and transformative process these men had gone through while connecting with self and others.

When I moved back to Los Angeles, back to the United States, I felt like an alien. Not only because I didn't have all the new apps or had never ever seen an episode of Game of Thrones; I felt different. I tried to assimilate. I was trying so hard. It didn't feel good.

When I took a step back and I looked around, I realized that everyone seemed as disconnected as I felt. We had so many walls up and I had fallen back into that so quickly. I tried to understand why. I had learned so much, but once I returned to where I came from, I wasn't using what I knew. I had built up my own defensive walls and created facades to make me appear all the ways I thought I *should* be. Our society encourages us to do that, telling us to chase unattainable goals, to look, to act, to work, to think and even to feel certain ways.

It's like we've forgotten that we're all human and that part of being human is being imperfect. We all know it, but for some reason when we walk outside, and we forget. We pull those walls back up and try to appear perfect again. It's hard work to build those walls and hold up those facades. Imagine what it would be like if we took that energy and channeled it into being present for the moments of our lives. Without exception, the most valuable, worthwhile and cherished moments of people's lives are always the moments of connection.

I knew I had to practice the same courage that I had seen so many of my clients role model for me. I had to let go of what I thought I *should* be and show up as exactly who I *was*. It didn't mean pouring out my deepest, darkest secrets, but it meant not pretending that I had it all together all the time. I started talking to friends and colleagues about what was really going on with me. I made a conscious decision to be vulnerable. I soon discovered that my sharing led to their sharing, which led to us connecting in meaningful ways. Everything began to feel better. We all have a story. Sharing it allows us to be present and enjoy the deepest moments of connection. Those moments give life its value. The ability to create these moments is what makes us effective conscious leaders.

Ignite Action Steps

It starts with a mindset change. We need to remember what it means to be human. First, reconnect with yourself by acknowledging yourself as you are. Give yourself permission to show up in all of your messy imperfection. It will require self-acceptance and vulnerability. It's not going to be easy. It will take practice. You can think about self-acceptance and vulnerability as working out. It won't be fun at first. You might not be good at it, but with time, we can get better. It'll become easier. Sometimes you will backslide, then you will start again. As you continue to do it, something amazing happens: You're not just doing it for you anymore. You start to connect with others through your own self-acceptance and vulnerability. They learn that they can do it too.

You become a role model; then others become role models when they start practicing it as well. Soon, it creates communities of people who are able to show up and be themselves, be seen for who they are, and spend their energy doing things of value

I propose that we all start exercising our vulnerability muscles. I believe that if we start to accept the things about ourselves that we think are negative, we'll start to see the positive aspects that actually exist. Learning happens and strength is built in moments of challenge. It's in the messiness that the unexpected beauty can emerge.

That is the exquisite mess that is being human.

Sara Feldman - USA
Social Worker, Psychotherapist, and Educator
www.exquisitemess.com

Katja Glöckler

"It is your birthright to grow."

I wish for you to know that you are not too much, nor too little. You are just right. You are beautiful. I hope my story helps you find the words you need and shows you how to bring them into your body. Of course, I want you to dance and never stop dancing; to experience feeling so alive and vibrant that you are in alignment with life. You are exactly "right" where you are. Stop figuring it out, dance it out.

Feel the Words You Need to Hear

As a child, life was nothing less than perfect. I was a little girl with blond, curly hair who loved everything pink and all shades of it. I was creative whenever I could be. I had a best friend and many girlfriends I played Barbie dolls with. I imagined I'd become an artist or a teacher when I grew up. But apart from all that, my biggest passion was dancing. Whenever I could, wherever I could — I danced. And I was happy.

I was the little girl who was raised in the generation that was strongly influenced by Twiggy and the fashion trends in the '60s. It was clear that you had to fit into a specific shape if you wanted to be perceived as a beautiful and confident woman. I wasn't thin enough to fit in. I was looked upon as "too much" to be perfect. I would certainly face the consequences later on if I didn't change as soon as possible. When I was eight years old, I was put on my first diet, which was followed by probably 100 more in the next 30 years. It was a decision made out of love, pure love, to protect me and to set me up for the best future, if I wanted to be a professional dancer.

"Don't eat so much. Avoid sweets and the food you love." I was told. The rules were easy. Eat as little as possible, less is always better, nothing is best if you want to truly dance. It was a time in society when one calorie was equal to the next calorie; and when the legacy of the first supermodels was passed on to the next generation. It was also when lite products entered the market. I remember asking my friends in school to share their lunch with me during the breaks — and how jealous I felt about the kids who could eat as much of whatever they wanted. I was supposed to be thin if I wanted to be on stage.

"Try harder. Strengthen your willpower. Be strong for the sake of becoming less." The message sank deeper and deeper into my mind until it grew into my cells, becoming a part of my DNA. A weird combination of "not being enough" because I was "too much." There was this constant desire for more: More food, more energy, more pleasure, more freedom, more love, and — most importantly — more life. Could I ever be satisfied? Could I ever get enough? Why was I always so hungry? I asked these questions over and over again until I was 40.

Driven by the desire to be satisfied, I acted secretly to get what I was craving, then developed this dangerous emotion. It was the "wanting more" and the "knowing that it was wrong." The emotion I am talking about is *guilt.*

It was the guilt that pulled me back when I wanted to go further. When I tapped on the gas to live my dreams. When I stepped outside of my comfort zone. When I took risks and when I said "YES" to growth. It was the guilt that created the self-doubts that led me to question myself, my decisions, and me, enjoying my life.

I remember them all: The moments I desperately asked myself, "Why can't I be happy without wanting more? Why can't I just be a regular, normal person?"

When I was 19, the expectations of society won. I gave up dancing. My rational mind told me that the time was just right and that I had more important things to focus on. I started to study at university. I made nothing else more important than focusing on my professional education. I needed to get ready for my future.

Except... I didn't enjoy what they told me to learn. I had lost the light I needed. I missed dancing. I gained more weight, which I saw as a sign that I had made the right decision in quitting dancing. I felt no one would want to watch me dance or have me on their dance team.

Six months later, I fell in love. He was the roommate of a friend I had met at university. It was a Sunday afternoon when I knocked on their apartment door and he opened it. I knew then and there that he was the one. He later became my husband and the father of my children. He was the first man in my life who didn't want me to change — to be less or more. He just wanted me happy and thriving.

We had many things in common; there was this deep connection right from the beginning, but dancing wasn't part of it. It was not part of his life, his interests or his passions. From time to time, I danced secretly; some steps, some moves, in my living room when nobody saw me. Often, I just danced internally while lying in bed before I fell asleep. Doing little movements that activated my mental, emotional and body memories. It was my very unique way of meditation back then. Dancing was inner happiness.

I didn't do it only to get quieter and to relax. I also did it to be more alive and to increase my ability to feel more. Activating the memories of expressive dancing lit me up like nothing else. It was like taking off a coat of dust, like drawing a curtain inside of me; to lay bare my senses and to increase my ability to feel; to honor me, to awaken pure beauty, to embrace perfection inside. It was very strange for my husband when I told him I was secretly dancing inside when we made love.

After graduating with two majors, entering work life, becoming a wife and mum of two wonderful boys, building my own business, and living abroad in Mexico for several years, I grew up massively. Of course, I had learned many things that only life can teach you — real truths, conscious truths.

I started several practices: Hypnosis, meditation and energy work. I began coaching. I read a million self-help books to understand myself so I could heal and grow. I was fascinated to uncover all the internal mechanisms of how past experiences shape our lives, burn emotions into our bodies, and keep us in never-ending loops of behavioral patterns. It was incredible to understand how we create self-doubts and negative beliefs out of our past, out of insecurities and always out of a perceived lack of love.

One of the most fascinating insights for me was how I could train my ability to live my dreams and to go forward towards my goals and desires. To get out of the never-ending loops of tapping on the gas to go forward and then stomping on the brakes and sabotaging myself, I had to slow down and go back to where I had come from.

This was definitely my time to learn. To start to heal, to allow myself to live my desires, to love myself and to create something bigger, to understand more and more who I truly was. Nevertheless, I was impatient with myself. (Believe me, this still hasn't changed today.) It's challenging to do the work, desperately wanting the breakthroughs of an Ignite Moment. I cried, shouted, even screamed in front of the ocean, begging the Universe, "What do I still have to do to get answers? When will it come? When will it happen?" I prayed, promising that I would do everything in my power to live the answers I would be given. That I would spread them by helping others open up their own consciousness to heal and energize the planet with loving and life-exciting energy.

My answer came in an off-handed way. A good friend convinced me to attend a Dance Festival. For 20 years, I had let go of my passion. Other things seemed more important than getting on the dance floor. Going against my rationalizations, I attended anyway. There was a broad offer of several classes and, on the dance floor, I was mesmerized by the instructor of the "Burlesque" class. She was beautiful, an absolutely perfect ballerina with a perfect dancer's body.

She welcomed us, saying, "Do you know *why* I love Burlesque so much? I often hear that I am too thin, that I don't have the shape of a woman, that I should be *more*. But when I dance Burlesque, I am just perfect. Take me as I am. Perceive my beauty or leave. This is me. I am beautiful. *So are you*. Every woman on this planet is perfectly divine, no matter her age, the size of her body, the color of her skin… You are beautiful as you are!"

There was a magical silence in the room when the music started and we made our initial moves. At first, it was nothing more than walking, but you could tell that the message sank into the bodies, past our minds, where it normally gets rejected. I felt it myself. I saw it in all the women… Like thirsty flowers being watered, these three words — *you are beautiful* — found the places inside each body where they were needed like missing pieces filling the gaps in a highly complex and wonderful structure. While we danced, the message became truth. Each woman in that 45-minute class had grown beautiful. No guilt. No shame. It was then I knew, "We are on this planet for one reason — to grow. *Without* the struggle of wanting more. Each tree, each fruit, each plant and Being grows from the moment of fertilization. There should be no status of *grown-up*, as if there's an end to growth. It is our birthright to keep growing."

The night, after the Burlesque class, I decided to bring my natural passion — dancing — back into my life, no matter what. When I danced, I realized it brought in the truth of the words that we all need to feel: *Beauty, Confidence, Strength, Passion, Power, and the encouragement to show up as we are.* I came to understand in that class that it was through personal expression and movement that we embody the essence of our true and authentic selves.

This was the beginning of RiseConfiDance, my vision and my purpose; a way to combine my natural passion for dancing with the transformational work that I'd learned. I use dancing to raise one's conscious confidence, to stand up, to grow, to feel one's power, to break free and to get into one's full potential and shining light. There it was. The answer — the clear sign from the Universe telling me: "Katja. This is your way. This is you."

Now you might think, "She got it;" or you might assume, "She completed her mission, she found the message. This is the end of the story."

Let me tell you: This isn't the end. After having this major insight, I wanted to bring everything together as soon as possible. Of course, when you've got the answer from the Universe, you don't want to procrastinate. You want to bring it into the world as quick as humanly possible. I started to work with a coach to receive support, to make it easier, and to be sure to stay inline and on track.

There was so much to do in such a short amount of time. I wanted it so desperately. Even though I knew it was "my" task and "my" mission to bring a transformational experience to other women on this planet, I struggled. I remembered my promise to the Universe that I would do everything humanly possible to bring this idea to others and to serve them. Yet... I still heard those judgments from when I was young.

"What, if it won't work? What if this was just the answer for you on this planet? What if you are totally crazy?" The words were as loud and clear as in the moment when everything made sense. How could this change and turn 180 degrees? It was a terrible heaviness, right there where I had experienced the ignite energy, the overall answer. "What if this was all bull-shit? What if this won't bring happiness? What if it was a waste of time and energy?" I knew if I couldn't transform this heaviness, it wouldn't just slow me down. It would make it impossible to make it all happen. During one of my coaching sessions, again, something channeled through me. My coach asked me, "Tell me... What you need to hear today, Katja?" I closed my eyes and I took this deep breath, to center, to feel and to localize the inner gaps, the missing pieces inside of me, the roots of the pain. I spoke my truth. When I opened my eyes, my coach had noted my answers read it back to me.

"You do not have to figure out everything before you are somebody. When you hear inspirational life stories, it appears that everyone else has it already figured out. They have the body, the money, the man, the life. And then, you may feel like you are in the middle and stuck and never going to get there — that you have only completed your mission on this planet when you have solved all the problems; when you don't hear the self-doubts anymore; when you've

won your final battle and hold the extract, the holy solution, in your hands.

Those stories might give you again the painful impression of not being good enough, but this is a lie. You are absolutely perfect where you are and all you need to do is keep putting one step in front of the other. We are ALWAYS in the middle of life. It is a journey, and it starts on day one and goes on until you die.

As long as you live, you are on a journey. As long as you live, you will face questions and challenges, and feel the pain of growth from time to time. Life is growing in relationship to your awareness; and, as you go, as you expand things, challenges become bigger, bolder and braver because it is the mirror of what has happened inside of you. Your story, your version, your wins. Not someone else's. YOURS.

Life means growth. It is progression, but that doesn't mean that you are only somebody when you have made the leap. You have come a long way. Since you arrived on this planet and no matter where you have been, you have always been in the right position of your journey. You are just right, exactly where you are, as long as you continue your commitment to grow and to rise, to find the answers, to seek the truth and to embody — and live — what you have learned. Remember... It is your birthright to grow as long as you live. This includes continuously learning and gaining wisdom for as long as you live. Never be afraid of the future. Be curious to find out what is waiting for you. You can always give and serve from where you are right now, as you go, as you grow, and as you find out more."

I opened my eyes, the tears still running down my face, and said "Thank you."

"No, thank yourself," my coach said. Without knowing it, I had experienced in a very powerful way the very words that I had needed to hear at that moment. I became the true message that filled me up from the inside out. I saw how the missing pieces of a wonderful and complex structure found its place. It was my conscious awakening of self and I danced freely after that session.

I am finally living my role as a conscious leader. Dancing was my way of bringing back vibrancy and the lost parts of oneself. I give words to go with the dance; words that our bodies are hungry to hear that food can never satiate. Words that bring in love. Words that can truly transform you, taking over the gaps and corners that self-doubts once filled. This is the way you support yourself. You don't just have it in your head, you have it in your body: The confidence to live your life, your dream, your vision.

These are the true powerful moments. The ones where we learn through our pain, thereby finding our way out of our pain. What we learn, we are compelled to give to others. We serve others so that they can find the words that they need to make them move and to fill them up; to let them heal, then rise and feel complete; to let them embody who they truly are. Trust that you are on your way, as long as you live, and as long as you breathe (while dancing).

Ignite Action Steps

Movement is always available to you. Dance is magical.

- **Put the music on at home and dance.** There is no way to do it wrong. Dance is movement and our bodies are meant to move.
- **Dance with your children.** Learn from their ease with moving their bodies.
- **Find a dance class.** Break free from any judgment; it can be fun.
- **Dance with yourself.** You do not need a partner. Dance with your own soul.
- **Do Secret Dancing.** Turn on the music in your head and make small movements, even when laying in bed. Secret dance when making love to your spouse.
- **Every answer is inside of you.** Don't be afraid. Just listen to the pain and tell yourself the words you need to hear. Dance them into your heart.
- **Create a safe space for your dance.** Allow yourself to expand. Movement brings clarity by taking you out of your head and bringing you into the feelings. When you hear self-doubts coming up, start to dance. Get into your body's powerful energy.

The time to dance is now.

Katja Glöckler - Germany
Confidence Ambassador
Transformational Dancer, Coach, Author & Speaker
www.katjagloeckler.com

NITASHA SARIN

"A true leader is not one who asks all to conform to their ideals, but one who embodies the humility to Master Self Love & Leadership in order to Optimally Serve Love & Leadership."

It is my intention to inspire you to Fall into Freedom and Redefine Success on your own terms. By sharing my story, you too will find clarity in "consciousness" and first create your own personal love, leadership and mastery. This will Empower you to *give* forward, serving the highest form of Leadership to those on their quests for personal freedom.

REDEFINING SUCCESS IN LEADERSHIP

"Conscious Leadership." Well, WTF do these words really mean?! When I was asked to be a part of this *"Conscious Leaders"* book, I'll be honest — I was torn. Delighted at the idea of anything *Leadership* related, but at the same time turned off by North American Western society's overuse of words such as "conscious," "functional," and "yoga" being slapped on every and any new marketable concept (i.e., Goat Yoga? Conscious parenting, conscious cooking, sleeping, shitting ...the list can go on and on).

Needless to say, I had a choice. Wallow in one-dimensional thought pattern of negativity over simple semantics and what society has done to such revered words, concepts & philosophies such as yoga, consciousness and leadership — OR open my mind to multi-dimensional thinking and take a stab at adding to the conversation with all the life experience and professional

294 / Nitasha Sarin

expertise I can offer. The latter prevailed.

So, I invite you to play with me a little. Here goes…

We all know Clarity is Mastery. So, let's start with clarifying the ambiguous concepts and make this some interactive, experiential fun, shall we? Stick with me here. Grab a journal and a pen. Write down the words CONSCIOUS and LEADERSHIP. Now, popcorn style, without thinking too much — vomit on the page. Let it all out, confusion and all.

Great. Done? There's no right or wrong answer, only subjectivity based on our own personal blueprints of life intertwined with opinions and experiences of others. That said, here's Webster's definition with my transposition below for the sake of being on the same page for this chapter at least — take it for what it's worth and, hopefully, you'll gain some useful golden nuggets to consider and put into action!

Con·scious /ˈkän(t)SHəs/ *adjective* — aware of and responding to one's surroundings.

Nitasha's Understanding: I like this one. I would look at Consciousness as also being a journey of evolution and enlightenment while being entirely tapped in to the Present Moment. Observing everything about the nuances of your 5 senses. There's nothing more present than your 5 senses — what do you see, hear, taste, smell, feel physically and emotionally? Ask yourself at any given moment while you're driving, walking, in the middle of a massive crowd. Do multiple 5-Sense check-ins throughout the day and then sit back and become super uber *Aware* of not only how you respond to your surroundings, but how you choose to breathe, act and then respond to the stimuli presented to you at any given moment. It's always shifting. Always changing. Become focused, become consciously aware; we'll start there and you'll see how this relates to self leadership and serving leadership.

Lead·er·ship /ˈlēdərˌSHip/ *noun* — the action of leading a group of people or an organization.

Nitasha's Understanding: Hmmm. I only partially agree with this one. Here's why… My thought pattern is 2-fold. On the one hand, in today's modern society where so much is based on the SELF (self-love, self-care, selfies, personal growth, personal branding, etc.), the ego and self-absorption seem to have taken on a wide-angle approach of ME in every area… except Leadership?!

All of a sudden the ME conversation of self-leadership has been overlooked and we as a society have been brain-washed into believing that we are Leaders only when WE are leading OTHERS. Fullstop. WHAT? Where do we get off leading others before building a solid base of roots, beliefs, commitments and convictions that we fully implement towards ourselves FIRST, prior to Leading others?

On the other hand, the ME is definitely coming up here — in society's skewed approach to defining success. WE are currently conducting Leadership in a *"LOOK AT ME... I have all the answers"* approach, wearing our ego-filled badges of honor and status titles of Manager, Supervisor, Team lead, Lord of the Manor, King of the Castle. This leads to misalignment of true self-happiness and internal profitability or intrinsic success.

So, how about we flip the script.

REDEFINING SUCCESS:

Now, in order to Redefine something, we definitely need to have a clear understanding of what our current definition and belief system is. Let's continue playing. Ready? Grab the journal and pen again.

What does Success mean to you?
Go for it . Free for all, write, doodle, sketch, draw.

What did you come up with?
*   White picket fence, 2.5 kids, a cottage, a C-suite "leadership" title, X amount of money in the bank account, the yacht, the Maserati, 3 universities degrees, New York Times Best-seller, front page of Forbes magazine?

While all these things are lovely accomplishments and accolades, they can too often define us rather than fuel us to take a candid and confrontational "TRUTH LOOK" INSIDE ourselves. Societies definition of Success — external admiration, recognition, meeting target numbers and checking off boxes on the race to the finish-line... has us wearing a mask of Fear, Conformity and Judgement, leading to our inability to truly express our messages to the world and lead others with credibility and integrity towards their own Balance and Personal Freedom.

So, let's Redefine Success, together.

This is a call to all Leaders and Visionaries. This is a call to YOU. You are the Leader of your Life. If you're reading this, I suspect you are driven and ready to up-level to new heights… You desire to create your Legacy and Impact on the world. However, you feel out of balance with lack of clarity and focus. The thought of more has you stressed, overwhelmed, unsupported, burnt out, and feeling suffocated — not FREE.

Why?

Because we are a dichotomous society. We live in a fast-paced world where chronic stress, overwhelm, and fear of change and the unknown are on the rise. We are at risk of losing our personal power and state of wellbeing as conformity and skewed definitions of success and happiness prevail over our Passion, Purpose, Freedom, Truth, Expression, Desires and, most importantly, Self Mastery.

We feel stuck, stifled, and suffocated with our circumstances, which has us succumbing to the up-rise of mental, physical, emotional, spiritual and financial blockages and prevents us from leading and performing at epic realms the way we know we are meant to. We are forgetting our voices. We crave to slow down, free our minds and be Present (conscious). But we don't know how.

Have you stopped for a moment to actually become a LEADER of YOURSELF? Can you clearly visualize your desires, passion and purpose? Are you genuinely ALIGNED with your mission, vision and LEGACY you wish to leave? What you want is to feel EMPOWERED. You crave balance, focus, vision, support and a clear plan that ignites your fire, supports the legacy and impactful message you desire to create, express, and serve. You DESIRE to dream, believe, achieve, and create with full authenticity and truth. But instead… stress, insecurity, doubt, frustration, conformity — our mental demons surface and take over.

So, make it STOP. Flip the switch.

We Crave BALANCE. The Ultimate LUXURY. Yet, we hide that craving by aiming to achieve external indicators of success, including leading others before leading ourselves! It's the classic which came first — chicken or egg? Did the Titanic allow recognition or understanding of the depths of power and enormity from the iceberg beneath the water's surface, or did the ego stand in the way and distract us towards the one-dimensional vision of overcoming superficial waters, surface obstacles, to attain solely external profitability and success?

Over my years of personal evolution, I've been influenced and inspired by learning from traditional Eastern Vedic Guru's and Buddhist philosophies, as well and leaders such as Nelson Mandela (whom I was fortunate to meet when I was 10 years old), Mahatma Gandhi, Martin Luther King Jr, Rosa

Parks, and Princess Diana, to name a few. I've also had the opportunity to work with, interview and coach more contemporary masterful thought leaders such as Robin Sharma, Paul Allen, Deepak Chopra, Arianna Huffington, Vishen Lakhiani, Wayne Gretzky and our newest athletic leader, Teen Tennis Champion Bianca Andreescu. All of these incredible souls have a common denominator: they have been Masters of themselves prior to the Masters of others. I've learned that all indicate *"Balance"* is the ultimate path to personal freedom and success. Now, I know there's a massive divide when it comes to the general population's acceptance of the word "Balance," so for the purpose of this... let's define again: Pen and journal ready? Let's do this. Ask yourself.

What do you visualize when you think of the word balance?
For most is a straight line. A place of solace and eventual outcome. I beg to differ.

Bal·ance /ˈbaləns/ *noun* — 1. An even, linear distribution of weight enabling someone or something to remain upright and steady. 2. A condition in which different elements are equal or in the correct proportions. 3. A static homeostasis.

Nitasha's Understanding: Umm. NO. For this, I will use the words "Balance" and "Personal freedom" interchangeably.

Repeat after me: *"There is NO Linear Approach to Balance."*

In life, there will always be moments of lightness and darkness. It's our choice to focus on either dancing with the flow of the highs and lows like waves of the water, or resisting them. It's your path. Your personal balance to define. Where do you choose to stand and play? Think about the flatline in a hospital — if that is your ultimate goal, it defines the dead. The ups and downs of life, the heartbeats, indicate the essence of being alive. Embrace it.

Going back to my list of inspirational souls, in essence, they have practiced and mastered the art of Balancing Internal and External Profitability to achieve their own Personal Freedom. What's that? I like to call it our WEALTH WELLNESS INDEX.

Internal Profitability: Empathy, Compassion, Forgiveness, Diversity, Tolerance, Adaptability, Personal Responsibility, Accountability, Passion, Purpose, Healthy Boundaries, Giving Forward/Social Impact.

External Profitability: Power, Monetary Profitability, Recognition, Awards, Accolades, Materials, Possessions, Numerical Data Driven Results, Societies Expectations

One without the other is impractical and unsustainable in achieving true Balance and Freedom. Take a mental measure — where are you focusing your energies? But the buck doesn't stop there. Our Masterful Leaders have taken it a step further and found even more internal peace, happiness and freedom by sharing and passing forward their knowledge and success to others in order for them to also create their own Balance and Personal Freedom. Being the light of strength, love and leadership for themselves first, then being the light of strength, love and leadership for others, who will in turn continue to be the Light for others still — and the rippling effect continues. So long as we shift the conversation and evolve our approach of education within "Conscious Leadership."

Over the past 20 years, I've led myself and teams within the corporate world, entrepreneurial ventures, consulting, coaching and leading teams on a global scale. During this time, I did take many moments to research, ask questions and learn from the best of the best of Leadership minds and souls. Inspired by my observations that the richest and wealthiest people in the world sitting in Monaco, Italy, Dubai and Singapore with all their material possessions were not happy; nor were the highly stressed out NYC Manhattan executives climbing their corporate ladders and living in overpriced shoeboxes of apartments.

With the noticed pressure of society's comparison to "keep up with the Jones'" or today's Kardashians, living the need to be recognized by a "like," a "heart," and number of followers as a false sign of leadership, I found myself falling into the same trap. Feeling suffocated myself, and on the edge of Burnout, I was ignited to prioritize my self-leadership and expand my consciousness.

I eventually rebranded my business and created Empowered360 Experiences. Because we were wrongly defining our own self-worth by society's metric of success. Empowered360 Experiences initially offers people a self-examination — to explore, experience, enlighten and evolve to a new level of living and being while redefining success. Creating solid roots, rituals and habits of Conscious Self-Leadership as a segue to Serving Leadership as an influential and impactful Global Leader of positive change.

The new success metric being Optimal Wellbeing derived through Personal Freedom, Balancing mental, emotional, physical, spiritual, financial and aspirational realms. I called these realms fitnesses and make up the 360 Intelligence

Approach. Super sexy words and concepts, the experiences are 1:1 private, in groups or teams, and also held as journeys around the world! I wanted to create space for high performers to get together, remove their perfectionist masks, and get raw and real. They learn methods and models that they practice on each other during a cultural immersion, a "work-ation" week, and return home with a strategic Empowered Mastery Blueprint in hand to implement.

This is my way of creating true conscious leaders.

Travelling from country to country, speaking on various stages, running several retreat experiences while still coaching and consulting the "wealthiest" to redefine success — I repeat, Health and Balance were the Ultimate luxury — I knew that if I didn't lead by example and implement my own Self-Leadership Rituals, I'd longer be able to lead effectively.

I have learned that in mastering these elements of Balancing Self Love and Leadership with Serving Love and Leadership, I am fulfilling my life's legacy of being an exemplary Conscious Leader. It has allowed me the freedom to be the best for myself and others. I believe the sooner you implement these ideas, the sooner you'll see the positive Shifts in your life! You have the Empowered choice to Reclaim your Personal Power and Balance. You have the Empowered choice to slow down, take in the present moment, Breathe. There is a deeper purpose to your Life. Start here. Start Now. And remember… Fear or Freedom wins. Be BOLD. Be CREATIVE. Be BALANCED. Be FREE. To your EMPOWERED Life.

Ignite Action Steps

SELF LOVE and LEADERSHIP (Leading the Self)

Basically, we have to take responsibility and do the work on ourselves first, starting with the process of Understanding Self Love and Self Leadership. Here are the four key self-leadership pillars to focus on:

Explore — *yourself in all areas of truth… Fears, Anxieties, Passion, Desires.*

Experience — *fun unraveling. Refocus on only one area to bring it into balance. Baby steps.*

Enlighten — *as you gain, you surrender control, fall into flow and accept the epiphanies and ignite moments during these new changes in life.*

Evolve — *elevate and thrive toward the upwards trajectory of personal growth and evolution.*

REPEAT.

SERVE LOVE and LEADERSHIP (Leading Others)

Going back to when we defined as "Conscious…" I invite you to become aware of your energetic movements and what makes you light up internally with passion and purpose so that, eventually, you can use those golden nuggets to serve love and leadership, and enable others to attain their own balance and personal freedom.

Express — *Confront, embrace unique qualities and Express your truth prevent any feelings of dis-ease turning to disease. It also helps us lead by example pathways of ease.*

Engage — *Lead by example by dropping your masks of perfection. Embrace vulnerability and imperfection as you engage with others to step into their truths.*

Empathize — *Practice the art of empathy as your team shares their powerful personal stories and professional desires.*

Encourage — *Inspire and empower others to live extraordinary lives, infinitely thinking beyond their natural dreams, and create strategic blueprints of balanced success together.*

REPEAT.

Below are a few simple *"Rituals and Shifts"* to help kickstart your path to Self Leadership and Serving Leadership:

RITUAL 1

ME TO WE: "Infinity Thinking" and Possibility Mindedness.

Here, we dive into elevating from victim-like, one-dimensional thinking to a multi-dimensional, enlightened Conscious Leadership Mindset. Review it, repeat it and tattoo it to your mind, body and soul. Most of the world's population, 90 percent of people, see their realities of life one -dimensionally. Let's aim to elevate this tunnel vision thought pattern.

- *Example:* If your boss or someone did something nasty to you, a one-dimensional approach would be Victim mentality: "Somebody hurt me. What a jerk." Let's take the same scenario and elevate it to "Infinity-Thinking" and Multidimensional Mindedness.

- "Somebody hurt me. What a jerk" — VICTIM
- "Perhaps I did something to contribute to that." — PERSONAL RESPONSIBILITY and ACCOUNTABILITY
- "Perhaps something happened to that person 10 minutes (or some time frame) ago and it has nothing to do with me." — EMPATHY and COMPASSION
- "Maybe this person was culturally brought up this way, educated in a certain manner and this is their way and their reality of what is right and wrong." — DIVERSITY and TOLERANCE.

- There you see and elevated mindset of conscious leadership; four of the infinite possibilities of why the situation took place.

  - Give silent space to yourself to be the Leader of your own life first. Then, extend the teachings of personal responsibility, accountability, empathy, compassion, diversity and tolerance. Allow space for others to evolve their own highest selves.

RITUAL 2

Embrace the Power of Choice

You have the Empowered Choice to step away from fear, stress, overwhelm and burnout. You can create your Life and Business filled with Passion and Purpose. Whether you're leading yourself, your family, your teams; scaling already existing success to heightened realms; or you're a new entrepreneur — you are not Alone.

The common question is, "How do I remain focused and balanced with my health and wellbeing when bombarded with a constant flow of demands, expectations, and excess responsibilities?"

- Choose Freedom over Fear
- Set healthy boundaries. Be clear in communication. Say NO more.
- Set realistic expectations of yourself and others
- Simplify and declutter your thoughts and environment

RITUAL 3

Define and Commit to your Non-negotiable Daily Practices (Rituals & Shifts)

- Breathe: Inhale positivity in the form of thoughts, emotions, oxygen as nutrients. Exhale out negative thoughts, emotions (stress and anxiety), physical ailments.
- Touch Nature: There is tremendous healing and grounding with time spent with any of the 5 elements — earth, wind, water, fire, ether.
- Befriend Failure: Do not dwell on the past. Learn from the experience and fail forward.
- Wake up early: You have the most amount of willpower first thing in the morning. Be disciplined in your ability to wake up early for silent Self-Mastery time.
- Speak beautiful words to yourself: Studies show positive self talk as key to mastery.
- Always be willing to give forward. There is no other greater intrinsic reward.
- Believe that the Journey is the Destination. Stay Present.

"For to be free is not merely to cast off one's chains, but to live in a way that respects and enhances the freedom of others"

Nelson Mandela

Nitasha Sarin MSc, MBA - Canada
nsarin@globalifegroup.com
Founder; Global Life Group & Empowered360 Experiences
Strategic Consultant, EQ:EI Leadership & Executive Wellness Coach
www.globalifegroup.com

A tremendous thank you goes to those who are working in the background, editing, supporting, and encouraging the authors. They are some of most genuine and heart-centered people I know. Their devotion to the vision of IGNITE, their integrity and the message they aspire to convey, is at the highest caliber possible. They too want you to find your ignite moment and flourish. They each believe in you and that's what makes them so outstanding. Their dream is for your dreams to come true.

BOOKS AND RESOURCES MEANINGFUL TO THE IGNITE YOUR LIFE FOR CONSCIOUS LEADERS AUTHORS

Ashley Avinashi
https://medium.com/@raisinghumanity, www.raisinghumanity.com

Amy O'Meara
www.lifemeant.com/book

Ana Cukrov
Holy Bible, I am enough - Marisa Peer, Conversations with God - Neale Donald Walsch

Beth Medved Waller
Visit www.whatmattersw2.com/ignite to watch the Youtube lyric videos and read the full song lyrics for the music referenced in BETH's story.

Catherine Malli-Dawson
www.chopracenter.com
The Path to Love - Deepak Chopra
The Seven Spiritual Laws of Yoga - Deepak Chopra and David Simon
The Power of Now - Eckhart Tolle
Mobile Meditation applications: Insight Timer, Ananda, Soulvana

Damian Culhane
www.damianculhane.co.uk/Map_Your_Purpose

Dana Shalit
Abraham Maslow's Hierarchy of Needs - Dr Karl Jung
Dark Side of the Lightchasers - Debbie Ford
Mama Gena School of Womanly Arts

Emily C. Ross
Daring Greatly - Brene Brown

Francesca Ciaudano
Source: Gallup. State of the Global Workplace Report, 85% of employees are not engaged or actively disengaged at work.
Note: this technique is also called Anapana. You can research more at https://www.vridhamma.org/What-is-Anapana

Ivana Sošić Antunović
You Are The Placebo - Dr. Joe Dispenza
The Conscious Parent - Dr. Shefali Tsabary

Katja Glöckler
RiseConfiDance, www.katjagloeckler.com

Lori Lennox
Start Close In by David Whyte, https://www.stevenkharper.com/startclosein.
html

Maggie Reigh
A Course in Miracles - https://acim.org/

Matej Šimunić
[1] IPCC, 2018: Summary for Policymakers. In: Global Warming of 1.5°C.
An IPCC Special Report on the impacts of global warming of 1.5°C above
pre-industrial levels and related global greenhouse gas emission pathways, in
the context of strengthening the global response to the threat of climate change,
sustainable development, and efforts to eradicate poverty [Masson-Delmotte,
V., P. Zhai, H.-O. Pörtner, D. Roberts, J. Skea, P.R. Shukla, A. Pirani, W. Mou-
fouma-Okia, C. Péan, R. Pidcock, S. Connors, J.B.R. Matthews, Y. Chen, X.
Zhou, M.I. Gomis, E. Lonnoy, T. Maycock, M. Tignor, and T. Waterfield (eds.)].
World Meteorological Organization, Geneva, Switzerland, 32 pp.

[2] Bock, L. and Burkhardt, U.: Contrail cirrus radiative forcing for future air
traffic, Atmos. Chem. Phys., 19, 8163–8174, https://doi.org/10.5194/acp-19-
8163-2019, 2019.

[3] Gerber, P.J., Steinfeld, H., Henderson, B., Mottet, A., Opio, C., Dijkman, J.,
Falcucci, A. & Tempio, G. 2013. Tackling climate change through livestock
– A global assessment of emissions and mitigation opportunities. Food and
Agriculture Organization of the United Nations (FAO), Rome.

[4] The global tree restoration potential
BY JEAN-FRANCOIS BASTIN, YELENA FINEGOLD, CLAUDE GARCIA,
DANILO MOLLICONE, MARCELO REZENDE, DEVIN ROUTH, CON-
STANTIN M. ZOHNER, THOMAS W. CROWTHER
SCIENCE05 JUL 2019 : 76-79

[5] Restoring forests as a means to many ends BY ROBIN CHAZDON, PEDRO BRANCALION SCIENCE05 JUL 2019 : 24-25

[6] Ornstein, L., Aleinov, I. & Rind, D. Climatic Change (2009) 97: 409. https://doi.org/10.1007/s10584-009-9626-y

[7] IPCC, 2011: Summary for Policymakers. In: IPCC Special Report on Renewable Energy Sources and Climate Change Mitigation [O. Edenhofer, R. Pichs-Madruga, Y. Sokona, K. Seyboth, P. Matschoss, S. Kadner, T. Zwickel, P. Eickemeier, G. Hansen, S. Schlömer, C. von Stechow (eds)], Cambridge University Press, Cambridge, United Kingdom and New York, NY, USA.

[8] Primary forest cover loss in Indonesia over 2000–2012 Nature Climate Change volume4, pages 730–735 (2014)

Meena Kumari Adnani
Well-Behaved Women Seldom Make History, written by Laurel Thatcher Ulrich
www.strongandshine.com

Michael D Lynch
A Mind at Home with Itself - Byron Katie
No More Mr. Nice Guy - Dr. Robert A. Glover

Nancy L. McFarland
As A Man Thinkest - James Allen
Big Magic: Creative Living Beyond Fear - Elizabeth Gilbert

Sam Beard
Go to the www.sambeard.org website. See: Change the World. How To. II.

Sherry Brier
DOORWAY TO ECSTASY: A Dancers Initiation - Sherry Brier

Vicki Graham
Vicki Graham, Holistic Integrative Therapist, Medical Intuit, Teacher and Coach. Author of "I can Breathe Again, My Inner Physician Revealed the Secret to Heal Myself" and composer of The CD, "The Sound of Balance, Vibrational Healing".
Director of Harmony Health Center
www.harmonyhealth.net

Upcoming Books in the
IGNITE SERIES
If you have story to share,
Please apply at www.igniteyou.life/apply